1993

The Warriors of Islam

The Warriors of Islam

Iran's Revolutionary Guard

Kenneth Katzman

Westview Press

BOULDER • SAN FRANCISCO • OXFORD

In memory of my father,
Marvin

This Westview softcover edition is printed on acid-free paper and bound in library-quality, coated covers that carry the highest rating of the National Association of State Textbook Administrators, in consultation with the Association of American Publishers and the Book Manufacturers' Institute.

Copyright © 1993 by Westview Press, Inc.

Published in 1993 in the United States of America by Westview Press, Inc., 5500 Central Avenue, Boulder, Colorado 80301-2877, and in the United Kingdom by Westview Press, 36 Lonsdale Road, Summertown, Oxford OX2 7EW

Library of Congress Cataloging-in-Publication Data
Katzman, Kenneth.
  The warriors of Islam : Iran's Revolutionary Guard / Kenneth Katzman.
    p.   cm.
  Includes bibliographical references and index.
  ISBN 0-8133-7890-7
  1. Sipāh-i Pāsdārān-i Ubqilāb-i Islāmī (Iran)   2. Iran—History, Military.   I. Title.
UA853.I7K38   1993
356'.16'0955—dc20

92-17902
CIP

Printed and bound in the United States of America

The paper used in this publication meets the requirements of the American National Standard for Permanence of Paper for Printed Library Materials Z39.48-1984.

10   9   8   7   6   5   4   3   2   1

Contents

Introduction

In Iran, the Islamic Revolutionary Guard Corps is everywhere. In the immediate post-revolutionary period, the Guard was a hastily gathered, disorganized, and ill-trained militia that helped Ayatollah Ruhollah Khomeini and his lieutenants solidify their hold on power in Tehran. During the eight-year war against Iraq, it also developed into an organized military, a monitor of popular conformity to Islamic law, and a key tool for the export of the Islamic revolution. In the Iran-Iraq war, it fought the war alongside Iran's regular armed forces, which were held over from the Shah's regime. Since the end of the Iran-Iraq conflict in 1988, the Guard has taken on a defensive military role and some civilian reconstruction duties as well.

The limited amount of research that has been done on the Guard thus far has tended to compare it to Iran's regular military. However, the Revolutionary Guard is far too unusual in its ideological outlook, method of operations, role functions in Iranian society and politics, and developmental history to conform easily to traditional approaches of politico-military analysis. Unlike Iran's regular military, the Guard is also a political force and thus must be analyzed more broadly. The regular military, reflecting its nationalist orientation forged under the Pahlavi dynasty, is generally apolitical—loyal to whatever regime is in power. This apolitical nature, in part, accounts for its ability to survive, albeit weakened and extensively monitored politically, under the Khomeini regime. The Guard, by contrast, sees involvement in politics as not only permissible, but as part of its mission to defend the Islamic revolution—a mission that is enshrined in the Constitution of the Islamic Republic.[1]

The relationship between the Guard and the clerical leaders of the Islamic regime who helped organize the Guard is just one among many aspects of the Guard that need discussion if one is to understand this organization. Fortunately, much work has been done on civil-military relations at the theoretical and empirical level, and this research will be a useful tool for analyzing the Guard's relationship with the Islamic government, its involvement in political disputes among factions of the regime, and its rivalry with the regular military.

Much work in political science, history, and sociology has been done on the causes and processes of revolution. Far less attention has been paid to the process of post-revolution institution building and the mechanisms by which major social revolutions consolidate their grip on power. An even smaller body of work, most notably by Katharine Chorley,[2] Jonathan Adelman,[3] and John Ellis[4] has examined the related issue of the development of revolutionary armed forces. It is this research on institution building and revolutionary armed forces as instruments of revolutionary consolidation that is most pertinent to an analysis of the Guard. This approach will involve useful comparisons between the Guard and other revolutionary armed forces, particularly the Soviet Red Army, the Chinese People's Liberation Army, and the French revolutionary army.

There are some basic problems in attempting to analyze the Revolutionary Guard, foremost among them the difficulty in obtaining information about it. Since the takeover of the U.S. Embassy in Tehran in 1979, there have been no diplomatic relations between the U.S. and Iran. Aside from the ongoing U.S.-Iran Claims Tribunal at the Hague[5] and bilateral contacts in the context of the U.S.-Iran arms affair in 1985-86,[6] there has been little official contact between the two nations. US diplomats, therefore, have had little access to Iranian officials or the Iranian political process.

The nature of the Iranian political system also restricts the amount and type of information that can be obtained by journalists. Access to Iran by foreign journalists is controlled by the government, and often appears to vary according to the prevailing political climate in Tehran. Access has tended to be poorer when the radicals are driving policy than when more pragmatic elements have the upper hand politically.[7] The ascendency of pragmatic leaders following the death of Ayatollah Khomeini in June 1989 accounts, therefore, for the more open press policies since his death. When journalists have visited Iran, the range of their access has often been limited. For example, very few reporters were allowed to visit the front during the war. When permission for such visits was granted, it generally followed a battlefield victory and was arranged to enable the government to support its claims and boast of its military achievements. During such press visits, government representatives accompanied the journalists involved, and independent confirmation and investigation was not generally allowed.[8]

A second major problem is the reliability of information on Iran. The Iranian regime is a divided one, and each faction has an interest in portraying its ideals, policies, leaders, and efforts in the best light possible. Information that can be gathered from inside Iran by journalists, therefore, has to be carefully evaluated or caveated in terms of the particular group, person, or faction that is providing the information.

The factionalism in the regime, however, also benefits researchers on Iran in that it tends to result in a greater availability of information. Just as each faction may tend to slant its view of events to benefit its own position, similarly, any one faction also has an interest in revealing information about a rival faction for the purpose of discrediting that competitor. In this process, information that would not otherwise be disclosed comes to light. An excellent example is provided by the revelations surrounding the 1986-87 "Mehdi Hashemi Affair." Mehdi Hashemi, a relative by marriage and aide to Ayatollah Hosein Ali Montazeri (who was forced out as Khomeini's designated successor in March 1989) was head of the "Office of Liberation Movements," originally a formal arm of the Revolutionary Guard[9] that coordinated Iran's efforts to export the Islamic revolution. A diehard radical, Hashemi leaked revelations of the U.S.-Iran arms deal to a Beirut newspaper *Al Shiraa*.[10] Hashemi's leak was intended to embarrass and politically weaken a key Iranian figure in the arms deal, then Majles (Consultative Assembly) Speaker Ali Akbar Hashemi-Rafsanjani (now Iran's President), who Hashemi felt had sold out the Islamic revolution by dealing with the United States.[11]

Outside the regime, a continuous stream of information is provided by Iranian exiles, some of whom have served under or support the former Shah's regime, others of whom once served in or supported the Islamic regime and have since broken with it. Examples of the latter include the first President of the Islamic Republic Abol Hassan Bani-Sadr, now in exile in France, and the voluble Mojahedin-e-Khalq (People's Warriors) Organization, based in Iraq. In general, it will not be possible to rely on these sources unless specific events or interpretations put forth by these exile sources can be independently confirmed. This caution would especially apply in using exile information to analyze affairs in which their organizations may be involved or would particularly benefit by adoption of their interpretation of events. Neither should exile reporting be rejected out of hand, however; it can often amplify or fill in gaps left by other reports and can contribute to the analysis of events and trends. Many exile reports about demonstrations or civil disturbances in Iran have been acknowledged, at least indirectly, by the Iranian government.[12]

Yet another difficulty in gathering information about the Revolutionary Guard is that there are few former Guardsmen living in exile and available for systematic interviewing. This is primarily because most Guards are supporters of the Islamic regime, even if they oppose many of Rafsanjani's pragmatic policies. An interview methodology that uses non-Guard exiles or former regular military personnel as a substitute would suffer from major limitations, in that these exiles are precisely those elements that would have an unfavorable bias against the Guard. Thus, systematic interviews can provide, at best, second hand accounts of Guard training, units, assignments, involvement in battle, unit leaders, and experiences.

The sources described above, fortunately, do not exhaust the available methods of obtaining information and formulating a comprehensive understanding of the Revolutionary Guard. The primary source, and, in many ways the most reliable, is the official Iranian press. Official statements by Iranian political leaders and senior Guard commanders generally provide accurate indications of the policy direction these leaders are advocating. Mobilization calls described in the Iranian press have yielded a wealth of data about the structure of the Guard and *Basij*, or popular volunteer troops, which it controls. The Iranian press has also often provided official biographies of newly appointed Guard Ministers, but not military commanders. Guard commanders also have occasionally given interviews to Iranian journalists and have discussed tactics, operations, and weapons used. The official press accounts of specific battles, however, are not reliable, especially in the inflated enemy casualty figures cited and the exaggerated, if understandable, claims of battlefield success.

The unofficial, but sanctioned, press is another highly reliable and wealthy source of information on the Guard. The Iran Press Digest and its related publication, the Echo of Iran, have run articles on key organizations that gave rise to the early Guard; reviews of the Guard's affairs, evolution, and involvement in military industries; and biographies of Iranian officials, which included their links to or service in the Guard. Another excellent source of information, although somewhat limited, as described above, is that provided by journalists. British and French reporters, especially, have occasionally been granted access to Iran. Arab newspapers also have often provided coverage of events in Iran, probably because of the proximity of and interest in Iranian developments on the part of many Arab governments. Western European and Arab news reports will be a particularly important source of information on the Guard's involvement in export of the revolution and terrorism. Foreign Broadcast Information Service (FBIS) provides translated versions of official press statements, editorials, and excerpts from Persian language magazines, including those published by or catering to the Revolutionary Guard.

A systematic description of specific battles in the Iran-Iraq war will not contribute significantly to assessing the Guard's evolution as a political institution. Detailed accounts and analysis of engagements in the war have been adequately covered by several researchers.[13] In some cases, however, the outcomes, tactics and weapons used, and analysis of certain battles will be needed to support assertions and analysis of the Guard's growth as an institution and as a powerful voice in key regime decision-making bodies.

In general, there has been an attempt to draw from as broad a base of sources as possible. However, it needs to be noted that the Iranian political system, largely due to its fragmented nature, is highly complex, and events and trends are often subject to several equally plausible interpretations.

Notes

1. *Constitution of the Islamic Republic of Iran,* reprinted in *The Middle East Journal,* Spring 1980, pp. 181-204
2. Katharine Chorley, *Armies and the Art of Revolution* (Boston: Beacon Press, 1973)
3. Jonathan Adelman, *Revolution, Armies, and War: A Political History* (Boulder, Co.: Lynne Rienner Publishers, Inc., 1985)
4. John Ellis, *Armies in Revolution* (London: Croon Helm Ltd., 1973)
5. "U.S. and Iran Move on Smaller Claims," New York Times; May 8, 1990, P. A7
6. *Report of the President's Special Review Board,* February 26, 1987
7. John Simpson, *Inside Iran* (New York: St. Martin's Press, 1988) pp. 89-91
8. Ibid, P. 285
9. "Mehdi Hashemi's Confessions," excerpted from Tehran The Islamic Republic in Tehran Akhbar, Vol. VII, No. 205; December 10, 1986
10. "Power Struggle Between Montazeri, Rafsanjani Groups Cited," London Keyhan in Persian; February 12, 1987, P. 16; "Lebanese Weekly on Hashemi, McFarlane" in FBIS; November 5, 1986
11. Ibid
12. "Clandestine Radio on Soccer Demonstrations," (Clandestine) Voice of the Mojahed in Persian; February 18, 1990 in FBIS; February 20, 1990, P. 51; "Nuri Comments on 'Amusing' Foreign Media Reports," Tehran IRNA in English; February 28, 1990
13. For an insightful analysis of the Iran-Iraq war, see: Anthony Cordesman, *The Iran-Iraq War and Western Security, 1984-87* (London: Jane's Publishing Co. Ltd., 1987); Shahram Chubin and Charles Tripp, *Iran and Iraq at War* (London: I.B. Taurus and Co. Ltd., 1988); Edgar O'Ballance, *The Gulf War* (London: Brassey's Defence Publishers Ltd., 1988); and Sepehr Zabih, *The Iranian Military in Revolution and War* (London: Routledge, 1988)

1

The Guard as Revolutionary Institution

Ayatollah Ruhollah Khomeini, the leader of the Islamic revolution in Iran, died on June 3, 1989, but his regime not only survived his death but apparently achieved a relatively orderly transition of power. This is largely because Khomeini institutionalized the Islamic revolution in Iran. One of the most important institutions the revolution has produced is the Islamic Revolutionary Guard Corps (IRGC; Pasdaran Enqelab-e-Islam). The Revolutionary Guard is one of the strongest institutions the Islamic revolution has produced; a primary instrument for promoting the goals of the Islamic revolution and Khomeini; and, unique among revolutionary armed forces formed in other major social revolutions, it has become a relatively complex and cohesive organization without losing its ideological zeal.

To analyze the Guard's strength as a revolutionary institution, a distinct framework of analysis is needed, one that will permit rigorous presentation of what is known and can be demonstrated to be true about the Revolutionary Guard.[1] Such a framework will facilitate the analysis of the Guard as a revolutionary institution and as a unique revolutionary armed force. It will be necessary to supplement the framework, where applicable, with work on the role of the military in politics and political development by other scholars.[2] Relevant as well, particularly for comparing the Revolutionary Guard to other revolutionary armed forces is the work on revolutionary militaries. For example, John Ellis measures the strength and success of such forces by the degree to which they were able to identify the personal interests of their fighters with the goals of the revolutions that produced them.[3] Jonathan Adelman argues that a revolutionary armed force, because of its zeal, is more militarily effective than its prerevolutionary predecessor.[4] For purposes of this analysis, however, the most important observer of revolutionary armed forces is Katharine Chorley, who delineates stages through which revolutionary armies must pass in order to defend the revolution's gains and prosecute revolutionary war.[5] Chorley argues that a revolutionary armed force inevitably becomes professionalized and loses its revolutionary zeal and ideological character. This is essentially an adaptation of Weber's concept of the routinization of charisma, in which the ideological zeal of an institution is dampened as the institution develops and becomes increasingly regularized and bureaucratized.[6] Others argue that the interests of the organization, although instrumental in perpetuating ideology, ultimately take precedence over ideology when ideological purity and organizational interests conflict.[7] It will be shown that the Revolutionary Guard, to some extent, refutes these latter assertions.

Whether or not one accepts Huntington's argument that the outstripping of institutionalization by mobilization leads to political breakdown, it can certainly be argued that the durability of the Iranian revolution has lain, in part, in its ability to create revolutionary institutions to absorb the many social forces that contributed to the overthrow of the Shah. Despite Ayatollah Khomeini's unquestioned personal authority, the regime undoubtedly would have been unable to handle the many challenges it has faced had it not established an institutional base. These challenges included rebellion by several ethnic groups, insurrection by a major urban guerrilla opposition group, bombings in Tehran that resulted in the death of several major leaders in 1981, and a major invasion by Iraq. To demonstrate this, the several other institutions produced by the revolution and their roles in strengthening the Islamic revolution must also be discussed.

By being able to organize, incorporate, and provide a channel for participation for the revolution's newly mobilized social forces, the Revolutionary Guard played a crucial role in defeating the above mentioned, as well as many other, severe threats to the revolution's very survival. Primarily, the Revolutionary Guard provided the hardline, pro-Khomeini nonclerics, many of whom had battled the Shah's regime as urban guerrillas in major cities, with an avenue for participation in the regime.[8] It can be argued that without the Revolutionary Guard to absorb these non-clerical elements, the Islamic revolution might otherwise have been seen, to a greater degree than it was, as a seizure of power by Iran's clerics. Had such a perception taken hold, the clerics might well have been left defenseless in the face of significant armed challenges and the revolution might have been very short-lived. It can be demonstrated, therefore, that the Guard was able to absorb Iran's newly mobilized social forces, especially those elements that were motivated by the revolution's ideology.

Political Resiliency

The first criteria of an institution's strength is that it is adaptable, or resilient, rather than rigid.[9] The resiliency of an organization refers to its ability to survive challenges or adverse changes in its environment. The

Guard's resiliency is demonstrated in its ability to incorporate not only revolutionary social forces but also social groups which do not necessarily share the Guard's revolutionary ethos. Its role in rallying the armed non-clerical militants to the defense of the clerical leaders was touched on briefly above. However, like other revolutionary armies that were forced to engage anti-revolutionary foreign powers, the Guard had to assimilate groups, such as conscripts, that did not identify with the Guard's zealous ideology or its battlefield strategy and tactics. The Guard needed these non-ideological groups, however, to provide manpower and skills for successful prosecution of the war.[10]

The Guard also provided an opportunity for advancement for ambitious youths who were less hardline than the typical rank and file Guard volunteer but viewed the Guard as a vehicle for upward mobility. The Guard's ability to resist dilution of its ideological commitment while incorporating these elements is a key indicator of its strength as an institution. As Chorley argues after examining several revolutionary armies, the development of a unified, disciplined structure that enables revolutionary armed forces to prosecute a revolutionary war also militates against revolutionary zeal and ideological commitment.[11] This is analagous to Weber's argument that, as modernization proceeds, charisma becomes routinized and dampened by bureaucratic patterns of organization.[12] The case of the Revolutionary Guard refutes these arguments to some extent.

Related to the Guard's ability to absorb less ideologically motivated elements was the ease with which it accommodated commanders and troops from different social backgrounds and recruitment networks into the core of the organization. The original organizers of the Revolutionary Guard, such as Abbas Zamani (better known by his nom de guerre Abu Sharif) were urban anti-Shah guerrillas, many of whom had trained in Lebanon with the PLO.[13] The core of the Guard then took on new elements from the private militias put together by the many revolutionary clerics from their mosque congregations.[14] About a year after its official inauguration the Guard took control of and responsibility for the *Basij Mustazafin*, or Mobilization of the Oppressed.[15] In general, the Basij was composed of very young and relatively old volunteers from the countryside and small towns, and were less well-educated than the somewhat more cosmopolitan core of the Revolutionary Guard.[16] The varied social composition of the Guard, aside from demonstrating the Guard's institutional flexibility, was nevertheless a key constraint in the running of the war.

A comparison of the history of the regular military and its role under the Shah and his father, Reza Shah (creator of the Iranian army), with the formation and role of the Revolutionary Guard, shows why the Revolutionary Guard emerged as a far stronger and important institution than the regular military. Although the regular military, to its credit, was flexible enough to survive the revolution and emerge as a separate institution despite many calls for it to be dismantled completely,[17] other prerevolutionary armies have carved out greater roles for themselves in their respective revolutionary armed forces' structures. For example, in contrast to the Iranian regular military, the officer corps and many units of the prerevolutionary French and Czarist armies were indispensable to the formation of unified and effective revolutionary armies in France and the former Soviet Union, respectively.[18] The Iranian regular armed forces also lost much of their prerevolutionary clout as an interest group in the regime and suffered repeated purges.[19]

The Guard's ability to make the transition to new missions is another indicator of its strength. Initially only an internal security militia, the Guard was able to later organize itself into military force to fight the war against Iraq. Moreover, once it had become a military force, the Revolutionary Guard was able to make some temporary pragmatic adjustments in its tactics in order to further its overall ideological goals. The Guard was able to modify its strategy and tactics for prosecuting the war according to such factors as tactical and strategic adjustments by the adversary, Iraq; infighting over war strategy among senior Iranian political leaders; and the US buildup in the Gulf in 1987. However, it will be argued that during the Iran-Iraq war and following the 1991 Persian Gulf war, the Guard tried to accomplish its overriding revolutionary objective—to answer Khomeini's call for the defeat of Iraq and the overthrow of Iraqi President Saddam Husayn.

The Guard also proved itself adept at parrying the several political challenges it faced during its existence thus far, especially during its early years. The Guard's resiliency is shown in its political struggles with the Islamic Republic's first Prime Minister Mehdi Bazargan, its first President Abol Hassan Bani-Sadr, and with senior political leaders immediately following the battlefield catastrophes that led to the end of the war with Iraq will be analyzed.[20] There are numerous examples in which the Guard teamed up with its political allies—or even acted alone—to undermine those political leaders whom the Guard leaders viewed as compromising the goals of the Islamic revolution. Perhaps the most critical test of the Guard's institutional flexibility was how it adjusted to the ending of the Iran-Iraq war and retained its importance even though its main mission, the defeat of Iraq, had ended.

Bureaucratization of Revolution

Another criteria for demonstrating institutionalization is complexity.[21] The multiplication and differentiation of organizational subunits and the diversity of the organization's functions indicate greater institutionalization. To a great degree, its acquisition of a progressively more complex organizational structure is an indicator of the Guard's institutional strength within Iran. Its ability to develop a complex and structured organization without sacrificing its revolutionary character distinguishes it from other revolutionary armed forces that similarly developed regular military structures and functions but sacrificed revolutionary zeal and enthusiasm.

It is instructive to compare the Guard with other Iranian revolutionary institutions, most notably the revolutionary committees (Komitehs) that, like the Guard, play a role in internal security. Not only did the Guard, unlike the Komitehs, assume a major military function, but the Guard also gained a measure of authority over the Komitehs even in internal security matters.[22] The Guard also came to play a greater role in export of the revolution than any other revolutionary institution that was involved in such activity, including the Islamic Propagation Organization and Ministry of Islamic Guidance, and it played a greater role in socializing Iran's youth into the ideology of the revolution than other Iranian revolutionary institutions.[23] It has been argued that adult socialization factors such as the workplace and private associations have been shown to be more effective than agents of childhood socialization, such as the schools and the family.[24] However, the process of socialization is enhanced somewhat when the regime's organs of indoctrination have access to the nation's youth and can supplement childhood socialization forces. The Guard, through its control of the young Basij, was uniquely placed within the regime to contribute to the socialization process. Accounts of the training the Guard provided to the Basij recruits support this argument.

Similarly, the Guard has played a role in enforcing adherence to Islamic practice among the population,[25] although this function is as much associated with the Guard's internal security mission as it is with its political socialization responsibilities. The Guard's Islamic morals police duty is a factor which helps distinguish the Guard from other revolutionary armed forces, which are often hesitant to perform internal policing functions.[26]

The Guard's functional diversity is greater than that of other revolutionary armed forces. A considerable body of evidence shows that the Revolutionary Guard plays a greater role in internal security and export of the revolution than that played by the Soviet Red Army or the Chinese People's Liberation Army.[27] Many of these roles the Revolutionary Guard plays in the Islamic Republic's power structure have been, in the Chinese and Soviet cases, played by separate secret police organizations and the Communist Party apparatus. In addition, the Guard performs an important role in mobilizing popular demonstrations of support for hardline government policies.[28] This function has generally been performed by the Communist Party apparatus in both China and the Soviet Union. Comparisons can also be made to the armed forces and volunteer popular militias (armees revolutionnaires) of the French Revolution.

The case for functional diversity of the Guard will also be supported by establishing the Guard's role, however, in the economy.[29] The analysis of the Guard's economic role, in turn, hinges on the degree of authority the Guard was able to wield over yet another revolutionary institution, the Construction Jihad (Jihad Sazendaghi), which was instrumental in implementing government economic policy, particularly in rural areas.[30]

Besides functional diversity, organizational complexity can also be demonstrated by the proliferation of the Revolutionary Guard's organizational subunits. It is especially useful to compare the Guard to other revolutionary institutions in Iran, in that these organizations developed within the same time period as the Guard. The Revolutionary Guard was initially an amorphous conglomeration of local, independent groupings of urban guerrillas, clerical militias, army defectors, and other pro-Khomeini militants that helped solidify the streets for Khomeini following the victory of the revolution.[31] It therefore initially had no formal command structure. However, the Guard leaders were able to clearly define and differentiate their individual roles and, on many issues, authority within the Guard command structure depended on position and not individual personalities. The Guard also developed its unit structure—corps, division, and brigades—along the lines of a conventional force, albeit with modifications, when it expanded its role into military operations following the Iraqi invasion.[32] A significant development along this line was its formation of separate air and naval services in 1985.[33] Moreover, the Guard developed a formal recruitment and training structure for frontline soldiers as well as agents of the Islamic revolution that attempted to spread revolution throughout the Arab world by all methods, including violence.[34]

The Guard also had to develop a logistical infrastructure to support its troops. It built a procurement organization separate from that of the regular military and even a defense industries capability to cope with the international weapons embargo against Iran.[35] An important indicator of the Guard's organizational differentiation and maturation is the increasing sophistication of the weaponry the Guard claimed to be producing indigenously. These support functions were overseen by one of the best examples of the Guard's organizational development—the Revolutionary Guard Ministry—which was formed in 1982 and was separate from the regular military's Defense Ministry.[36] The Guard also created specialized units to handle more sophisticated weaponry, such as armor, air defense systems, missiles and other systems, an indicator of increasing institutional complexity.[37] It is widely known that the Guard began the Iran-Iraq war with only light arms.

Integrated but Independent

Another criterium by which to analyze the growth of the Revolutionary Guard as an institution is its autonomy. Autonomy is measured by the extent to which the institution has and can protect its own values and interests that are distinguishable from those of other institutions and social forces.[38] Increasingly, the Revolutionary Guard's power as an organization became dependent on its intrinsic structure and procedures, rather than on the continued incumbency of any one particular Guard leader or group of leaders.

The Guard's first two and a half years until the appointment of Mohsen Reza'i in September 1981 were characterized by a rapid turnover in the leadership—one commander was tentatively appointed only to withdraw himself within days—yet the Guard continued to develop as an organization.[39] After 1981, the Guard experienced relatively stable leadership with one exception—the removal of Minister of the Revolutionary Guard Mohsen Rafiq-Dust in 1988.[40] Rafiq-Dust's removal did not lead to an immediate, significant decline in the capabilities or functional scope of the Guard as a whole nor even the Ministry which he built and led since its establishment in 1982. He was quickly replaced by longtime Guard stalwart and deputy Guard commander Ali Shamkhani. The Ministry as a whole, however, was damaged by allegations of corruption in weapons procurement during the war, which ultimately led the post-Khomeini Majles to approve a merger with the regular military's Defense Ministry into a new Ministry of Defense and Armed Forces Logistics.[41]

The strength of the Guard as a revolutionary institution stands in contrast to other Iranian revolutionary organizations that collapsed or were seriously weakened by leadership failure, turmoil, or change. For example, the concept of velayat-e-faqih (rule by a supreme Islamic jurisprudent), which was intended to serve as a permanent revolutionary institution, is a far less powerful institution since Khomeini died. Another comparison will be drawn from the dissolution of the Islamic Republican Party which, it will be argued, suffered from the temporary political weakness of its chairman, former President (now supreme leader) Ali Khamene'i.[42]

Further evidence of the Guard's autonomy is that the Guard was not dominated by a particular family, tribe, ethnic, or regional grouping within Iran. Being free of such subordination allows the institution to develop procedures and issue positions based on the interests of that institution, rather than on the interests of the group that controls the organization. In this respect, it is useful to compare the Revolutionary Guard to other armies in the Middle East, such as those of Iraq and Syria, that tend to be dominated by families and sectarian groupings of the leaders of those countries.[43]

The Guard's autonomy is also exhibited by its role in regime decision-making. This is not necessarily to say that the more the Guard acted on its own, or even in defiance of civilian authority, the stronger it is in comparison to other revolutionary institutions. However, the Guard managed its own internal affairs and its interests had to be taken into account in formulating regime policy. The Guard also often sought to advance its own organizational interests even when those interests may have conflicted with the general welfare of the regime or society as a whole. Establishing the Guard's strength as an interest group is complicated by the fact that Khomeini defined the revolution's interests and that no senior politician ever publicly contradicted Khomeini once he had set policy. Therefore, the only way to explore the Guard's role as an interest group is to analyze case studies of regime decisions in which there was a difference of opinion between the Guard and senior political leaders in decisions in which Khomeini did not express a strong policy preference. Such examples are drawn from accounts of policy debates in the leadership and within the Supreme Defense Council, Iran's highest military decisionmaking body during the war.[44]

Any discussion of the Guard as an interest group in revolutionary regime politics naturally leads to a discussion of the Guard's role in regime factional infighting. Particularly relevant are the specific examples in which the Guard may have formed policy alliances with certain regime leaders and acted contrary to the wishes of or with the intention of politically subverting more moderate regime leaders.[45] Such analysis will also be crucial to establishing the Guard as the principal organizational bastion, protector, and implementer of the ideals of the Islamic revolution, as defined by the charismatic leader, Khomeini. The Guard's role in factional infighting and degree of political subordination can also be compared to that of other revolutionary armed forces in history, and to Iran's regular armed forces. Absent from the Iranian political system, much to the benefit of Revolutionary Guard autonomy, is the highly disciplined, structured, and institutionalized civilian political party organizations characteristic of the former Soviet and the Chinese Communist parties. Indeed, it will be shown that the Soviet Army and the PLA generally sought to abstain from political involvement and clearly recognized the primacy of the Communist Party in determining the direction of the revolution and preserving revolutionary ideology.[46] Although still young compared to both the PLA and Soviet Army, the Revolutionary Guard views involvement in politics as not only permitted but as a necessary part of its mission to defend the purity of the Islamic revolution.[47] To this extent, it can be argued that the Revolutionary Guard has played a greater role in internalizing and perpetuating the ideology of the leader of the Islamic revolution than either the Soviet Red Army or Chinese PLA did for Lenin and Mao, the leaders of the Russian and Chinese Communist revolutions, respectively.

Another basis for comparison is the degree to which the Guard is penetrated by the civilian authorities. The involvement of political commissars in the Soviet Red Army and Chinese PLA has been widely discussed,[48] and can be compared with the imposition of clerical political officers into the Guard organizational structure to perform a similar commissary function.[49] However, clerical penetration of the Guard has been far less comprehensive or authoritative than that of the Communist parties of China or the former Soviet Union. The relative freedom from organized political control makes the Guard no more or less an institution than either the Soviet Army or the PLA. However, the Guard's successful resistance to civilian penetration does indicate that the Guard's potential for exercising its armed force outside of civilian political authority is that much greater, and thus poses a potential threat to Ayatollah Khomeini's successors if these political leaders break sharply with the late Ayatollah Khomeini's ideals.

An additional means for demonstrating the institutional strength of the Guard is to assess its ability to place its members or achieve appointment of its close allies to high government positions. The Guard's ability to resist the appointment of antagonists to Guard leadership positions argues for the Guard's strength, and it will be shown that top Guard personnel assignments remained firmly under control of the Guard itself. There is also a considerable body of data that illustrates that Guardsmen and members of organizations that work closely with the Guard have indeed achieved influential positions in the government structure and the Majles.[50] In addition, to contrast the Guard with the institution closest to its own command structure, the regular military, there are instances in which the Guard was responsible for the removal of certain regular army commanders from their command positions.[51] It can be shown, correspondingly, that pressure from the regular armed forces was at no time a factor in determining personnel shifts in the Guard.

Another factor indicating that the Guard developed into an autonomous and not a subordinate organization is its provision of an avenue for advancement within its own ranks, even below the top command level. The alternative in a subordinate organization would be that another institution, such as an organized political party, would be responsible for determining promotions or vetting candidates for key positions. Throughout most of the history of the Soviet Army and the PLA these functions have been performed by the Communist Party and/or security services.[52] In Iran, there no longer is an organized ruling party, there is no evidence that the one that existed until 1987 (the Islamic Republican Party, or IRP) was ever organized or powerful enough to have played such a role, and the Revolutionary Guard is itself the most powerful security service in the country. Moreover, the Guard itself controlled its own personnel assignments at virtually all levels of the command structure.[53]

Holding Together

Another measure of the strength of an institution is organizational coherence. In many ways, and although they represent different trends in political theory, Huntington's coherence as a measure of institutionalization corresponds to Weber's observation that political authority building involves the progressive centralization of military power from private armies to a national armed force.[54] Both of them would agree that, for rational authority to exist, rules and procedures that are set down for one segment of the organization—in this case a military force—must apply to all parts. A corollary is that orders from the top leadership of the organization must be transmitted and implemented faithfully because the organizational leadership is viewed as legitimate, even if an organizational level or department does not agree with each individual decision or command.

The concept of coherence is particularly relevant to the study of the Revolutionary Guard because of its widely cited factionalism.[55] This factionalism can assume many forms—political, ideological, personal, and organizational. It is understandable that extensive factionalism is still attributed to the Guard since Guard factionalism was prominent, widely reported, and easy to measure when the Guard was first formed. At least one early Guard commander blamed factionalism as a major part of his decision to resign.[56] Yet another opted not to accept an appointment as commander in part because, in his view, factionalism made the Guard essentially uncontrollable from above.[57]

Not only was the Revolutionary Guard's early factionalism observable, it was also explainable. The Revolutionary Guard was formed from the bottom up, not the top down. Unlike the Soviet Red Army and the French revolutionary army, the Guard was not formed with extensive participation of officers and units from the prerevolutionary monarchical army; it was created almost totally from revolutionary elements.[58] Even the Chinese People's Liberation Army, although it did not contain prerevolutionary components, was not, as the Guard was, formed essentially spontaneously. The PLA, which began to take shape after the Communist Party altered its revolutionary strategy from urban insurrection to guerrilla warfare in the 1930s, had a well defined organizational and command structure when the Communists formally assumed control of the mainland government in 1949.[59] The Guard, therefore, unlike other revolution-

ary armed forces, did not have the structure of a prerevolutionary or conventional army to provide organization and coherence from the beginning. These other revolutionary armed forces quickly assumed a regular
structure and organization even though they, at first, shunned such regularization as a contradiction of their initial revolutionary charisma, fervor,
and enthusiasm.[60]

Guard factionalism has progressively decreased, even if it has not disappeared since the revolution. The Guard not only is far less factionalized
than it was in its early years but it is less factionalized than the senior
regime leadership.[61] The evidence for this is that the Guard itself is
relatively cohesive in its commitment to radical ideology and policies and
that it now acts as a unit with a well defined chain of command. This is
in notable contrast to the conflicting policy directions and actions of
elements within the senior leadership.[62]

Guard factionalism at the rank and file level is difficult to approach
because it is less easy to observe than the senior command. Actions undertaken by various Guard units in contradiction to the pronouncements of
senior political leaders below Khomeini cannot be taken as conclusive
evidence of Guard factionalism. This is because the senior Guard leadership itself often obliquely criticized, disagreed with,[63] or acted contrary to
the wishes of senior political leaders below Khomeini and have used their
command of individual units to subvert distasteful government policies.[64]
However, we can point to actions undertaken by lower level Guard units
that were deliberately contrary to the statements or policies of the senior
Guard leadership as evidence of factionalism. Aside from citing instances
in which senior Guard leaders' orders were deliberately disobeyed, a useful means of demonstrating rank and file factionalism is to analyze Guard
actions following the dismissal of senior regime actors. An example is the
fall of designated Khomeini successor Ayatollah Montazeri in March
1989.[65] Such analysis would indicate whether or not personalistic factions
still exist in the Guard.

Since factionalism can also be ideologically based, it is possible to observe rank and file Guard reaction to perceived ideological shifts in overall Guard policy. An indicator of this type of factionalism would be unrest
in the Guard triggered by Guard policy deviations. An example of such a
policy deviation would be the U.S.-Iran arms dealings in 1985-6, in that
accepting weapons from the U.S. was clearly contrary to the often stated
and demonstrated hostility toward the U.S. that characterized all levels of
the Guard. Regional factionalism is difficult to distinguish from personalistic factionalism inspired by prominent clerics, many of whom wield particular influence in their home provinces. Nonetheless, if individual
Guard units can be shown to profess loyalty to local commanders at the
expense of the national Guard leadership, this will be taken as evidence

for the continued existence of local factionalism. This type of factionalism was a prominently mentioned complaint of the early Guard commanders who were trying to impose organizational structure on the initially chaotic Guard.[66]

Factionalism, although an important variable, does not exhaust the possible measurements of organizational coherence. In an organization such as the Revolutionary Guard, discipline and professionalism are crucial factors determining the Guard's ability to act as a unit. There is an analytical problem, however, in that it is difficult to separate indiscipline from factionalism. The only relatively reliable method for making this distinction is to examine press statements of Guard and senior political leaders. These leaders have made several pronouncements on the need to improve Guard discipline.[67] Since press statements from Tehran have often referred to factionalism as "discord,"[68] we can therefore take public references to Guard indiscipline at face value and, with reasonable certainty, infer that these statements are not, in fact, referring to Guard factionalism. The issue of Revolutionary Guard discipline and professionalization is ultimately inseparable from the more general understanding of its zeal, morale, religious and revolutionary commitment, and role as implementer and enforcers of the Islamic revolution as defined by Ayatollah Khomeini. It also is integral to any comparison of the Guard with other revolutionary armies.

Much of the literature on civil-military relations argues that there is a tradeoff between professionalization and political involvement.[69] Janowitz, however, raises the possibility that a more professional military has greater capabilities than an ill disciplined force, thus giving professional officers the confidence and resources to intervene successfully.[70] In general, however, there is somewhat more evidence to support those who argue that professional armed forces are likely to be generally conservative forces loyal primarily to the nation, willing to intervene in politics only when asked to do so by civilian leaders. According to several observers, these arguments apply even to the revolutionary armed forces of Communist regimes, even the PLA which, like the Guard, was not formed from the structure of the prerevolutionary army.[71] These forces are also considered reluctant to engage in internal security duties that are likely to make them unpopular.[72]

The Guard has clearly shown no such restraint or commitment to professionalization. It has clearly chosen to preserve its political role at the expense of the military effectiveness and efficiency that accompanies professionalization, even if it recently has instituted formal ranks and expressed its interest in procuring sophisticated weaponry. The Guard has not only intervened in politics willingly, but even when civilian leaders, sometimes including Khomeini, opposed such interference.[73] It has not yet become a conservative force—it still clearly identifies with the radical line in the Islamic regime. It considers itself loyal primarily to the Islamic revolution, which, according to Khomeini, should spread beyond the borders of the Iranian nation. Lastly, the Guard has welcomed, not opposed, its internal security role that it sees as legitimizing its function of preserving a purely Islamic society and combatting the regime's internal adversaries.[74]

Even in its purely military role, the Guard has generally placed revolutionary purity ahead of military tactical efficacy and rationality. The tactics the Guard and Basij used in the Iran-Iraq war, such as "human wave" offensives, were militarily unsound as practiced but fulfilled the Islamic forces' commitment to martyrdom in the service of Islam.[75] Moreover, the tenacity with which the Guard prosecuted the war even after it became clear that the war was essentially unwinnable—in clear contrast to conventional strategy of professional armed forces—relates to its commitment to answering Khomeini's call for the defeat of Iraq.

The experience of the Guard in war shows that there need not be a direct tradeoff between revolutionary fervor and military effectiveness, although the argument that revolutionary fervor increases effectiveness does not necessarily hold true for the Guard either.[76] Despite its clear commitment to remaining the guardian of revolutionary purity, the Guard did develop sufficient unity, cohesiveness, complexity, and structure to prosecute a long, full scale war against an adversary that had significant advantages in sophisticated weaponry and training. Moreover, the Guard did not need to be replaced by or incorporated into a unified, professional army that could prosecute revolutionary war.[77] The Guard made itself sufficiently structured and cohesive to bear the brunt of the fighting in the long all-out revolutionary war against Iraq. It sacrificed professionalism and efficiency in exchange for preserving its role as the zealous guardian of the ideology of the Islamic revolution. In doing so, and thereby limiting its cooperation with the regular army, the Guard ultimately bears much of the responsibility for the major defeats in 1988 which cost Iran the war.

Notes

1. The framework for the analysis is derived from Samuel Huntington. See Samuel P. Huntington, *Political Order in Changing Societies.* (New Haven and London: Yale University Press, 1968). Chapter One.
2. See especially Morris Janowitz, *The Military in the Political Development of New Nations* (Chicago: University of Chicago Press, 1964); John Johnson, *The Role of the Military in Underdeveloped Countries* (Princeton:

Princeton University Press, 1962); and Lucien Pye, *Aspects of Political Development* (Boston: Little, Brown, and Co., 1966)

3. John Ellis, *Armies in Revolution* (London: Croon Helm LTD., 1973)

4. Jonathan Adelman, *Revolution, Armies, and War: A Political History* (Boulder, Co.: Lynne Rienner Publishers, Inc., 1985

5. Katharine Chorley, *Armies and the Art of Revolution* (Boston: Beacon Press, 1973) Chaps. 11, 12

6. H.H. Gerth and C. Wright Mills, *From Max Weber: Essays in Sociology* (New York: Oxford University Press, 1946)

7. Samuel H. Barnes, "Ideology and the Organization of Conflict: On the Relationship Between Political Thought and Behavior" in *The Journal of Politics* Vol. 28, No. 3, 1966

8. Sepehr Zabih, *The Iranian Military in Revolution and War* (London: Routledge, 1988) P. 217

9. Huntington, op.cit.

10. Shahram Chubin and Charles Tripp, *Iran and Iraq at War* (Boulder, Co: Westview Press, 1988)

11. Chorley, op.cit.

12. Gerth and Mills, op. cit.

13. "Who's Who in Iran," Tehran: Echo Publications, January 13, 1980) P.20

14. Zabih, op.cit.

15. Schahgaldian, op.cit.

16. Ibid., pp.90-91

17. Nader Entessar, "The Military and Politics in the Islamic Republic of Iran" in Hooshang Amirahmadi and Manoucher Parvin eds., *Post Revolutionary Iran* (Boulder and London: Westview Press, 1988) P.62

18. Ellis, op.cit.

19. Entessar, op.cit. pp. 62-65

20. Shaul Bakhash, *The Reign of the Ayatollahs* (New York: Basic Books, Inc., 1984) Chaps. 5, 6; "Iran Guards Leaders Slain in Violent Purge," Washington Times; March 23, 1989; P. A7

21. Huntington, op.cit.

22. "Reza'i Wins Battle for Control of Guards," London, Iran Press Service; May 12, 1983 in JPRS 83763, June 24, 1983; pp. 6-7

23. Schahgaldian, op.cit., pp.87-98

24. Gabriel Almond and Sidney Verba, *The Civic Culture* (Princeton, New Jersey: Princeton University Press, 1963) Chap. 12

25. Ronald Perron, "The Iranian Islamic Revolutionary Guard Corps" in *Middle East Insight* (June-July 1985) P. 37

26. Jonathan Adelman ed., *Communist Armies in Politics* (Boulder, Co.: Westview Press, 1982)

27. Ibid; and Roman Kolkowicz and Andrzej Korbonski eds., *Soldiers,*

Peasants, and Bureaucrats (London: George Allen and Unwin Ltd., 1982) Chaps. 5,6

28. Schahgaldian, op.cit.
29. Ibid P. 75
30. "Iran's Military Chief Says War Could Resume," Reuters; December 6, 1988
31. Schahgaldian, op.cit.
32. Entessar, op.cit. P. 66
33. Ibid
34. Robin Wright, *Sacred Rage: The Wrath of Militant Islam* (New York: Simon and Schuster, 1985, 86) pp. 33-35
35. Anoushiravan Ehteshami, "Iran's Domestic Arms Industry" in Echo of Iran 16; February 23, 1989 pp. 20-24
36. "Interview with IRGC Minister Mohsen Rafiqdoost," Iran Press Digest; November 20, 1984, pp.14-17
37. Press excerpts from Jomhuri Islam in Akhbar Vol. IX, No.141 September 17, 1988, Take 6
38. Huntington, op.cit.
39. "Mission, Record of Revolution Guard Corps Reviewed," Iran Press Digest in English; June 15, 1982 in JPRS - 81258; July 12, 1982 pp. 38-39
40. "New IRGC Officials Appointed," Tehran IRNA in English; February 1, 1989
41. Ibid
42. Robin Wright "Wily Speaker Excels at Iran's Political Game," The Christian Science Monitor; August 27, 1987, P.1
43. Christine Helms, *Iraq: Eastern Flank of the Arab World* (Washington, D.C.: Brookings Institution, 1984); Martha Kessler, *Syria: Fragile Mosaic of Power* (Washington, D.C.: National Defense University, 1988)
44. "Tehran Attempts to Balance Guards' Zeal, Dangers of War," Washington Post, August 23, 1987. p. A1
45. "Iran's Armed Forces, the Battle Within," Christian Science Monitor; August 26, 1987. p. 1
46. Kolkowicz and Korbonski, eds., op.cit
47. Entessar, op.cit. p. 66
48. Timothy Colton, *Commissars, Commanders and Civilian Authority: The Structure of Soviet Military Politics* (Cambridge, Mass. and London: Harvard University Press, 1979); Jonathan Adelman, 1982, op.cit.
49. "History and Present Status of IRGC," Iran Press Digest; August 7, 1984, p.15
50. "Who's Who in Iran," op.cit.
51. "On Changes in Military Command" Iran Press Digest Special Review; August 12, 1986, P.2
52. Jonathan Adelman, 1982, op.cit.

53. "New IRGC Officials Appointed," op.cit.
54. Gerth and Mills, op.cit., P. 49
55. "Iran Guard Leaders Slain in Violent Purge, " op.cit.
56. "Commander of Iranian Guards Resigns," Washington Post; June 18, 1980
57. "Interview with Kazem Musavi-Bojnurdi," in Jomhuri Eslam, reprinted in The Flame; July 1, 1980
58. Zabih, op.cit.
59. Ellis, op.cit.
60. Chorley, op.cit. Chaps. 11,12
61. "Tehran Attempts to Balance Guards Zeal, Dangers of War," op.cit.
62. "Signs of Split Seen in Iran's Counterattack on US Navy," Christian Science Monitor; April 21, 1988, P.7
63. "The Present Position of the Revolutionary Guards," Tehran, Echo of Iran; October 18, 1988
64. "Killings in Austria, Emirates Laid to Iran," Washington Post; August 3, 1989, P.A1
65. Safa Haeri, "Arrests and Executions in Purge by Khomeini," The London Sunday Times; April 16, 1989, P.21
66. "Interview with Kazem Bojnurdi," op.cit.
67. "Hashemi-Rafsanjani, Others on IRGC Post-War Role," Tehran Television Service in Persian; September 15, 1988
68. "Ex-Majlis Deputy Released From Prison," Tehran Islamic Republic News Agency in English; February 28, 1989
69. Samuel P. Huntington, *The Soldier and the State* (Cambridge, Mass.: Harvard University Press, 1959); David Rappoport, "The Praetorian Army," in Kolkowicz and Korbonski, op.cit.; Morris Janowitz, op.cit.
70. Janowitz, op.cit. pp. 35-37
71. Amos Perlmutter, "Civil Military Relations in Socialist Authoritarian and Praetorian States: Prospects and Retrospects," in Kolkowicz and Korbonski, op.cit.; Timothy Colton, op.cit. P.286
72. Janowitz, op.cit. P.37
73. "Iran Guard Leaders Slain in Violent Purge," op.cit.
74. Ronald Perron, op.cit.
75. "Iran's Armed Forces, the Battle Within," op.cit.
76. Adelman, 1985, op.cit.
77. Such a transition is envisioned in Chorley's third stage in the development of a revolutionary armed force. See: Chorley, op.cit. Chaps. 11,12

2

The Political Environment

Part of the task of demonstrating the Guard's unique strength as an institution in Iran and as a revolutionary armed force involves comparing the Guard's formation and early growth with other institutions produced by the revolution and with its principal institutional competitor, the regular armed forces. Particular emphasis needs to be placed on comparing the regular military's history to that of the Revolutionary Guard. As for the regular military, the factors that need to be analyzed are its historical roots; the reasons for its weaknesses; and an explanation of its apparent rapid collapse in the face of the revolution, despite its training, organization, discipline, and armaments. These factors will be compared with the Revolutionary Guard's origins in the revolution, its rapid emergence as a powerful interest group in the regime, its social composition, the sources of its ideology, and its linkages to other revolutionary groups and organizations. Comparing the two armed forces—revolutionary and pre-revolutionary—helps place in relief the unique features of the Revolutionary Guard as an armed force.

A comparison of the Guard with other revolutionary institutions in Iran also shows that the Guard, more than any other institution in revolutionary Iran, has been the principal bastion and perpetuator of revolutionary purity. This can be accomplished by comparing the Guard's role in consolidating and defending the revolution to that of other institutions. Other institutions failed, became powerless or irrelevant, or, in some cases even became subordinate to the Revolutionary Guard itself. Moreover, placing the Guard within a more general institutional context will facilitate an understanding of its position in the overall Islamic republican political structure and its incorporation into the governing style of the clerical leadership.

The Regular Armed Forces

The regular armed forces of Iran, the roots of which can be traced, albeit tenously, to Cyrus the Great (6th century B.C.),[1] was an excellent

.come institutionalized by the
flaw was that, under the Shah,
ous organization. Donald Vought
. that the Iranian army was consid-
.n power and that its "loyalty [was]
.tution," and that "institutionally, per-
.velopment of institutional loyalty and
.at is, the Shah's army, not the nation's

.slamic revolution, in which the army virtu-
. mass popular uprising, Kazemi pointed out
. of the military, his attempts to cement military
loya.,   rewards, and his policy of dividing security re-
sponsibi..   .mpeting organizations did not ensure commitment to the S..   .ime throughout the junior ranks.[3] Entessar argues
that the Iranian arm, was viewed as an illegitimate tool of U.S. interests in
Iran and that the Shah's tactic of forbidding private communication
among senior commanders (ostensibly to prevent any coup plotting) paradoxically contributed to the inability of the commanders to cooperate to
save the throne from the revolution in early 1979.[4]

In addition to lack of autonomy, therefore, coherence and organizational adaptability, as well as legitimacy, were clearly lacking in the Shah's
army; these weaknesses largely explain why the regular military collapsed even though the very existence of the organization and the physi-
cal survival of many of its members were at stake. The regular military
was a weak institution despite its advanced chronological age, a factor
which usually suggests substantial institutionalization. The Iranian army
can be loosely traced to Cyrus the Great and through periods of dissolution and subsequent recentralization under the Sassanians, the Safavids
(especially Abbas the Great), Shah Nadir Quli Afshar (Nadir Shah), the
Qajars, and finally the Pahlavi dynasty.[5]

Contributing to the end of Qajar rule early in this century was the complete unraveling of the dynasty's already relatively weak national army
into tribal and provincial components, leaving three separate major
forces, each of which was under the control of a different European power.[6]
These three forces were: the Swedish-controlled gendarmerie, established
in 1911; the South Persian Rifles, which dominated southern Iran for the
British from 1916; and the Persian Cossack Brigade, created by the Rus-
sians in 1879 during the reign of the Qajar monarch Nasr ad-Din Shah.

Tensions between Britain and Russia in the wake of the 1917 Bolshevik
revolution led the British to seek greater influence in Iran. Britain dis-
placed Russia as patrons of the Cossack Brigade and encouraged the overthrow of the Qajar dynasty in 1921 by the pro-British Sayyid Zia ad-Din

Tabataba'i.[7] However, the real power behind the coup and, subsequently, the government, was a Cossack Brigade officer Reza Pahlavi, who became War Minister under Tabataba'i, Prime Minister in 1923, and ultimately the first Pahlavi monarch in 1925, Reza Shah.

After his emergence as leader of Iran, Reza Shah succeeded in centralizing political authority, in large part by disbanding local and subnational armed units in favor of a new national army, which he used to crush all local resistance. He forged and modernized this force by standardizing its equipment, forming a General Staff that issued written orders, establishing staff colleges, sending promising young officers to France, Germany, and Russia for training, and making military service compulsory.[8] Reza Shah also established an air force and a navy. First and foremost, Reza Shah was a nationalist, and his efforts to centralize authority in Iran and build up the national army were not only to consolidate his own position as monarch, but to make Iran less vulnerable to manipulation by foreign powers. Still, he was unable to resist the Allied invasion of Iran in 1941, which led to his abdication in favor of his son Mohammad Reza.[9]

Developments in the postwar period made the new Shah highly reliant on the army to maintain his grip on power. Shortly after the Soviet withdrawal from Iranian Azerbaijan and Kurdistan in 1946, he sent in the armed forces to reclaim those provinces from their pro-Soviet puppet regimes. In the early 1950s, the Shah found himself in a power struggle with the popular nationalist Prime Minister Dr. Mohammed Mosadeq; only a U.S.-backed coup by pro-Shah military officers saved the Shah's throne. He had briefly fled the country in August 1953 when his initial bid to oust Mosadeq by force failed.[10] Following his restoration, the Shah, in 1954, had to root out a serious infiltration of the military by the pro-Soviet Communist Tudeh Party, which found fertile ground for recruitment among the younger, middle class, lower-ranking military officers.[11] Then, in 1963 the Shah was faced with mass rioting led by a coalition of nationalists and clerics protesting the Shah's land reform program and his granting of extra-territorial rights to U.S. military personnel. The uprising, which was crushed by the military, witnessed the rise to prominence of Ayatollah Ruhollah Khomeini, then a teacher in a major Islamic seminary in Qom; Khomeini was subsequently exiled to Iraq.[12] Although some groups in the Islamic revolutionary coalition can be traced to pro-Mosadeq elements, the 1963 uprising represented the beginning of the Islamic revolution that would lead to the Shah's downfall fifteen years later.

Ever more dependent on the armed forces to maintain his rule, the Shah continually expanded its size and materiel resources. This buildup coincided with and was supported by U.S. efforts to bolster the Shah as a protector of U.S. interests in the Persian Gulf. For example, the size of the armed forces increased 11% annually—from 191,000 to 300,000 person-

nel—during 1972-76.[13] Moreover, the percentage of the national budget
allocated to defense increased from about 26% in 1964 to over 30% in
1972.[14] Qualitatively, during the 1970s the U.S. allowed and encouraged
the Shah to purchase some of the most advanced U.S. military technology
that could be exported, including the F-4 and F-14 aircraft, an advanced
surveillance system, Spruance Class destroyers, and sophisticated tanks
and helicopters.[15] Much of the equipment was financed through U.S.
grant aid. The Shah, with the help of European firms, also built a domestic
arms industry.[16]

The Shah's reliance on the military to save his throne in each of the
crises he faced made him all the more aware of his vulnerability to potential military conspiracy. However, the very steps the Shah took to guard
against military plotting virtually guaranteed that the Shah would not
survive his most serious challenge, the Islamic revolution. Primarily, the
Shah's identification of his dynasty with the military ensured that revolutionary anger was as much directed against the military (and the security
apparatus, SAVAK) as against the Shah and his policies. This perceived
equivalence between the Shah and the army doomed the military government he established in late 1978 to regain control of the streets from the
revolutionaries.

Just as significantly, the Shah's control over the communications and
activities of the senior officers,[17] though successful in preventing collu-
sion, prevented them from collaborating in an effort to salvage his reign
after the Shah left Iran in January 1979. Because of his fear of military
conspiracy, the Shah rewarded officer loyalty, not independence, competence, or individual initiative.[18] The Shah prosecuted ambitious senior officers for alleged corruption. In 1976, for example, Navy Rear Admiral
Ramzi Abbas Ata'i was found guilty, along with ten other officers, of em-
bezzlement.[19] He also delegated overlapping responsibilities to different
organs. Moreover, he placed relatives in key commands; for example, his
brother-in-law, Gen. Mohammad Khatemi, was Air Force Commander
until his accidental death in 1975 and Captain Prince Shafik was a high
ranking naval officer.[20] Therefore, the officer corps he left behind when he
departed Iran was composed of generally weak leaders who were unable,
by themselves, to formulate a decisive response to the massive uprising
facing the government of Prime Minister Shahpur Bakhtiar that the Shah
installed when he fled.[21]

For the rank and file, the lack of coordination and confidence of the
senior officers undoubtedly contributed to the lack of will on the part of
most units to resist the revolutionary forces. Moreover, the departure of
the Shah—coupled with the obviously growing strength of the revolutionary coalition throughout late 1978 and early 1979—gave all but the most

dedicated of the Shah's military followers the impression of imminent revolutionary victory. At that point, the rational decision for any officer or soldier to make was to withdraw from the struggle or even pledge allegiance to the revolution in order to avoid potentially fatal punishment once the revolutionary forces had triumphed. A similar dilemma has faced military forces in almost all major revolutions, and serves to reinforce the professional and moral reluctance among most militaries to engage in battle against civilian nationals.[22] While in power, therefore, the Shah's personal strength depended on his building a subordinate and not autonomous military. The Shah's political strength, however, was the military's key weakness, and when the military was most needed to compensate for the erosion of the Shah's authority, the military's institutional shortcomings robbed it of the ability to rescue the monarchy.

How and Why the Regular Military Survived

If many soldiers and officers chose collaboration with the revolutionary forces as the revolution reached "critical mass," then the survival of the regular military as an organization is understandable. Those who fought the revolution to the end were either defeated by armed revolutionaries or imprisoned or executed after the revolution's victory.[23] Those who did collaborate or refused to suppress the revolution could, to a large extent, be trusted by the new government. In part, this is because the revolutionary leadership undoubtedly understood that any plot by these units to eventually subvert the new government would surely have less chance of success after the revolution triumphed than before. It was inconceivable that the bulk of the Shah's army was merely pretending to cast in its lot with the revolution, with the intention of overthrowing it at some future point. After the revolution took power in February 1979, therefore, eliminating the residual threat from the Shah's army and SAVAK had become a matter of purging those elements that, despite the risks, may have nonetheless considered plotting against the new regime. It was not necessary to weed out every soldier who may have continued to harbor pro-Shah sentiments. The new regime also was able to use other well known mechanisms for ensuring its control of the regular military, most notably strict surveillance and the appointment of revolutionary loyalists to oversee the military structure.[24] Despite the contention of Gregory Rose that the post-revolution purges of the regular military were less significant than generally believed, there is no doubt that some purges indeed took place.[25]

In addition, it must be recalled that the new regime required formal, organized means for national defense. The Revolutionary Guard was as yet highly disorganized, and the revolutionary committees (Komitehs), which helped topple the Shah and then assumed some of the authority vaccuum left by the collapse of his regime, were neighborhood-specific, highly undisciplined, and incapable of coordinated national action.[26]

Absent an external threat to the authority of the new regime, the regular military might well have been expendable as an organization, especially since it could never be regarded as politically trustworthy by ideological purists in the Islamic regime. However, there were such threats, most notably the rebellions by several ethnic groups seeking greater autonomy. These revolts, which were undertaken by the Kurds, who inhabit northwest Iran, Arabs in the southwestern province of Khuzestan, and Turkomans in the northeast, were seeking to take advantage of the collapse of central authority caused by the Shah's fall. The uprisings began as early as a month after the victory of the revolution.[27] These rebellions not only threatened to create the impression that the new government was weak, but also had the potential to deny Tehran access to vital transportation routes and resources, especially the oilfields of Khuzestan.

Aside from providing the new government with the need to retain the regular military as a functioning organization within the revolution, the local ethnic disturbances provided the regular military commanders with a unique opportunity to prove their loyalty to the revolution. In particular, three officers who were later to hold top positions in the regular military and play influential roles in the running of the war against Iraq first proved themselves to the Islamic regime by fighting the most serious of the ethnic revolts, the Kurdish rebellion. The most prominent among those regular officers has been Ali Sayyid Shirazi, an artillery officer under the Shah and now a Brigadier General, who rose to Commander of the regular Ground Forces (1981) and then became a representative of Ayatollah Khomeini to the Supreme Defense Council in 1986. His role in fighting the Kurds and support for the growth of the Guard gained him support from leading clerics, including Khomeini, throughout most of the war with Iraq.[28] Maj. Gen. Qasem Ali Zahir Nejad, Iran's highest ranking officer, was also instrumental in subduing the Kurds and later in organizing Iran's defense against the Iraqi invasion as commander of the Ground Forces. He rose to Chief of Staff of the regular military's Joint Staff in 1981 and, in 1984, he became a representative of Khomeini to the Supreme Defense Council. Although trusted by Khomeini, Zahir Nejad was removed from the command structure in 1984 because of his perceived reluctant to prosecute the war aggressively.[29] Finally, Brig. Gen. Esmail Sohrabi also proved his mettle in Kurdistan and rose rapidly thereafter. During 1981-84 he commanded the 1st Armored Division and was Zahir Nejad's replacement as Chief of the Joint Staff in 1984 until his sidelining as a scapegoat for Iran's loss of Al Faw in 1988.[30] (Al Faw was seized from Iraq in

February 1986). Sohrabi graduated from the Tehran Officer's Academy in 1964.

Another key figure in the early years of the revolution was Mostafa Chamran, the Islamic Republic's first Defense Minister, who died on the war front in 1981. He was not a professional military officer, but rather a guerrilla leader trained in Lebanon; he therefore had more in common with the Guard leaders than the regular officers. As Defense Minister, Chamran played a major role in helping solidify clerical control over the regular military, in part by overseeing a purge of pro-Shah regular army elements. He even admitted that the purge would have been more extensive had the new regime not been faced with the Kurdish rebellion.[31] Not confined to regular military responsibilities, Chamran also apparently led his own Revolutionary Guard militia which controlled Tehran airport until 1981.[32]

The Regular Military and Revolutionary Politics

We cannot ignore the role that revolutionary politics played in Khomeini's decision to retain the regular military in the Islamic Republic. This decision, which could have been reversed at Khomeini's pleasure at any time, was made in April 1979, a full year and a half before the Iran-Iraq war broke out; the army's retention therefore cannot be attributed to the Iraqi invasion.[33] In explaining this decision, it must be noted that the revolutionary forces that toppled the Shah represented a broad coalition of mutually suspicious groups. The sometimes violent infighting that characterized the first few years of the Islamic Republic in fact represented an attrition process by which the strongest revolutionary grouping— Khomeini, his cleric disciples, and their allies—emerged dominant.

The liberal nationalists, represented by the first Prime Minister of the Islamic Republic Mehdi Bazargan, were toppled when the takeover of the US Embassy in Tehran in November 1979 exposed their impotence and triggered the resignation of Bazargan and his government.[34] Abol Hassan Bani-Sadr, who was elected the first President of the Islamic Republic in early 1980, represented the relatively moderate, non-clerical, technocratic wing of the regime. Bani Sadr and his supporters, like Bazargan before him, ran afoul of the clerics and was eventually ousted in 1981.[35] The Mojahedin-e-Khalq (People's Fighters) Organization (MEK) was similarly defeated in its late 1981 armed rebellion. The MEK, which will be analyzed in greater detail later in this chapter, represented the Islamic Marxist non-clerical wing of the regime and unsuccessfully revolted against what it perceived was increasing monopolization of the revolution by the clerics.[36] Another major group that was devoured by the revolution it supported was the pro-Moscow Communist Tudeh Party. Like the MEK, this group was never trusted by Khomeini and his supporters, and it was crushed by the Revolutionary Guard in 1983, a year after Iran had eased the external threat it faced by pushing Iraq off its territory.[37]

A common denominator among these early power struggles is the degree to which they pitted the clerics, who dominated Khomeini's inner circle, against non-clerical elements that dominated the pro-Bazargan, pro-Bani-Sadr, MEK, and Tudeh forces. Paradoxically, to defeat the challenges posed by these opposition groups, the clerics relied heavily on the Revolutionary Guard. However, the Guard was also dominated by non-clerics, many of whom had had past ties to some of these opposition groups, especially the MEK. For example, the Guard's first official commander, Abbas Zamani, was a supporter of the clerics' nemesis Bani-Sadr.[38] Therefore, it can be argued that there were undoubtedly mutual suspicions between the clerics around Khomeini and their non-clerical protectors in the Revolutionary Guard, despite the Guard's role in helping the clerics consolidate the revolution. Further evidence for such suspicions will be presented in the discussion of the formation of the Revolutionary Guard and its precursors.

Given such tensions between the ruling clerics and the non-clerics in the Guard, revolutionary politics mandated that the regular military be retained as a potential counterweight to the well-armed non-clerical revolutionaries that were dominant in the Guard. This argument does not contradict that made by many observers, and which is also correct, that the Guard was built up as a counterweight to the politically suspect regular military.[39] More precisely, the two forces were maintained and built up as deterrents to any potential bids for power by the other. Indeed, such factional balancing was a hallmark of Khomeini's ten year rule.[40] Moreover, the political need to juxtapose the two forces helps explain why they had to be kept separate. Such separation between the regular military and the Guard, in turn, will, in later chapters, help explain how the Guard was able to resist ideological dilution despite its need to adopt a rationalized and complex organizational structure.

The Historical Precursors of the Revolutionary Guard

Because the post-revolution role of the regular military has been partly a function of the formation and development of the Revolutionary Guard, a detailed analysis of the roots and early formation of the Guard is needed. An assessment of the Guard's precursors also is required in order to explain why the Guard's fervent ideological zeal has survived the various political and social forces that have diminished the fervor of similar revolutionary armies.

At the time of the revolution, the Guard represented a melding of several social and political elements. The first, which drove the Guard's formation and still dominates the Guard, is the lower middle class urban guerrillas that had been fighting the Shah for many years.[41] The second grouping was composed of somewhat more opportunistic but similarly militant youths, both urban and rural and centered around local clerics and their mosque congregations, that joined the revolution in its final stages.[42] The combination of these two major groupings to form the Guard followed the exact framework laid out by Chorley in her work on revolutionary army formation.[43] Because of the key role of the former grouping in forming the Guard, it is necessary to examine in greater detail the origins of the longtime urban guerrilla groups that formed the core of the Guard.

It is impossible to precisely fix the origins of the future Revolutionary Guard. Some future Guard organizers began their anti-Shah activities in the Mosadeq era.[44] However, most relevant to the Revolutionary Guard is when organized *armed struggle*, not merely peaceful political opposition began. The Islamic Nations Party was the first armed guerrilla group to spring up in the wake of the 1963 uprising against the Shah.[45] Four prominent leaders of the party subsequently went on to play key roles in the early Revolutionary Guard, but subsequently lost power to younger, more radical Guard leaders.

The first unofficial Guard commander, Javad Mansuri, as well as its first official Operational Commander, Abbas Zamani (aka Abu Sharif) were members of the Islamic Nations Party.[46] After release from jail in 1967 (he was arrested for his anti-Shah activities with the party), Abbas Zamani and another Islamic Nations Party colleague, Abbas Duzduzani, formed the Divine Party. The Iran Press Digest reports that Duzduzani subsequently joined the Mojahedin-e-Khalq Organization, another Guard precursor discussed below.[47] According to his autobiography, for a brief period in early 1980, Duzduzani was Commander-in-Chief of the Revolutionary Guard, with Zamani as Operational Commander.[48] The founder of the Islamic Nations Party was Kazem Bojnurdi, who was asked by Bani Sadr to command the Guard after Abbas Zamani's ouster in 1980.[49] Bojnurdi, who cast his lot in with the IRP after the revolution, refused the appointment because of the factional struggles for control of the Guard that he felt rendered it uncontrollable.[50] Although they all moved on to other positions in the Islamic Republic, all four of these early guerrillas had effectively lost their roles in the Guard by mid-1980, probably in part because they themselves did not hold together as a cohesive group. All four of them had either joined other groups, formed splinter groups, or, as in the case of Abbas Zamani, tied themselves to an unsuccessful politician.

A more significant precursor of the Revolutionary Guard was, ironically, to be one of its greatest nemeses after the revolution. This group is the Mojahedin-e-Khalq Organization (MEK). This little known connection between the MEK and the Revolutionary Guard is obtained from careful study of the biographies of two men who were to play crucial roles in the formation of the Guard—Behzad Nabavi, Minister of Heavy Industries during 1981-89 and Mohsen Reza'i, Commander-in-Chief of the Guard since 1981. In his autobiography, Behzad Nabavi, after detailing his involvement in the three nonviolent National Front Organizations that opposed the Shah, talks about his decision to take up armed struggle against the Shah.[51] Like Abbas Duzduzani, Nabavi joined the MEK in about 1970 because, by his own admission, he was attracted to its leftwing, anti-imperialist, and Islamic platform and the group's pursuit of armed struggle.[52] He was imprisoned in 1972 for anti-Shah activities with the group.

Nabavi reveals a key turning point for the militant non-clerical wing of the Islamic revolutionary coalition. He explains how, while in prison in 1975, he broke with the MEK when the organization began to emphasize Marxist rather than Islamic ideology.[53] Nabavi describes how the split then widened between the MEK leadership and those like Nabavi who rejected Marxism and emphasized Islamic ideology.[54] Interestingly, two of Nabavi's prisonmates who similarly broke with the MEK were Abbas Duzduzani, mentioned above, and Mohammad Ali Rajai, the future Prime Minister (1980) and President of the Islamic Republic (1981).[55] This split, which began in the Shah's prisons, did not prevent tactical cooperation between the MEK and its former members, as will be shown below. Revolutionary Guard Commander Mohsen Reza'i similarly described this split within the leftwing non-clerical armed opposition to the Shah. He explains that he, too, broke with the MEK when it "became eclectic," i.e., when the group began to integrate Marxism into its Islamic ideology.

The Islamic militants who broke with the MEK subsequently formed the most important Guard precursor, the Mojahedin of the Islamic Revolution (MIR). A special report on the MIR in the Iran Press Digest supports the biographic and autobiographic analysis that the MIR was founded by former MEK members who, in contrast to the MEK, strongly supported the Islamic character of the revolution.[56] Although unofficially in existence since about 1977, the MIR, which was composed of about seven minor groups, publicly declared itself as an organization in April 1979. MIR fighters, the guerrillas who had fought the Shah for years and many of whom had trained with the PLO in Lebanon, not only effectively battled the Shah's forces before and during the revolution, but also helped secure the streets for Khomeini after the regime collapsed.[57]

The significance of the MIR for the formation of the Revolutionary Guard is wide-ranging. Although O'Ballance overstates the case when he asserts that the MIR actually became the Revolutionary Guard,[58] the Iran Press Digest more accurately states that the MIR "was instrumental in organizing the Islamic Revolutionary Guard Corps (IRGC) and a large number of IRGC members held dual membership in the MIR too."[59] Essentially, the MIR was the core of the early Guard, the organized force of longtime guerrillas around which the rest of the Guard crystallized. The MIR was that core grouping of longtime guerrillas that Chorley postulates is necessary for the formation of all revolutionary armed forces.[60]

Many MIR members also helped form local revolutionary committees that eventually became, or furnished additional fighters for, Revolutionary Guard units. For example, MIR founder Behzad Nabavi joined a Tehran Revolutionary Committee and eventually became a Tehran Guard Commander before joining the new government.[61] Longtime Guard Deputy Commander, former Guard Minister, and now Navy Commander Ali Shamkhani, an MIR member, formed a revolutionary committee in his home province of Khuzestan and he subsequently became Guard commander of that province before becoming Reza'i's deputy when Reza'i became overall Guard Commander in 1981.[62] As mentioned previously, the revolutionary committees, many of which formed around local mosque congregations, provided the outer layer for the MIR core in the formation of the Guard. Even if not a full MIR member, former Guard Minister Mohsen RafiqDust certainly cooperated closely with the MIR. He underwent guerrilla training with the PLO in Lebanon, was a prison-mate of Behzad Nabavi, helped organize and arm anti-Shah demonstrators before the revolution, and was instrumental in organizing the Guard.[63]

At its formation, the Guard was an almost totally unstructured force, lightly armed, and heavily factionalized. Its function was primarily to solidify Khomeini's hold on the country and root out and, in conjunction with the revolutionary courts, punish collaborators of the former regime. To this extent, the early Guard paralleled the *armees revolutionnaires* of the French Revolution, as analyzed by Richard Cobb.[64] Even the Guard's early leadership was unclear; Abbas Zamani has been identified as the Guard's first official commander, but his appointment was never formally announced in conjunction with the Guard's official inauguration in May 1979. Moreover, a series of short-tenured political and clerical supervisors, including Ayatollah Lahuti, Mostafa Chamran, Iran's current supreme leader Ali Khamene'i, and Rafsanjani were assigned to oversee the Guard during its first year, but none gained firm control over the organization,[65] primarily because they were viewed as outsiders imposed on the Guard.

Despite the disarray in the revolution's new armed force, the Guard was still the best means preferable for solidifying the revolution's grip than other available sources of armed force. The remnants of the regular army were not necessarily a major threat to the new regime but certainly could not be trusted to work enthusiastically to entrench the new government either. The Komitehs, the Guard's sister internal security apparatus, were even less structured than the early Guard, locally organized, and virtually uncontrolla-ble.[66] In fact, the Guard was probably chartered as an official force in part to gain a measure of control over the Komitehs. Moreover, the clerics around Khomeini probably calculated that the political benefits of legitimizing the Guard's de-facto existence outweighed the costs of trying to suppress its formation; such suppression might have driven the nonclerical militants that formed the Guard to turn against the regime.

The Guard, the MIR, and the IRP

The crucial role played by the MIR in the formation of the Guard means that to fully understand the ideology and political views of the Guard we must first carefully analyze the MIR's ideology and political platform. In its special report, the Iran Press Digest describes, in detail, the political program of the MIR as follows: "belief in supporting the oppressed (ie. lower classes); a greater role of government in the economy; reforms to-ward more economic justice; strong campaigning against the U.S. and Soviet Union; support for liberation, and especially Islamic movements; strong campaigning against the liberals and groups opposed the Islamic Republic of Iran to the point of military encounter; and opposition to the increasing influence of conservative clerics and their supporters in the government bodies."[67]

Although future President Abol Hassan Bani Sadr addressed the first publicly acknowedged meeting of the group shortly after the revolution, it is clear from the MIR's platform,[68] particularly its opposition to liberal policies, that the MIR did not form a natural base of support for Bani Sadr. The MIR, in fact, helped mobilize against Bani-Sadr when his break with the clerics became more open in 1981 and eventually led to his ouster.[69] Moreover, the MIR's opposition to the influence of conservative clerics provides further evidence that tension existed between the hardline non-clerical militants that dominated the MIR (and subsequently the Revolu-tionary Guard) and many of the clerics below Khomeini. In addition, some press reports suggest that most MIR members wanted to limit the direct participation of *all* clerics, conservative and hardline, in govern-ment.[70] This tension was aggravated somewhat in 1982 when the clerics, having failed to install one of their own as an effective Guard superviser, attempted to gain greater control over the MIR by having Khomeini appoint a clerical representative to oversee the MIR. Resistance to this clerical intrusion continued until, in 1986, Khomeini officially disbanded the MIR and key MIR members formally disavowed their membership in the organization.[71] However, by 1986, the MIR had already served its purpose in forming the Guard and in placing its members and sympathizers in key government posts, as well as the Guard.

The non-clerical militants that formed the Revolutionary Guard and the MIR were fanatically loyal to Khomeini as the charismatic figure who, against long odds, had defeated their enemy, the Shah, and whose radical political ideology generally corresponded to theirs.[72] However, it is also evident from the MIR political platform that support and reverence for Khomeini as a charismatic leader did not automatically translate into support for Khomeini's clerical disciples, especially those who tended to be generally conservative politically (ie. favoring private enterprise, preservation of relations with the West, export of the revolution by example rather than force, and, later, opposition to pursuit of the war against Iraq until victory.) Ironically, not only could most clerics in Iran be generally categorized as conservative, but the clerical organization that subsequently dominated the regime—the Islamic Republican Party (IRP)—was itself controlled by clerics who were, if not conservative, certainly not nearly as radical as the non-clerical militants or Khomeini himself. These IRP leaders would include Rafsanjani, Khamene'i, former Chief Justice Abdol Karim Musavi-Ardabili, and the late IRP chief Ayatollah Hosein Beheshti, who was killed in a bombing of IRP headquarters in 1981.[73]

Since these clerics who rode to power on Khomeini's coattails knew that they were not nearly as popular with the non-clerical militants as Khomeini was, the IRP clerics quickly set out to cement the radical nonclerical wing of the revolutionary coalition to the IRP through political means. The IRP clerics undoubtedly wanted to ensure that the nonclerical militant wing of the regime would remain their allies should Khomeini, who was already about 79 when he took power, leave the scene suddenly. There is substantial evidence the IRP and the nonclerical radicals, as represented by the MIR and the Guard, came to a political agreement for mutual benefit shortly after the revolution. In August 1980, Mohammad Ali Rajai, a key founder of the MIR as well as one of the most important nonclerical members of the IRP, was supported by the IRP to become Prime Minister under Bani Sadr over the latter's opposition.[74] When he took office, Rajai brought his former cellmate, MIR founder Behzad Nabavi, into the new government as Minister of Executive Affairs (essentially Rajai's top aide).[75] Other nonclerical militants were brought into the Cabinet as well to implement a generally radical, redistributive, political program.[76] For example, Mohammad Salamati, Nabavi's cellmate and a cofounder of the MIR, came into the Cabinet as Deputy Minister of Labor.[77]

There are other indicators of a political marriage between the IRP and the MIR/Revolutionary Guard. In early Majles election campaigns, the MIR publicly supported candidates on the IRP slate.[78] The Guard was also formally given the leading role both in defending and exporting the revolution, a recognition of legitimacy the Guard had wanted, when the Guard was officially formed by Khomeini in 1979.[79]

The political strength of the alliance between the clerics and the radical non-clerics was further evidenced during the Islamic Republic's early power struggles. The first of these struggles was brought to a head with the takeover of the U.S. Embassy in Tehran from November 1979 to January 1981. The seizure helped the clerics and their non-clerical allies in the MIR and the Guard defeat an early major opponent, the Islamic Republic's liberal nationalist first Prime Minister Mehdi Bazargan. The actual takeover of the Embassy was perpetrated by radical youths (non-clerics) calling themselves the "Students in the Line of the Imam," implying their complete loyalty to the principles of Ayatollah Khomeini.[80]

Closer examination of the Students reveals their similarities and close links to the MIR and the Revolutionary Guard, as well as their integral relationship to the overall post-revolution power struggle. The Embassy takeover occurred a few days after Bazargan met publicly with then U.S. National Security Adviser Zbigniew Brzezinski to discuss the post-revolution U.S.-Iran relationship.[81] The meeting gave the Students justification for their action by bolstering their claim that Bazargan was insufficiently revolutionary to govern. Although Khomeini's lieutenants who dominated the Revolutionary Council had been maneuvering to undermine Bazargan from the beginning, the Embassy takeover sealed Bazargan's fate by exposing his complete lack of control; he and his like-minded Cabinet resigned within days.[82] In Crane Brinton's terms, the reign of the moderates had ended.[83]

Nonetheless, there is substantial evidence that the Embassy takeover was not a spontaneous act by angry students, but rather a planned and coordinated act. The Christian Science Monitor, quoting a former Student, reported that the seizure was planned well in advance by hardline clerics, the Students, and at least one top official in the Revolutionary Guard.[84] Further evidence and background supports the report. The Revolutionary Guards stationed around the Embassy had previously prevented a similar takeover by a militant leftwing, anti-US, but anti-Khomeini group in May 1979, yet the Guards did nothing to stop the Students that rushed the Embassy on November 4, 1979.[85] Once the Embassy was seized, the Students officially thanked the Revolutionary Guard, essentially for not preventing the takeover.[86] A daily chronology of the hostage crisis compiled for the House Foreign Affairs Committee claimed that, after the failed U.S. rescue mission in April 1980, the hostages were moved to Revolutionary Guard installations around the country.[87]

The involvement of certain major figures in the hostage crisis provide further insights into the organic linkages between the Students, the Guard, and the political motivations of the takeover. For example, the Guard's first, albeit unofficial commander Javad Mansuri ran for the Majles in 1980 as a "Student in the Line of the Imam" candidate on the IRP coalition slate.[88] Several of the Students subsequently joined and became commanders in the Guard; one Student leader, Hosein Sheikh-ol-Eslam, became a key Foreign Ministry undersecretary who worked closely with the Guard in export of the revolution and placing Guard agents in Iranian embassies abroad.[89]

MIR founder Behzad Nabavi was a key figure in the hostage crisis. A biography of Nabavi reports that many of the Students were MIR members and followers of Nabavi.[90] This would explain his appointment in late 1980 as chief negotiator for Iran in the hostage crisis. As founder of the MIR and a major player in the militant non-clerical wing of the regime to which the Students clearly belonged, Nabavi was the one government official with sufficient credibility with the Students to ensure that the Students would comply with the terms of a deal for the U.S. hostages' release. By the same token, even though the Embassy takeover furthered Nabavi's hardline political agenda, he was credible to the U.S. as Iran's interlocutor since he was a formal government official and had close ties to Prime Minister Rajai. Rajai, in turn, was well connected with the IRP clerics and, thus, Khomeini.[91]

Institutional Context

Having contrasted the formation of the Revolutionary Guard with the pre-revolution regular military, the Guard's strength as an institution in Iran cannot be fully demonstrated without discussing other major organizations and institutions produced by the revolution. An overview of these institutions will help place the Guard in the overall context of the Islamic Republic's governing style. Although the strengths and effectiveness of each institution vary, the interactions of all institutions as a system have given the regime considerable resiliency. Most notably, the regime has survived the political turmoil associated with initial regime consolidation; the Iraqi invasion in 1980; the battlefield defeats and acceptance of a ceasefire in 1988; and the death of the charismatic leader Khomeini in 1989. It can be argued that any one of these factors alone could have toppled the regime had it not institutionalized its rule.

The Islamic Republican political system can be viewed as a balance of power among contending political and ideological forces. This model held even during Khomeini's rule, even though Khomeini's unquestioned authority could have enabled him to establish a more hierarchical regime.

In general, the pre-revolutionary national institutions, such as the Foreign Ministry and regular military, have formed a support base for more pragmatic leaders, while the revolutionary institutions, such as the Guard, Komitehs, Construction Jihad, and Foundations have supported the radicals. The pragmatists and radicals have competed for popular support as well as within the higher level decisionmaking institutions, including the Majles, Council of Guardians, Council for Expediency Discernment, Assembly of Experts, and Supreme Defense Council (now the Supreme Council for National Security).[92] Sitting atop the infighting has been the *velayat-e-faqih*, or supreme leader, a position created and first held by Khomeini and now occupied by Ayatollah Ali Khamene'i. The *velayat-e-faqih* has been crucial in determining political outcomes by shifting the political balance toward one side or the other.

The first institution that merits discussion is without question the most important: the institution of *velayat-e-faqih*, or rule by the supreme Islamic jurisprudent. This position was created for and first held by Ayatollah Khomeini as supreme leader of the Islamic revolution. As Ramazani aptly states, Khomeini's powers as *faqih*, which reflected his unquestioned authority as religious and political guide, were codified rather than granted by the Islamic Republic's Constitution.[93] The position of *faqih*, as originally conceived, was to be held by a cleric who was a religious source of emulation (*marja taqlid*), eminently qualified as an Islamic jurist, an efficient administrator, and who "enjoyed the confidence of the majority of the people as leader."[94] In Article 110 of the Constitution, the *faqih* was granted sweeping powers to appoint other high ranking officials; approve Presidential candidates and dismiss incompetent incumbents; serve as Commander-in-Chief of the Armed Forces (regular and Guard); appoint and dismiss regular and Guard commanders; and organize the Supreme Defense Council, Iran's highest military decisionmaking body.[95] It was intended that this melding of supreme religious and political authority would ensure Islamization of the government and society.

In practice, Khomeini held these and many other powers by virtue of his overarching authority as the charismatic founder of the Islamic Republic. He set overall policy direction and arbitrated factional disputes among his subordinates, by both privately and publicly indicating his policy preferences.[96] Khomeini's public pronouncements were invariably greeted with declarations of support by politicians and organizations spanning the political and ideological spectrum.

As an institution, *velayat-e-faqih* has, at least formally, survived Khomeini's death. However, inhabited now by Ayatollah Ali Khamene'i (formerly Iran's President during 1981-89), the institution is far weaker. In the new Constitution, ratified on July 28, 1989 (about two months after Khomeini's death), new formal powers had to be added to the position of *velayat-e-faqih* to compensate for the Khamene'i's diminished personal authority as compared to Khomeini.[97] Currently, Khamene'i's pronouncements are not greeted with automatic support, he has not been able to contain infighting as Khomeini did, and he is viewed by many as less politically skilled and effective than President Rafsanjani, to whom Khamene'i is formally superior.[98]

The position has also suffered on religious grounds. Khamene'i was promoted to Ayatollah when he succeeded Khomeini, a clear violation of the original intent that the *faqih* hold unquestionable religious credentials. As an admission of the weakness of Khamene'i's religious credentials, a separate supreme religious guide, Grand Ayatollah Araki, was designated after Khomeini's death.[99] The institution of *velayat-e-faqih* therefore ranks low on a key criteria of institutional strength—autonomy. The strength of the institution apparently depends largely on the personality occupying the position rather than its own intrinsic capabilities within the regime structure.

What the institution of *velayat-e-faqih* has lost from Khomeini's death, the Presidency has undoubtedly gained. In the new Constitution, this office has also gained broad new powers over executive affairs—powers it had previously shared with the abolished position of Prime Minister.[100] As an institution within the Islamic Republic, however, the Presidency is still plagued with much the same drawbacks as the office of *velayat-e-faqih*; its strength is dependent on the person occupying the position. The past weakness of the Presidency resulted as much from former President Khamene'i's personal political inabilities as it did from its conflict with the office of the Prime Minister (held by hardline non-cleric Mir Hosein Musavi during 1981-89). Moreover, not only is the Presidency's new strength due to Rafsanjani's skills and prestige, but he, in part, engineered the new formal powers allotted to the office before the election in which he was the overwhelming favorite.[101]

Another important institution, a carryover from the Shah's regime, is the Consultative Assembly, or Majles. The Majles was almost completely powerless under the Shah but received new life under the Islamic Republic. The Majles has been influential in the budgetary process, it reviews appointed Cabinet officials, conducts investigations, and helps implement economic and some military policies.[102] As an important hallmark of institutional strength, it has maintained its formal powers and integrity through four consecutive elections, and it has been able to accommodate a diverse range of opinion within its ranks. Even ousted Prime Minister Bazargan led a small loyal opposition block within the Majles for many years after his removal.

The Majles, however, has suffered from the same weakness as the previous two institutions discussed—its dependence on strong personalities rather than structural factors internal to the institution itself. Press reports indicate that the post of Majles Speaker, long held by the powerful Rafsanjani, was somewhat less influential within the regime under the more radical but less politically skilled Mehdi Karrubi, the former Deputy Speaker.[103] After Rafsanjani was elected President in 1989, 210 of the 270 Majles deputies, recognizing that Rafsanjani's departure from the Majles Speakership would weaken the institution, unsuccessfully attempted to persuade Ayatollah Khomeini's son Ahmad—an important and generally radical figure—to take Rafsanjani's Majles seat and presumably the Speakership, according to the English language newspaper Tehran Times.[104] This petition to Ahmad Khomeini amounted to a virtual admission that the Majles' strength indeed depended heavily on a major regime leader occupying the post of Speaker.

A separate but related organization created by the revolution and enshrined in the Constitution is the 12 man Council of Guardians, which reviews Majles legislation for conformity to Islamic principles. It was intended to enshrine Islamic law as the predominant legal basis for regulating society. The Council is composed of six Islamic theologians who are appointed by the *velayat-e-faqih* and six Islamic lawyers. Since the revolution, the Council has been dominated by senior, generally conservative clerics who have been viewed as blocking radical reforms and limiting state control of the economy.[105]

The institution, however, has suffered from rigidity and inflexibility. Its refusal to back radical social legislation, such as land reform, foreign trade nationalization, and wealth redistribution led to successful efforts by radicals to weaken the Council. In 1988, regime radicals who were then ascendant were able to persuade Khomeini to set up a new body, the Council of Expediency Discernment, to resolve legislative disagreements between the Majles and the Council of Guardians.[106] The intention and net effect of the new council was to curb the conservative influence of the Council of Guardians, and weaken its independence and influence.[107]

Yet another organization initially held much promise of becoming a strong institution for perpetuating clerical rule. The Islamic Republican Party (IRP), was instrumental in the first years of the Republic in consolidating the clerics' grip on power, translating Khomeini's directives into policy, and furnishing many of the major officials and Majles deputies for the regime.[108] However, the IRP, although it did admit and ally with nonclerics, was not able to broaden its base sufficiently to ensure its viability, let alone establish itself as a powerful mass party. It provided a base of political support for party chairman and President Ali Khamene'i, but in 1987 Khamene'i's weakness, coupled with factional infighting within the party, caused Khomeini to formally disband the IRP.[109] Rafsanjani reportedly was instrumental in the official dissolution of the party, perhaps in an effort to undermine his political competitor, Khamene'i.[110] As an institution, therefore, the IRP failed on several counts, particularly in its inability to incorporate new social elements, adapt to the changing political environment, or increase its cohesiveness.

Another group of organizations that were created by the revolution was instrumental in helping the regime shore up its support among the masses, particularly the urban lower classes. These are the major Foundations, primarily the Martyr's Foundation and the Foundation of the Oppressed, that were set up to provide financial assistance and employment to the urban poor. The Martyr's Foundation, until recently headed by former Majles Speaker Mehdi Karrubi, was originally set up to help the families of those killed in the revolution and later became charged with caring for the families of war dead and arranging treatment abroad for the wounded.[111] The Foundation of the Oppressed has been responsible for handling the property confiscated from the royal family and exiled elite during the revolution and redistributing the proceeds to lower class families in need.[112] By 1982 the Foundation ran 200-300 factories, 100 construction companies, 91 agricultural enterprises, and over 1,000 office or apartment buildings.[113]

In the early years of the revolution, the Foundations worked closely with local Revolutionary Guard units in helping Iranian peasants and workers seize land and businesses owned by the former elite. The significant funds and assets administered by the Foundations also provided the regime with the financial resources with which to mobilize and educate the masses politically and ideologically.[114] The Martyr's Foundation, for example, is said to fund political activities in addition to its formally constituted activities.[115]

Paradoxically, the principal institutional weakness of the Foundations resulted from their key strengths—control over funds and, therefore, patronage. The funds controlled by Foundation leaders bred substantial corruption and almost every Foundation has been plagued by allegations of wrongdoing and frequent investigations.[116] According to Huntington, vulnerability to corruption virtually defines a subordinate, and therefore weak, institution. As an affirmation of the corruption within the Foundation of the Oppressed as well as its links to the Guard, former Guard Minister Mohsen RafiqDust was appointed head of that Foundation after his ouster as Guard Minister; he was publicly tasked with preventing misuse of the Foundation's funds.[117]

Another organization, the Construction Jihad (Crusade for Reconstruction), became a home for many young, skilled revolutionary technocrats and engineers who wanted to serve the revolution but were not sufficiently motivated to engage in actual combat as were the Guards and Basijis. The purposes of this organization were essentially to extend the regime's authority into the countryside, develop rural infrastructure, and help build support for the regime among the peasantry.[118] Just after the revolution, Jihad members worked closely with the Guard and the Foundations in helping the peasantry seize land. Jihad members, in some cases, became land distribution agents and loan administrators.[119] After the war broke out, it served as the Guard's "Corps of Engineers," setting up defensive emplacements, building roads and bridges for tactical operations, and developing Iran's indigenous military production capabilities to circumvent the international arms embargo against Iran.[120]

There are other similarities and linkages between the Jihad and the Guard; paradoxically, these connections are also the Jihad's weakness as an institution. Like the MIR, the Guard, and the Students who held the U.S. Embassy, the Jihad was formed originally by young, nonclerical militants; Gholam Reza Foruzesh, Minister of the Construction Jihad, was himself one of the students that held the U.S. Embassy officers hostage.[121] Several other Student hostage holders subsequently joined the Construction Jihad as well.[122] One of the early leaders of the Jihad, Ali Reza Afshar, was also member of the Revolutionary Guard and later became the Guard's official spokesman and Chief of Staff to Commander Reza'i; Afshar now commands the Basij.[123] Shortly before Khomeini's death, the Ayatollah's representative to the Jihad, Hojjat ol-Eslam Abdollah Nuri, was made concurrently the representative to the Guard, probably to mollify the Jihad's sense of inferiority and subordination to the Guard.[124] The chief weakness of the Jihad is precisely its subordination—it has become almost an appendage of the Guard, and has lost much of its independent identity. In the eyes of the population and ruling elite, Jihad members never achieved the heroic status that the Guards did as willing martyrs for the revolution.

Several major problems have plagued one final major revolutionary organization, the nationwide system of Revolutionary Committees (Komitehs). The Komitehs, as previously explained, constituted a major early building block of the Guard, furnishing militant fighters, armed with weapons seized from the Shah's armories, for the new revolutionary force. The Komitehs sprang up around neighborhood mosques and powerful clerics as the Shah's authority eroded, fulfilling the administrative functions performed by the former regime. Although they gave up their administrative tasks when the Islamic government took shape, the Komitehs persisted as local security forces.[125]

Because of their local organization, there was little coordination or structure connecting the individual Komitehs, and the Komiteh guards (not to be confused with Revolutionary Guards), like many similar internal security forces, have been excessively brutal, have acted outside the law, and have become highly unpopular.[126] The regime has reined in the Komitehs in several ways. In the mid 1980s the regime created a national structure for the Komitehs, appointed a national Commander, and placed them formally under the Ministry of Interior.[127] Moreover, the regime gave the Guard greater authority over the Komitehs by mandating that Komiteh guards serve tours at the front under Revolutionary Guard command.[128] The most severe blow to the Komiteh came in 1990 when the regime, after long debate, voted to merge the Komitehs with the police and gendarmerie, although it is widely believed that the Komitehs informally have maintained their independence.[129] The merger of the Komitehs is especially significant since both the Komitehs and Revolutionary Guard started from the same baseline in 1979; they formed from the same social elements (lower middle class urban nonclerical militants) and had similar duties. Moreover, the Guard, unlike the Komitehs, has successfully resisted its incorporation into a unified national army.

Implications

The foregoing analysis is not meant to convey the impression that the revolution would necessarily have failed without the development of the Revolutionary Guard, nor that the Guard is without some of the flaws that have been identified for other revolutionary institutions. However, in demonstrating the institutional strength of the Guard, it is useful to bear in mind how it was able to avoid many of the pitfalls and setbacks that plagued other revolutionary institutions. Ultimately, this will help explain how the Guard has become the vanguard of the principles of the revolution to a greater degree than other similar forces have for their respective revolutions.

Notes

1. Donald Vought, "Iran" in Richard Gabriel ed., *Fighting Armies: Antagonists in the Middle East, A Combat Assessment* (Westport, Conn. and London: Greenwood Press, 1983)
2. Ibid P. 90
3. Farhad Kazemi, "The Military and Politics in Iran," in Elie Kedourie and Sylvia G. Haim eds., *Iran: Towards Modernity—Studies in Thought, Politics, and Society* (London: Frank Cass, 1980)
4. Nader Entessar, "The Military and Politics in the Islamic Republic of Iran" in Hooshang Amirahmadi and Manoucher Parvin eds., *Post Revolutionary Iran* (Boulder and London: Westview Press, 1988)
5. Vought, op.cit. pp. 85-90
6. Kazemi, op.cit.; Entessar, op.cit.; Vought, op.cit.
7. Fred Halliday, *Iran: Dictatorship and Development* (Middlesex, England and New York: Penguin Books, 1979) P. 66

8. Kazemi, op. cit.; Vought, op. cit.
9. Vought, op. cit. P. 90
10. Kazemi, op. cit. P. 223; Halliday, op. cit. P. 70
11. Kazemi, op. cit. P. 224
12. "Ayatollah Ruhollah Khomeini: The Mullah Who Transformed Iran," Washington Post, June 5, 1989 P. A26
13. Robert Graham, *Iran: The Illusion of Power* (New York: St. Martin's Press, 1980) P. 185
14. Kazemi, op.cit., P. 234
15. Graham, op.cit., pp. 184-8
16. Ibid, P. 186
17. Halliday, op. cit.
18. Vought, op. cit. P. 90
19. Graham, op.cit., P. 184
20. Ibid, P. 183
21. Halliday, op. cit. P. 69
22. Morris Janowitz, *The Military in the Political Development of New Nations* (Chicago: University of Chicago Press, 1964) P. 37
23. Entessar, op. cit. P. 63
24. Nikola Schahgaldian, *The Iranian Military Under the Islamic Republic*, (Santa Monica, California: Rand Corporation, 1987)
25. Gregory F. Rose, "The Post Revolutionary Purge of Iran's Armed Forces: A Revisionist Assessment," in *Iranian Studies*, Vol. XVII, Spring-Summer 1984, No. 2-3; Entessar, op.cit. P. 63
26. Shaul Bakhash, *The Reign of the Ayatollahs: Iran and the Islamic Revolution* (New York: Basic Books, Inc., 1984) pp. 56-59
27. Schahgaldian, op.cit. pp. 123-125
28. "Fervor, New Leaders Propel Iran's Army," Washington Post; April 8, 1982, P. A1
29. "On Changes in Military Command," Iran Press Digest; August 12, 1986
30. "Hardliner Gets Top Military Command - Iran," Associated Press; May 12, 1988
31. Schahgaldian, op.cit., P. 22
32. Ibid, P. 66
33. "Khomeini Says Iranian Army Must Be Kept Strong," Reuters; April 17, 1989
34. "Chronology of the Hostage Crisis," Associated Press; November 25, 1979
35. Bakhash, op.cit.
36. Ibid
37. Autobiography of Behzad Nabavi, in Iran Press Digest; March 13, 1984

38. *Iran Yearbook 1988,* published by Mazda Publications, Costa Mesa, California, 1988. P. 570
39. Schahgaldian, op.cit.
40. "Internal Turmoil Roils Iran," Washington Post; July 10, 1988, P.A1
41. Sepehr Zabih, *The Iranian Military in Revolution and War* (New York and London: Routledge, Chapman, and Hall, 1988)
42. Ibid
43. Katharine Chorley, *Armies and the Art of Revolution* (Boston: Beacon Press, 1973) Chaps. 11, 12
44. "Autobiography of Behzad Nabavi," op.cit., P. 19
45. Biography of Abbas Duzduzani, Iran Press Digest; September 8, 1980
46. *Iran Yearbook 1988,* op.cit.; Islamic Republican Party slate of Majles candidates, published in the Iran Press Digest; April 3, 1984, P. 18
47. Biography of Abbas Duzduzani, op.cit.
48. Autobiography of Abbas Duzduzani, in Iran Press Digest; March 6, 1983, P. 14
49. "Who's Who in Iran," in *Iran Almanac 1987* (Tehran: Echo of Iran, 1987)
50. The Flame, July 1, 1980; 1984 Islamic Republican Party slate, op.cit.
51. Autobiography of Behzad Nabavi, op.cit.
52. Ibid
53. Ibid
54. Ibid
55. Ibid
56. "Organization of Mojahedin of Islamic Revolution," Iran Press Digest Special Report; March 5, 1985 pp.3-6
57. Ibid
58. Edgar O'Ballance, *The Gulf War* (London: Brassey's Defence Publishers, Ltd., 1988) P. 21
59. "Organization of Mojahedin of Islamic Revolution," op.cit.
60. Chorley, op.cit.
61. Autobiography of Behzad Nabavi, op.cit.
62. "IRNA [Islamic Republic News Agency] Carries New Ministers' Biographies," Tehran IRNA in English in FBIS; September 20, 1988
63. "Autobiography of Behzad Nabavi," op.cit.; Robin Wright, "A Reporter at Large," in *The New Yorker,* September 5, 1988
64. Richard Cobb, *The People's Armies* (New Haven and London: Yale University Press, 1987)
65. Schahgaldian, op.cit.
66. Bakhash, op.cit. P. 63
67. "Organization of Mojahedin of Islamic Revolution," op.cit.
68. Ervand Abrahamian, *The Iranian Mojahedin* (New Haven and London: Yale University Press, 1989) P. 219

69. Ibid
70. "Opposition to Behzad Nabavi," Iran Press Digest; June 8, 1982, P.28
71. BBC report on the dissolution of the MIR, in Akhbar (News); Volume VII, No. 154; October 7, 1986
72. "Organization of Mojahedin of Islamic Revolution," op.cit.
73. Bakhash, op.cit., P.67
74. "Iranian Rightists Assail Bani-Sadr Over Conduct of the War with Iraq," New York Times; January 5, 1981, P.A1
75. "Chief Negotiator Nabavi Profiled," Cyprus Mail in English; January 11, 1981, P.3
76. "Infighting Among Ruling Clergy Reported," Christchurch The Press in English; January 18, 1984, P.18
77. Iran Yearbook 1988, op.cit.
78. "Candidates of Tehran Bazaar and Guilds and Islamic Revolution's Mojahedin Organization for Islamic Majles Elections Nomination," Jomhuri Eslam in Akhbar (News); April 7, 1984, Vol V., No. 9
79. "Revolutionary Guard Corps Established in Iran: Aims and Responsibilities," Tehran Domestic Service in Persian; May 6, 1979
80. "Iran Militants Planned to Hold U.S. Embassy Only Days, Student Claims," Christian Science Monitor; December 31, 1980
81. Ibid
82. *The Iran Hostage Crisis: A Chronology of Daily Developments,"* Report for the U.S. House of Representatives Committee on Foreign Affairs; Washington, U.S. Gov't Printing Office, March 1981, P. 170
83. Crane Brinton, *The Anatomy of Revolution* (New York: Vintage Books, 1965)
84. "Iran Militants Planned to Hold U.S. Embassy Only Days," op.cit.
85. "Ayatollah, Aide of Khomeini Shot," Washington Post; May 26, 1979
86. "Praise for Revolution Guards," Tehran Domestic Service in Persian; November 4, 1979
87. *The Iran Hostage Crisis: A Chronology of Daily Developments,* op.cit.
88. Slate of IRP candidates, op.cit.
89. "Emigre Paper: 27 Participants of US Embassy Takeover Killed," London Keyhan in Persian; December 5, 1985, P.5; "Iran's Agents of Terror," US News and World Report; March 6, 1989 pp.23-24
90. "Opposition to Behzad Nabavi," op.cit.
91. "Iranian Rightist Assail Bani-Sadr," op.cit.
92. Bakhash, op.cit.
93. "Document: Constitution of the Islamic Republic of Iran," introduction by Rouhollah K. Ramazani, in *The Middle East* Journal, Spring 1980, pp 181-183
94. Ibid P.189
95. Ibid pp.198-199

96. "Ayatollah Ruhollah Khomeini: The Mullah Who Transformed Iran," op.cit.
97. Tehran Times in English; June 21, 1989, P.2
98. "Divided Iranians Seem Unable to Settle on Firm Policy Course," New York Times; October 10, 1989, P.A1
99. "Ayatollah Araki Reconfirms Sharia Payments," Tehran Domestic Service in Persian; June 11, 1989
100. "Radio Program Examines Constitutional Reform," Tehran Domestic Service in Persian; July 20, 1989 in FBIS; July 24, 1989
101. "Rafsanjani Emerging Stronger Than Ever From Chaos in Iran," Reuters; April 23, 1989
102. "Document: Constitution of the Islamic Republic of Iran," op.cit., pp.194-197
103. "Hardliner to Lead Iran's Parliament," Washington Post; August 17, 1989
104. "Khomeini's Son Predicted as Speaker," IRNA in English in FBIS; June 28, 1989
105. Robin Wright, "A Reporter at Large," op.cit., P.61
106. "Internal Turmoil Roils Iran," op.cit.
107. Ibid
108. Bakhash, op.cit.
109. "Wily Speaker Excels at Iran's Political Game," Christian Science Monitor; August 27, 1987, P.1
110. Ibid
111. Abrahamian, op.cit., P. 50
112. Bakhash, op.cit., P. 243
113. Ibid, P. 184
114. Ibid, P. 243
115. "Hardliner to Lead Iran's Parliament," op.cit.
116. Bakhash, op.cit., pp. 102-3
117. "RafiqDust Named Chairman of Oppressed Foundation," Tehran Domestic Service in Persian in FBIS; September 7, 1989
118. "Three Year Record of Construction Crusade Lauded," Keyhan International in English; June 17, 1982
119. Bakhash, op.cit., Chap. 8
120. "Iran's Military Chief Says Gulf War Could Resume," Reuters; December 6, 1988
121. "IRNA Carries New Ministers' Biographies," op.cit.
122. "Emigre Paper: 27 Participants of U.S. Embassy Takeover Killed," op.cit.
123. "Accomplishments, Plans of Construction Jihad Reviewed," Keyhan International; June 13, 1982, P.8
124. "Khomeini Appoints Nuri His IRGC Representative," Tehran Domestic Service in Persian in FBIS; March 9, 1989

125. John Simpson, *Inside Iran: Life Under Khomeini's Regime* (New York: St. Martin's Press, 1988) P.81
126. "Revolutionary Guards," Iran Press Digest; March 13, 1984, P.5
127. Robin Wright, "A Reporter at Large," op.cit.
128. "Revolutionary Guards," Iran Press Digest, op.cit.
129. "Bayan Comments on Merger of Security Forces," Tehran Bayan in Persian; 22 June - 22 July 1990, pp 16,17 in FBIS; 30 August 1990

3

The Resiliency of the Revolutionary Guard

As has been shown, several institutions produced by the Islamic revolution—especially the IRP—were insufficiently flexible or adaptable to establish themselves as strong institutions within the Islamic republican political structure. The IRP was disbanded in 1987 and another revolutionary institution, the Council of Guardians was partially superceded by the formation of the Expediency Discernment Council in 1988.[1] These two organizations were unable to adapt to a changing political environment, either by assuming new functions, altering their organizational structures, assimilating new social elements, or responding effectively to political challenges. However, these organizations were unable to fulfill a crucial requirement of institutional strength—the achievement of a union between the interests of the membership and the functional and ideological norms of the organization.[2]

To a large degree, the Revolutionary Guard's strength as an institution in revolutionary Iran has resided in its ability to adapt to changing and difficult circumstances and to parry the challenges leveled against it since its formation in 1979. The Guard's ability to overcome the obstacles to its growth in size and political influence, as well as its functional development, are even more significant when the Guard is compared to other revolutionary armed forces. Unlike the Soviet Army, the Chinese People's Liberation Army, and the French revolutionary army, the Guard was forced to compete for influence with another armed force—the Iranian regular military—within the same political structure. The Guard, in essence, needed to expend significant organizational and political resources merely to gain and maintain its position as the dominant armed force in Iran, a resource drain that few other revolutionary armed forces experienced.

The Guard's organizational adaptability and did not translate into ideological flexibility. None of the challenges the Guard has faced, either from within the organization, from other organizations or political and

social forces within Iran, or from outside Iran, has yet succeeded in damp-
ening the Guard's ideological commitment to the hardline principles of
the Islamic revolution. The Guard's zealous ideological character has, in
fact, prompted several attempts to curb the Guard's power. To a greater
degree than other institutions within Iran and other revolutionary armed
forces in history, the Guard has emerged as an armed vanguard of the
principles of the revolution that created it.

Analyzing Guard Resiliency

The concepts of organizational adaptability, flexibility, and resiliency
are imprecise. An organization like the Revolutionary Guard can be considered adaptable for its ability to integrate members of varied social
backgrounds, yet at the same time rigid in its inability to innovate new
doctrines, tactics, or strategies that will produce objective successes such
as battlefield victories. The measures of resiliency which can encompass
the most relevant and precisely focused developments and characteristics
of the Revolutionary Guard are (a) political, (b) social, and (c) structure-
functional resiliency.

The measurement of political resiliency refers to the Guard's ability to
repulse the several political challenges to its growth and development.
Fearing the Guard's influence in the regime and ability to bolster its political allies in the leadership, various politicians have sought to confine the
Guard's responsibilities, control its leadership, and prevent its growth.[3]
The analysis of the Guard's political resiliency therefore will focus on the
degree of success the Guard demonstrated in outmaneuvering its adversaries in the leadership. This analysis will also help explain the Guard's
role as the principle institutional vanguard of the Islamic revolution as
defined by Ayatollah Khomeini.

Analysis of the Guard's social resiliency will focus on the process by
which the Guard has been able to integrate members from diverse social
backgrounds, experiences, and interests into its ranks and to mobilize
these groups toward the Guard's goals. The ability to do so is a key criteria of institutionalization and, according to Ellis, crucial to the success of
revolutionary armed forces.[4] Within this analysis, it will be shown that the
Guard was able to accommodate and effectively mobilize even those social elements that lacked the zealous ideological motivations of the
Guard's radical core, without suffering dilution of its revolutionary character. These less hardline elements were, nonetheless, crucial to the
Guard's efforts to prosecute the revolutionary war against Iraq.

The last aspect of resiliency that must be explored is structure-functional
resiliency. This refers to the Guard's ability to perform new functions and

develop the appropriate structures in order to respond to external pressure, fulfill its mission, and strengthen its institutional position vis-a-vis competing institutions in Iran. An important requirement of this analysis is to examine the success of the Guard—initially only a revolutionary internal security militia—in organizing itself as an army when Iraq invaded Iran in 1980. It is also important to assess the organizational adaptations the Guard made to perform its mission as chief instrument of Iran's attempts to export the Islamic revolution. After the war ended, the Guard had to adopt a primarily defensive military posture and assume some reconstruction duties, tasks that were much less directly related to fulfilling Khomeini's ambitions to spread the revolution throughout the Islamic world.

Political Resiliency

There was opposition to the Guard's very formation in 1979, and, once formed, the Guard was nearly dismembered by political competition for control over it. Before Khomeini officially inaugurated the Guard in May 1979, liberal nonclerical politicians led by the Islamic Republic's first Prime Minister Mehdi Bazargan, recognizing the Guard's militance, sought to prevent the Guard from becoming an independent armed force.[5] Bazargan and his allies wanted to incorporate the militia into the police and regular army.[6] As further evidence of dispute over the Guard's birth, Khomeini's official announcement of the Guard's formation occurred one week after Bazargan's statement that the Guard (and Komitehs) would be dissolved following the establishment of a formally elected government.[7] In late April 1979, Bazargan had also criticized the Guards and Komiteh members for resisting the authority of his Provisional Government and for their vengeful retribution against Khomeini opponents and supporters of the former Shah's regime.[8]

Despite Bazargan's objections, the Guard was created on May 5, 1979, formally reporting to the Revolutionary Council, the secretive body of Khomeini confidants that ruled Iran in all but name during the early years of the Islamic regime.[9] If one assumes that Khomeini and his close aides intended, from the outset, to eventually displace Bazargan and his liberal colleagues, then it directly follows that the Revolutionary Council members found the Guard a convenient tool for undermining Bazargan. The takeover of the U.S. Embassy in Tehran, exemplified this tacit Guard-Revolutionary Council coalition against Bazargan. Although the Revolutionary Council's patronage was undoubtedly instrumental in shielding the Guard from Bazargan, the Guard's firm hardline ideological grounding and its refusal to submit to Bazargan's authority also contributed to its success in repulsing this early political challenge.

A better case for the Guard's political resiliency can be derived from its early ability to develop and expand despite the attempts by various political factions to gain personal and political control over the Guard. The factional battle for influence in the Guard aggravated its early divisions along regional and personal lines and nearly fractured the young militia before it had solidified as an organization.[10] This early turmoil represented a disadvantage that the Guard's counterparts in the French, Russian, and Chinese Communist revolutions did not face. The French revolutionary army was constituted in large part from the prerevolutionary one and its direction and leadership was especially clear during the Napoleonic phase of the revolution.[11] Similarly the Red Army was steadily and ably constructed under the strong tutelage of Leon Trotsky, a leading Bolshevik, and the revolutionary army of the Chinese Communist Party was already a cohesive force when it brought the Communists to power in China in 1949.[12]

Because the Guard intially was a patchwork of local militias and revolutionary groups, segments within the young Guard were necessarily susceptible to political appeals from a wide range of different politicians. Nonetheless we can discern several themes in the early power struggles for control of the Guard. At the most basic level was the effort by the clerical political leadership to impose its authority on the Guard. This manifested itself in the establishment of the official position of IRGC (Guard) Superviser (downgraded to "Khomeini's Representative to the Guard" after 1982), a position generally held by a cleric. The Superviser was to be nominally superior to the Guard Commander and empowered to approve Guard leadership decisions and ensure that the Guard's actions conformed to Khomeini's guidelines.[13]

On another level was the competition within the civilian political structure for control of the Guard. For example, the first IRGC Superviser, Ayatollah Hasan Lahuti, was a generally liberal cleric; his views were in line with those of Bazargan and Lahuti was undoubtedly trying to bring the Guard into Bazargan's fold.[14] Lahuti was clearly not politically compatible with the hardline militants in the Guard. Predictably, Lahuti was removed as Guard Superviser in October 1979, one month before hardliners, including the Guard, ousted Bazargan by seizing the U.S. Embassy in Tehran.[15]

The demise of the moderate Bazargan government led to the political ascendancy of his opponents—the IRP clerics who dominated the Revolutionary Council. (The Council took control of Iran after Bazargan's resignation.) After Lahuti's resignation as IRGC Superviser, two leading IRP clerics (and currently the two top political leaders in Iran), subsequently served in succession as Guard Superviser—the mid ranking clerics Ali Akbar Hashemi Rafsanjani, now President, and Ali Khamene'i, now supreme leader of Iran.[16] Although, as key IRP and Revolutionary Council members Rafsanjani and Khamene'i were important in cementing the IRP's alliance with the Guard/MIR/nonclerical militant wing of the regime, neither was enthusiastically supported by the Guard as Superviser. Rafsanjani served in the position only one month (Oct-Nov 1979) until being succeeded by Khamene'i, who a Stockholm newspaper claimed "was reluctantly accepted as [the Guard's] new leader."[17] Although both were more radical than Lahuti, they were undoubtedly viewed as political commissars imposed on, rather than from, the Guard itself. Neither was successful in imposing structure or discipline on the still disorganized Revolutionary Guard.

Ali Khamene'i's tenure as Guard Superviser lasted through the early 1980 election of the generally moderate noncleric Abol Hassan Bani-Sadr as the Islamic Republic's first President. Bani Sadr's substantial popular majority (76 percent of the vote), coupled with his opposition to direct clerical rule and some hardline tenets of the revolution, virtually ensured conflict between him and the IRP clerics, who were backed by their militant nonclerical allies in the Guard, MIR, Komitehs, Construction Jihad, and Students in the Line of the Imam (U.S. hostage holders).[18] Bani Sadr's Presidency was therefore a pivotal event in the organizational development of the Guard and a key test of its ability to survive in politically hostile circumstances.[19] Had Bani Sadr succeeded politically, the Guard may have suffered an abbreviated organizational lifetime, reduced responsibilities, and attenuated influence in the regime. However, the involvement of the Guard in defeating Bani Sadr both reflected and accelerated the Guard's development as an institution and resulted in policies more in line with the Guard's militant ideology.

In addition to personally opposing the hardline ideology espoused by the Guard, as a politician Bani-Sadr undoubtedly calculated that circumscribing the power of the Guard was essentially to undermining the power base of the Guard's political patrons, the IRP clerics. Bani-Sadr's battle against the Guard, which began almost as soon as he took office, was given early support from an unlikely source—Ayatollah Khomeini. About a month after Bani Sadr took office, Khomeini, seeking to stabilize the fledgling Islamic government, appointed Bani-Sadr Commander-in-Chief of the Armed Forces, giving the new President formal control and appointment powers over both the Guard and regular military.[20] Although Khomeini was fully supportive of the Guard as the revolution's own Islamic army, Bani-Sadr was close to Khomeini in the early days of the revolution, and he apparently prevailed on Khomeini the need for a unified military command under the duly elected President of the republic. The effects of Bani-Sadr's Presidency on the Guard are best captured in a 1982 press interview with the Guard's unofficial first Commander (now an Ambassador) Javad Mansuri:

Bani-Sadr's being made Commander-in-Chief of the Armed Forces was the hardest blow struck on the [Islamic Revolutionary Guard] Corps during its existence, but it was able to escape the danger which threatened it. This danger even brought the Corps more solidity. Bani-Sadr's command caused strong disunion within the Corps and among many good, pious forces for whom work inside the Corps had become impossible, and Bani-Sadr often said openly that such people should be expelled from [the] IRGC. The relations between the IRGC and the [regular] army were also very bad, which prevented the Corps from spreading and reaching full growth. I remember how often I asked Shadmehr, head of the common (regular army and Guard) Staff at the time of Bani-Sadr, to give the Corps the necessary equipment in proportion to the operations it is commissioned to make, and he used to answer frankly that they gave no arms to the Corps, and the Guards had to arm themselves by disarming the enemy (Iraq) only.[21]

In addition, as another major Guard leader Ali Shamkhani points out, Bani-Sadr attempted to exert sway over the Guard at its leadership level.[22] In May 1980 Bani-Sadr requested and received additional authority over the armed forces from Khomeini.[23] Shortly thereafter Bani-Sadr, claiming approval from top Guard commanders, named his ally Abbas Zamani (a key early founder and organizer of the Guard) as permanent Guard Commander. (Zamani had been serving as operational commander and de-facto Guard Commander since the Guard's official formation; Zamani's appointment, therefore, was in reality only a formal strengthening of Zamani's position.)[24] This effort to subdue the Guard from the top failed, however. Zamani, who had had substantial legitimacy in the Guard as a hardened, longtime anti-Shah guerrilla, became tainted by Bani-Sadr's prominent patronage, giving Zamani's and Bani-Sadr's opponents in the Guard command structure sufficient ammunition to force Zamani's resignation as Guard commander the following month.[25] By withdrawing support for, and thus toppling Abbas Zamani as its leader, the Guard was able to counterattack against Zamani's patron, Bani-Sadr, without directly contradicting the assertion of the Guard's charismatic father figure, Khomeini, that Bani-Sadr run Iran's military affairs.

Despite the fall of Zamani, Bani Sadr continued—and the Guard continued to scuttle—his efforts to name his personal choice to the top Guard post. Following Abbas Zamani's resignation he asked Kazem Bojnurdi, Zamani's co-founder of the Islamic Nations Party, to head the IRGC. After a few days of "deliberation" in which the most powerful elements within the Guard (the MIR) undoubtedly expressed opposition to Bojnurdi, he declined the appointment, obliquely admitting that Guard factionalism would make the organization difficult for him to control.[26] With Bani-Sadr's inability to dominate the Guard clearly exposed, the IRP subsequently backed the appointment of an ally, Morteza Reza'i, as Guard Commander in July 1980.[27] In conjunction, another supporter of the IRP, Hojjat ol-Eslam Fazlollah Mahallati, a veteran of the PLO guerrilla camps that trained many future Guardsmen, was named Guard Superviser.[28] Also that summer, Bani-Sadr suffered another major political setback when the IRP forced him to name Ali Rajai, a former teacher and a co-founder of the MIR (the Guard's principal precursor) as Prime Minister.[29]

In addition to solidifying the MIR-Guard alliance with the IRP, Prime Minister Rajai was instrumental in checking Bani-Sadr's efforts to weaken the Guard. After the Iran-Iraq war broke out in September 1980, Rajai, along with the IRP dominated Majles, opposed Bani-Sadr's injunction against arming the Guard with heavy weapons.[30] More importantly, it was Rajai who coined an oft-repeated assertion in support of the Guard that "a maktab (ideologically pure) army is better than a victorious one."[31] As brief yet significant as it is, Rajai's position, which has largely continued to hold as Guard policy, is in disagreement with the principal argument of revolutionary armed forces scholar Jonathan Adelman. Adelman argues that there is no tradeoff between revolutionary zeal and objective military effectiveness, but, to the contrary, the revolutionary experience invariably adds strength and military effectiveness to the lackluster and ineffective armies of the former regimes.[32]

The Guard's alliance with the IRP clearly proved an effective tool in its political battle against Bani-Sadr. In addition, the Guard's political strategy included the selective use of its own internal security and military responsibilities to undermine the President. Even before the Iran-Iraq war began, the Guard openly defied the President's authority by aggressively prosecuting the war against rebellious Kurds despite Bani-Sadr's announcements that ceasefires with the Kurds had been negotiated.[33] Throughout Bani-Sadr's presidency, the Guard clearly attempted to underscore, where possible, his ineffectiveness by cooperating with the holding of the U.S. hostages (Bani-Sadr apparently favored their release) and by tacitly endorsing the takeovers and ransacking of the headquarters of opposition groups in Tehran.[34] In July 1980 the Guard and its political allies used a minor failed regular army coup to give the Guard command of army units and bases allegedly involved in the plot, to accelerate the purging of regular army officers, and to argue that Bani-Sadr's power base in the regular military constituted a threat to the revolution.[35]

Despite Khomeini's injunctions that all military forces and political leaders rally around Bani-Sadr following the Iraqi invasion, the Guard and its political allies nonetheless continued to undermine him. In early 1981, a speech by Khomeini's heir apparent Ayatollah Hosein Ali Montazeri and a telegram from southern front "revolutionary organs" (a term denoting the Guard, revolutionary committees, and other hardline elements) criticized Bani-Sadr for failing to organize a counteroffensive against Iraq.[36] When Bani-Sadr responded by organizing a counterattack against the invaders, these same political elements excoriated Bani-Sadr and the regular military for the counteroffensive's failure.[37]

The political infighting during the first year of the war clearly demonstrates that politics preceded military effectiveness. It was in the broader interests of both the regular military and Bani-Sadr on the one hand, and the Guard and the IRP clerics on the other, to cooperate in organizing a successful drive against Iraq. Nonetheless, the unwillingness of either group to allow its antagonist the possibility of military, and thus political, success prevented sufficient battlefield cooperation. Paradoxically, this polarization between political groupings was perhaps greater than at any time in the eleven year history of the revolution, even though the objective threat to the still fledgling revolution posed by the Iraqi invasion was also at its peak and therefore demanded maximum cooperation.

Politically, the Guard continued to aid and abet the deterioration of Bani-Sadr's position during 1981. The Guard broke up pro-Bani-Sadr demonstrations, becoming progressively more aggressive in doing so as Khomeini's backing for the President waned.[38] Revolutionary Guardsmen even arrested members of Bani-Sadr's staff just before his ouster in June 1981.[39] Although many political groups contributed to toppling Bani-Sadr, in helping oust him, the Guard had proven its resiliency by winning an important political battle that no major revolutionary army had fought—a battle for its very survival against a major regime leader, a Commander-in-Chief of the Armed Forces of the revolution that spawned that revolutionary army. Although there were political differences over the composition, leadership, control and roles of the French, Soviet, and Chinese Communist revolutionary armed forces, the very existence of these forces within their regimes had never appeared to be in doubt.

Bani-Sadr's fall reversed the effects of his Presidency. This was best summarized in 1982 by the Guard's unofficial first Commander Javad Mansuri:

> After Bani-Sadr was removed, the [Revolutionary Guard] Corps began a fresh life. It now had the opportunity to wage an open battle against armed leftist groups and suppressing them. On the battlefronts, the Corps were supplied with adequate arms and weapons, their relations with the army improved, and they were able to demonstrate their ability in defending the country and the Islamic regime.[40]

The defeat of Bani-Sadr essentially left the IRP clerics in control of Iran and the alliance between those clerics and the Guard remained generally intact throughout the remainder of the war. In addition to demonstrating its resiliency, the Guard's battle with Bani-Sadr clearly showed that the

Guard viewed itself as a political and not a disciplined and professional force, and that it considered its involvement in politics as not only permitted but as an integral part of its mission and charter. Unlike the involvement of the Red Army and Chinese People's Liberation Army in several succession struggles in the USSR and China, respectively[41], the Revolutionary Guard did not await invitation from civilian leaders before becoming involved in internal political struggles. The Guard viewed Bani-Sadr not only as a threat to its organizational survival, but as a traitor to the principles of the revolution the Guard helped bring to power. Paradoxically, the Guard even appeared to be more intensely opposed to Bani-Sadr than did the revolution's charismatic leader, Khomeini, whose ideals Bani-Sadr was subverting and who tolerated Bani-Sadr almost until his political end.[42]

The Guard's involvement in the political power struggle against Bani-Sadr also greatly bolstered its influence with its patrons in the IRP. To the IRP, the Guard had proven had proven to be a useful element in helping the clerics solidify their control. Less positively, the clerics were undoubtedly rendered fearful of the Guard's likely reaction should these clerics, for whatever reason, attempt to moderate the direction of the revolution in the future. This is a scenario that some of the leading regime clerics indeed faced seven years after the fall of Bani-Sadr.

The Guard vs. Its Patrons

In 1982, when the Iranians expelled Iraq from Iranian soil, the war was transformed from one of national survival to a true revolutionary war in which the power of the Islamic revolution to spread beyond Iran's borders was at stake. From 1982 to 1988, a period corresponding to Iranian battlefield progress, Khomeini's support for the war forced a consensus among his clerical subordinates, the Revolutionary Guard, and, to a lesser extent, even the regular military, to prosecute the war against Iraq until victory.[43] Victory was usually defined as the overthrow of Iraqi President Saddam Husayn and the Ba'thist regime and the establishment of an Islamic Republic in Iraq. This consensus ended in the summer of 1988 when Iran's armed forces—both regular and Guard—were overrun in a series of Iraqi offensives and driven off Iraqi territory, and Iraqi troops again seized territory inside Iran. In the infighting that accompanied the July 17, 1988 decision (endorsed by Khomeini) to end the war by accepting U.N. Security Council Resolution 598, the alliance between the Guard and many of its longtime supporters, especially the chief champion of a negotiated settlement, Rafsanjani, was badly damaged.[44]

In 1988 the Guard's zealous commitment to the war, a conflict which had been virtually synonymous with the revolution itself for eight years, became a liability to many of the same politicians who previously had used the Guard's militancy to their own political benefit. Moreover, that the Guard opposed those clerics who were willing to compromise the hardline principles of the revolution demonstrates that the Guard's political support was only available to those politicians who remained faithful to the tenets of the revolution.

Press reports and Khomeini's message to the September 1988 gathering of Guard commanders in Azadi Stadium suggest that, despite the battlefield catastrophes, the Guard opposed the acceptance of a ceasefire.[45] Rafsanjani and his cohorts probably realized that the zeal the Guard had directed against Iraq could similarly be turned against these clerics if the Guard perceived them as deviating from the revolution's principles or, just as critically, manipulating Khomeini into ending the war. It can therefore be argued that Khomeini's official statement taking responsibility for the ceasefire decision[46] was a crucial act in blunting the intended backlash from the Guard and its militant allies in the regime.

There is a considerable body of evidence that, as Iran's military fortunes began to collapse in 1988, Rafsanjani, anticipating the impending need to sue for peace and the likely attendant unrest in the Guard, set out to weaken the Guard politically. In doing so, he provided the Guard its most serious political challenge since the fall of Bani-Sadr. Following consecutive Iranian defeats at Al Faw and East of Basra (Iraq's second largest city) Rafsanjani, who had been playing a key role in running the war as Khomeini's Representative to the Supreme Defense Council, was tasked by Khomeini to act for him as Commander-in-Chief of the Armed Forces.[47] He was mandated to reverse Iran's military slide in part by improving cooperation between the regular military and the Guard.[48] Rafsanjani was subsequently able to convince or compel Guard Commander Mohsen Reza'i to appear on television to accept personal blame for Iran's defeats, thus politically weakening the Guard leader and demoralizing the Guard.[49]

As part of his mandate from Khomeini, Rafsanjani set up a General Headquarters that combined the command staffs of the Guard and regular military.[50] Rafsanjani also appointed longtime Reza'i subordinates Ali Shamkhani and Ali Reza Afshar as deputy chiefs of Operations and Intelligence and Human Resources, respectively, in the General Headquarters,[51] an apparent attempt to isolate Guard Commander Reza'i. In early September (six weeks after the acceptance of the ceasefire), he apparently allowed the Majles to oust longtime Guard Minister (and Rafsanjani ally and reported brother-in-law) Rafiq-Dust,[52] even though as Majles Speaker he probably could have intervened on Rafiq-Dust's behalf. Rafsanjani's dominance of the Majles suggests that he probably sponsored or tacitly backed legislation to merge the Guard and Defense Ministries,[53] an action which touched off rumors that the Guard and regular military forces would eventually be merged.[54] The Guard has consistently sought to remain independent from the regular military.

The Guard Retaliates

Unlike the earlier political struggles against Bazargan and Bani-Sadr, the Guard had few political allies with which to counter Rafsanjani. Many of the clerics in the regime agreed that war had to be abandoned and apparently saw the loss of the war as both necessitating and creating an opportunity for weakening the political influence of the Guard.[55] Moreover, Khomeini himself had publicly endorsed the abandonment of the war effort, thereby leaving the Guard and its hardline allies isolated. The Guard, therefore, had to draw upon its intrinsic institutional resources to repulse the post-war political challenge, without appearing disloyal to the Islamic government or, especially, the Guard's charismatic father figure Khomeini.

In rebuking the challenge, the Guard leaders, in late September 1988, convened a major meeting of national and local Guard commanders throughout Iran in Tehran's Azadi Stadium in which the commanders would, according to Reza'i, "survey their future plans for guarding the Islamic revolution."[56] The huge gathering was essentially a show of strength by the Guard—an implicit threat to Rafsanjani and the political leadership that the Guard would resist a serious effort to undermine it. Subsequent statements by the Guard commanders were similarly ominous; Guard Spokesman Ali Reza Afshar stated that the failure of the clerics to preserve the ideology of the revolution would constitute a threat to the revolution itself.[57] Even more alarming, a respected Arab newspaper reported that, in connection with the dispute over the Guard's post-war role, Guardsmen made several attempts on Rafsanjani's life.[58]

The Guard's resort to political brinkmanship succeeded to a large extent. All those political leaders who addressed the Guard commanders' gathering pledged that the Guard would remain as a separate military force and prime guardian of the revolution. Simultaneously, Reza'i's hardline ally Ali Shamkhani was named to replace Rafiq-Dust as Guard Minister.[59] The Majles also postponed deliberation on legislation to merge the Guard and Defense Ministries for six months.[60] (The merger was approved following Khomeini's death about a year later.[61]) Moreover, Khomeini publicly issued a statement of support for the Guard, directing political leaders not to take any steps to weaken it.[62]

If the Guard had, at least temporarily, resisted its suffocation at the hands of its longtime political superiors and patrons, the clerics kept up their efforts to alter the Guard's zealous revolutionary character. Rafsanjani and then President Ali Khamene'i were at the forefront of the effort to operationalize the concept that professionalization of an armed force reduces its propensity to involve itself in politics. In a major speech to the Guard in October 1988, Rafsanjani called on the Guard to improve its discipline, establish a clear "hierarchy" (ie institute formal ranks), focus on training and proficiency in conventional military techniques, and to abandon export of the revolution through force.[63] According to Rafsanjani, it is "one of the responsibilities of the IRGC Commanders to think and to change their organization into a military one, a completely military organization. And it is the responsibility of the IRGC personnel to accept that. They should feel that they are members of a serious military organization."[64] Khamene'i echoed a similar theme, seconding the call for the Guard to improve its discipline and to stay out of "petty politics."[65] However, there is virtually no evidence that the Guard leadership or rank and file have responded to these efforts to professionalize and depoliticize the organization. The Guard clearly has not abandoned its efforts to export the revolution by force; the institution of conventional military ranks in 1990 has not led to a broader professionalization effort, and the Guard has continued to mobilize popular support for hardline policies.[66]

The Guard's resilience in the face of these challenges demonstrates its firm roots in the revolution and clearly distinguishes the Guard from weaker, less adaptable, and less resilient revolutionary institutions such as the IRP, the several Foundations, and the revolutionary committees. These institutions either collapsed or were seriously weakened in the course of the Islamic regime's perpetual power struggles. Even the institution of velayat-e-faqih, which probably best symbolizes the Islamic revolutionary political system, has barely survived one transfer of power.

The Guard's ability to retain its revolutionary militance and organizational strength in the face of regime attempts to weaken it also distinguishes the Guard from its historical counterparts. Neither the French revolutionary army, the Chinese PLA, or the Soviet Red Army faced threats to their initial formation by key leaders of their respective revolutions, even though, as revolutionary organizations, these armies were naturally subject to some infighting for influence within them.

The popular armies of the French revolution, which possessed many of the characteristics displayed by the early Guard, were disbanded when their militance began to outrun and therefore threaten the revolutionary leadership in France.[67] The PLA, although unquestionably still a major interest group in the Chinese Communist regime, has succumbed to civilian attempts to professionalize it. By the time of the Cultural Revolution, it had become a sufficiently conservative force to act as a restraining element on the Red Guard militants who were exceeding their mandate from Mao.[68] Conventional military ranks have been instituted in the PLA, as they have been in the Guard, but the PLA, unlike the Guard, suffered the replacement of hardline veteran revolutionary commanders by competent, professional officers.[69] The Red Army had similarly become a relatively obedient servant of the Communist Party that created it. The professionalization and depoliticization of the Red Army was a key goal of Trotsky and the early Bolshevik regime precisely so that it would never pose a political threat to the Communist Party.[70] The Red Army was unable or unwilling to resist Stalin's replacement of revolutionary commanders, notably Voroshilov and Budienny, with more professional officers during World War II.[71] More recently, as evidence of its lack of ideological commitment, the Red Army failed to emerge as an institutional base of opposition to the collapse of Communism and the Soviet Union itself; this was exemplified in the military's divided, half-hearted, and abortive participation in the hardline coup in the former Soviet Union in August 1991.

Social Resiliency

Just as the Guard was forced to fend off assaults on its organizational integrity and hardline ideology from the political environment, it similarly had to cope with constraints and challenges emanating from its own social structure. The Guard's social structure, in turn, was partially determined by the demands of the war against Iraq. Although the Guard's social composition never threatened to destroy the Guard as an institution, some of the social groups the Guard had to accommodaate within its ranks could have dampened its revolutionary zeal. These groups did not do so. A corollary is the Guard's ability to integrate various social groups that, although radical, nonetheless complicated the Guard's ability to perform its mission. It will be shown how the Guard succeeded in overcoming the operational limitations posed by such groups.

The social core of the Revolutionary Guard was primarily comprised of lower middle class urban guerrillas that had been fighting the Shah since at least the early 1970s. Longtime Guard Minister Mohsen Rafiq-Dust, one of the older members of the inner circle that helped form the Guard in 1979, was active against the Shah since shortly after the 1963 uprising in which Khomeini played a prominent role.[72] Many of the Guard leaders and organizers were students or practitioners in technical fields. Mohsen Reza'i, whose father was a pro-Khomeini minor bazaar merchant, worked briefly in the oil industry in southern Iran. Ali Shamkhani, referred to in a 1980 Iranian press report as Engineer Shamkhani, was one of the better educated of the Guard leaders; he studied at an agricultural college in southern Iran.[73] MIR founder Behzad Nabavi was an electronics technician who studied at the Tehran Polytechnic Institute.[74] To the inner circle of guerrillas were added hardline militants from lower middle class social backgrounds who became armed and active during the revolution itself.

Opportunists

In addition to the militants that joined the Guard for ideological and political reasons and formed the core of the organization, the Guard incorporated within its ranks a category of recruits that can be described as "opportunists." The opportunists were those who joined the Guard primarily because of self-interest. They were sympathetic to Guard ideology and its often brutal tactics but were not as fervent in their support of the Guard's ideals as those who formed or first joined the organization; they viewed Guard membership as a tool for personal advancement. As Bakhash points out, "tens of thousands of youths, drawn from the unemployed and lumpen elements of the urban slums, found jobs in the Revolutionary Guard and committees."[75] Similarly, an Indian newspaper described a "push-pull effect"—the combination of a poor domestic economy, the closing of the universities, and the Guard's prestige in the new regime and employment opportunities—as accounting for the emergence of the Guard as a popular avenue for advancement.[76]

To ambitious youths, the Guard's effectiveness as a vehicle for upward mobility in revolutionary Iran was demonstrated by several notable examples of success. About two years after helping form the Guard, Javad Mansuri became a Foreign Ministry undersecretary.[77] Mohammad Qarazi, another organizer of the early Guard, became Governor General of Khuzestan, Minister of Oil, and then Minister of Posts, Telegraph, and Telephone.[78] Mohsen Reza'i became Commander of the Guard, and thus a national figure, at age 27; Shamkhani became his deputy at age 26.[79] The examples provided by these Guardsmen, coupled with the image of the Guard as part of Iran's new elite, undoubtedly served as a strong incentive for young Iranian youths to volunteer.

In addition to the intangible factors of prestige and upward mobility, there were more concrete, immediate rewards for joining the Revolutionary Guard. Foremost among these was undoubtedly the higher pay accorded rank and file Guardsmen compared with that of regular military soldiers.[80] Moreover, some international press sources have reported that Guardsmen also received parcels of land that were confiscated from wealthy landowners who fled the revolution.[81] Given the high rate of unemployment in Iran throughout most of the war and the material benefits of Guard service, it is not difficult to understand the strong attraction of Guard membership.

Although not contributing to the militant ideological character of the Guard, the opportunists were nonetheless indispensable to the Guard's ability to build its numerical, and therefore institutional strength. These organizational goals, although subordinate to the Guard's ideological goals, undoubtedly explain why the Guard was willing to offer substantial material incentives to its recruits. The key drawback provided by the opportunists is that their commitment to the institution is only as great as the material and intangible benefits provided. When such benefits are withdrawn or exceeded by other institutions, opportunists, virtually by definition, will desert the organization. Yet another problem posed by this grouping is that the opportunists viewed the Guard as a stepping stone to more prestigious positions in the Majles and national and provincial government, and therefore did not contribute to the development of organizational loyalty.

Despite the negative effects of opportunists on the Guard, neither the organization nor its radical ideology was weakened by their presence. Just as opportunistic Guardsmen used the Guard, so too did the Guard make use of its ambitious soldiers to build up its ranks in absolute terms and relative to the regular military. Moreover, to the extent that opportunistic Guardsmen viewed the organization as a means of advancement, they had incentive to conform to the principles and codes of conduct of the Guard and to succeed according to the Guard's definition of success. This utilitarian motivation, therefore, limited the adverse effects of the opportunists on the Guard.

Conscripts

Considerably more adverse to the Guard's role as vanguard of the revolution were the conscripts which became a progressively larger percentage of Guard ranks as the war dragged on. According to unconfirmed estimates, by end of the war in 1988, conscripts comprised about 80% of the Guard's frontline troops.[82] This figure does not, however, include the Guards vast internal security forces or Basij fighters. Although the Guard probably began to use conscripts in the mid 1980s, in 1987 the Guard officially announced that it would begin drafting eligible males for the war effort.[83] In addition, the official announcement of the conscription policy warned of a strict crackdown on Guard deserters, essentially confirming that not all Guard soldiers had joined the organization of their own volition.[84]

The need for a draft in the Revolutionary Guard can be viewed as a contradiction of the very essence of the Guard—a zealous, ideological force of volunteers willing to die for Khomeini, the revolution, and Islam. Nonetheless, the same fanaticism that manifested itself operationally in the use of high casualty "human wave" assaults against the better armed Iraqis, resulted in a depletion of many of those Guardsmen most supportive of the Guard's ideology and tactics.[85] This high rate of manpower depletion, in turn, accounts for the Guard's acceptance of conscription. The draft alone did not solve the Guard's manpower problems, and the Guard supplemented this approach by gradually shifting the lead role in the human wave offensives to the more plentiful and pliable Basij. The Guardsmen reserved for themselves the less risky role of unit commanders and follow-on forces to the leading edge Basij attack waves.[86]

In contrast to the opportunists, whose personal interests coincided with the institutional interests of the Guard, the conscripts posed a greater problem for the Guard's fulfillment of its role as armed vanguard of the revolution. Like conscripts in any army, the Guard's conscripts were forced to serve and therefore they were the least supportive of the Guard's ideology of any grouping within the Guard. The Guard's high casualty tactics and commitment to prosecuting the war until victory undoubtedly made its conscripts particularly disgruntled when compared to those in Iran's regular military and those of other conventional armies. Available evidence suggests that the Guard's willingness to pursue war until victory—even as the war effort collapsed in 1988—was not shaken by the high percentage of conscripts within Guard ranks. Nonetheless, the heavy use of conscripts indirectly weakened the Guard's ability to prevent a ceasefire by contributing to the battlefield collapse. Press accounts suggest that, despite statements from the Guard leaders to hold fast in the face of Iraqi offensives, even Guard units fled the battlefield in huge numbers.[87] The territory East of Basra that took Iran two months and tens of thousands of casualties to capture in 1987 was recaptured by Iraq in 1988 in a nine-hour battle.[88] Such capitulation was uncharacteristic of the Guard's previous performance; Guardsmen fought to the death under similar military pressure in the initial Iraqi invasion and throughout most of the war.[89] Although many factors, including improved Iraqi battlefield performance and possible use of chemical weapons, may account for the Guard's rapid military unraveling in 1988,[90] the high percentage of conscripts within its ranks undoubtedly contributed to the relative lack of resistance. The military collapse, in turn, severely weakened the Guard leaders' ability, if not their attempts, to prevent the Iranian government decision to end the war.[91]

One potential contradiction that requires explanation is the Guard's need to institute conscription even though Basij volunteers remained relatively plentiful throughout the war.[92] The Basij volunteers, unlike Guard rank and file soldiers, were not fixed forces. The Basij volunteered for three month tours, usually corresponding the periods of high military activity, and then returned home.[93] Guard conscripts, therefore, were needed to replace the fixed, permanent, forces that were depleted at a high rate during the war. It must also be considered that the Guard's internal security responsibilities spread its ranks thin, and the Guard could not easily assign its most committed members to the front without sacrificing its internal security capabilities.[94] The Guard's domestic role, as will be shown later, has been a key additional source of its power and influence in the regime.

On balance, the Guard's use of conscripts was an unavoidable drawback to its military role in the prosecution of revolutionary war. The conscripts did help fill out the Guard's continually depleted ranks, but the conscripts' weak commitment to the war and the hardline principles of the revolution contributed to the Guard's poor military performance when Iraq applied serious battlefield pressure in 1988. Despite the adverse impact of the use of conscripts, however, the Guard retained more than enough political strength to prevent political leaders from converting the Guard's battlefield defeats in 1988 into its political emasculation.

Experts and Bureaucrats

As a result of the Guard's growing complexity and demands placed upon it throughout the war, the Guard also had to integrate two other groups into its structure—administrators and technical experts. These two groups were, to a significant extent, contradictions of the Guard's revolutionary character. As postulated by Weber, the Guard's bureaucrats, who were needed to handle the Guard's growing payroll, weapons procurement apparatus, logistical support needs, and relations with the civilian bureaucracy, could have been expected to temper the Guard's revolutionary zeal by introducing rationality and regularization of procedure into the Guard's operations.[95] The Guard's technical experts were recruited to develop its domestic arms production capabilities and to improve battlefield logistics through technology, such as communications systems.[96] Some engineers and technicians performed these functions for the Guard indirectly throught service in the Construction Jihad, which also develop weapons systems and provided logistical help for the Guard.[97] As in the case of Guard bureaucrats, the technical experts could have been expected to dampen the Guard's revolutionary enthusiasm by introducing the contrary principles of decisionmaking through rational scientific examination rather than emotion.

Contrary to expectations, the Guard's experts and bureaucrats did not make it more conservative, rationalized military force. Rather, these groups gave the Guard greater capabilities with which to prosecute the revolutionary war it did not want to abandon. Although the technical experts and administrators enabled the Guard to make use of progressively more sophisticated conventional weapons and tactics, the Guard never abandoned the hallmark of its revolutionary fervor—the human wave offensive. Rather, the Guard used complex conventional weapons to improve the effectiveness of its near suicidal tactics.[98]

Interaction with the Regular Military

The issue of Guard cooperation and interaction with the regular military is broad, but the Guard's use of regular military expertise is relevant to the discussion of the Guard's ability to adapt and absorb the impact of weakly or non-revolutionary social groupings. Although the Guard and regular military remained separate as institutions with their own chains of command, the Guard accepted training from the regular military and allowed some regular military officers to direct selected Guard units in specific major offensives.[99] As in the Guard's use of technical experts, the Guard was able to accept the knowledge and talents of the regular military without compromising its hardline goals and principles. The conventional military training and limited battlefield integration did not cause the Guard to abandon its use of unconventional tactics such as the human wave offensive. This was even the case during the 1986 Al Faw offensive—Iran's most successful assault—in which the Guard and regular military achieved their highest degree of coordination ever.[100]

The Guard's ability to resist ideological dilution despite tapping into the expertise of the army of the prerevolutionary regime separates the Guard from the Soviet Red Army. The Red Army reintegrated former Czarist officers, referred to as "military specialists" into command positions in the Civil War, relying even more heavily on them in WWII.[101] Unlike the Guard and in part due to the influence of these "military specialists," the Red Army opted for professionalism over revolutionary zeal and competent officers ultimately gained greater influence than dedicated revolutionaries within the Red Army structure.[102] Rather than spawn a completely new army, the French revolution paved the way for competent officers to advance beyond the traditional aristocratic military elite.[103] In structure, tactics, and strategies the French revolutionary army was a conventional, professional armed force, even as it enthusiastically prosecuted revolutionary war under Napoleon.[104] Although history does not provide confirmation, it can be argued that the French army's commitment to revolutionary conquest was due more to the charismatic military and political leadership of Napoleon than to the intrinsic ideology of the French revolutionary army. Had Napoleon decided to end the war he prosecuted, it is doubtful that he would have incurred significant opposition from the officer corps and rank and file of the French army.

Thus far the discussion of the Guard's social resiliency has been confined to the analysis of groups within the Guard that were neutral, unenthusiastic, or possibly even opposed to the Guard's ideology. The overall analysis, however, must also include the Guard's ability integrate social groups that enthusiastically supported the Guard's ideology but whose presence imposed practical limitations on the Guard's ability to carry out its mission. The Guard's degree of success in coping with such constraints is as credible a test of Guard resiliency as is the examination of Guard efforts to absorb non or anti-ideological groups within its ranks.

The Basij

The primary example of a social group that posed operational but not ideological problems for the Guard is undoubtedly the *Basij Mustazafin* (Mobilization of the Oppressed), the volunteer popular forces which are commonly referred to as the Basij. The Basij was composed of very young (under the 17 years of age required for normal military service and often as young as 10 or 11 years old) and elderly volunteers (many were senior citizens), usually from rural towns and villages.[105] The Basij volunteers were almost always highly motivated ideologically and religiously, as were their brethren in the Guard proper, and were generally more poorly educated than most Guardsmen; many Basij were illiterate.[106] Basijis were also recruited from among high school and unversity students, government bureaucrats, and factory workers.[107] Like the Guard, the Basij contained technical specialists within its ranks.[108]

Although the Basij, as an organization, was formally separate from the Guard during the Iran-Iraq war and has its own commander, in actuality has always been an integral part of the Guard itself. It was formally placed under Guard control on 1 January 1981[109] and officially constituted as a fifth Guard service in 1990. The Guard has recruited, organized, trained, and commanded all Basij units, and the longtime Basij commander, the hardline cleric Ali Rahmani, was appointed by Reza'i in 1984.[110] In January 1990, Reza'i's longtime ally and Guard spokesman Ali Reza Afshar was appointed Basij commander, on Reza'i's recommendation, thus virtually eliminating what little independent command authority the Basij ever possessed.[111]

Many accounts of the war correctly describe the Basij fighters as virtual "cannon fodder" for the Revolutionary Guard, going into battle lightly armed and in human waves, crossing minefields to reach entrenched Iraqi positions, in essence paving the way for follow-on attacks by the more experienced and heavily armed Guardsmen.[112] The Basijis, already highly motivated by their commitment to the revolution, were further encouraged by religious and revolutionary indoctrination by the Guard and its radical clerical instructors.[113] The military training of the Basij by the Guard consisted of a two week instruction program in the use of hand grenades and automatic rifles, heavily infused with the promise that death in the war would provide automatic acceptance in heaven.[114] Plastic keys were hung around each Basiji's neck; each was told that the key would open heaven's gates.[115] Prayers, Koranic readings, songs, and fiery speeches by the Guard commanders comprised much of the training program and life at the frontline.[116]

Although the ideological commitment of the Basij remained beyond question, its very nature imposed substantial problems for the Guard. The Basijis were volunteer and not fixed forces. They served a brief, generally three month tour, and then returned to their homes and jobs.[117] Basij volunteers signed up for service in response to annual or semi-annual mobilization calls by the Guard and political leadership. Because Basij fighters constituted the majority of the rank and file infantry soldiers in Guard operations, this short term of service limited the time period in which Iranian forces were at sufficient strength to launch offensive operations. The Guard also had to cope with uncertainty over the number of volunteers that would respond to each mobilization call and the inability to organize sufficient numbers of fixed units that trained and fought together throughout the year.[118] Addressing the inherent limitations of reliance on volunteer forces, Chorley notes the frustration of American revolutionary General George Washington, whose need to rely on volunteers substantially complicated his efforts to plan operations against the British.[119]

There is also an important relationship between the social composition of the Basij and the constraints the Basij imposed on the Guard. Because a large percentage of Basijis hailed from rural Iran, the three month tour that best accommodated the Basij was the December-March time frame, which allowed the Basijis to return to their villages in time for the start of the agricultural season, and students to return to school in time for spring exams.[120] The Guard's window of maximum strength, and therefore the period of major offensive operations, was thus limited to the winter season, when the Basij could best be mobilized. The Guard's official spokesman Ali Reza Afshar confirmed this relationship and explained that Iraqi offensives and counteroffensives generally occurred in the spring when the level of Basij dispatches to the front was at its annual low point.[121] In one unsuccessful effort to alleviate this problem, the Guard attempted to institute a phased dispatch program to ensure a constant, predictable presence of Basij at all times and thus to better enable the Guard to organize offensive operations at the times of its choosing and in optimum conditions militarily.[122]

Although Iran's loss of the war ultimately proved the Guard unsuccessful, the Guard attempted, with some initial success, to circumvent the constraints imposed upon it by its need to rely heavily on volunteer manpower. Essentially, the Guard was able to achieve a synthesis between its war strategy and the prevailing patterns of Basij mobilization. The Guard did so by launching its offensives coincident with maximum advantages of terrain and weather conditions, given its timing and manpower constraints. At the height of Iranian manpower availability (December to March), the terrain of southern Iraq, which contained predominantly Shia Iraqis presumed to be least favorably disposed toward the Sunni dominated Iraqi government, favored the lightly armed, manpower intensive attacks pioneered by the Guard and Basij. The southern Iran-Iraq border areas, particularly around Iraq's second largest and largely Shia city of Basra, are characterized by marshlands which, in the wet conditions, hindered the movement of Iraq's tanks and heavy artillery.[123] The rough weather also hindered the operations of Iraq's crucial air power. In winter, which corresponded to the time of maximum Iranian manpower mobilization, Iraq's military advantages were minimized and Iran's strengths magnified.

This coincidence of maximum Iranian manpower availability, weather and terrain advantages, and the location of politically strategic targets inside Iraq largely explains the patterns of Iranian major offensives during the war. Major Iranian offensives in the Hawizeh Marshes in 1984 and 85, at Al Faw in 1986, and East of Basra in 1987 were all launched in the marshy terrain near, and with the intention of isolating and ultimately seizing, Basra.[124] This war strategy was based on the assumption that capturing Basra would precipitate the fall of Iraq's Ba'th regime by inspiring an uprising among Iraqi Shias. The war plan also enabled the Guard to achieve another of its goals—upstaging the regular military. The strategy achieved this aim by minimizing the need to adopt more conventional tactics which are the key strengths of the regular military. Despite heavy Iranian casualties, particularly among the Guard and Basij, these offensives, especially the 1986 capture of Al Faw, placed heavy pressure on the Iraqi government, and significantly bolstered the military decisionmaking influence of the Guard.[125]

By 1988, however, many of those Guard and Basij fighters who were eager to die for Islam and the revolution had done so. The high Iranian casualties and apparent inability of the Guard's strategy to topple Saddam Husayn apparently weakened Iranian morale and rendered it unable to mount a major offensive in 1988. All Iran was able to muster was a relatively insignificant offensive in non-strategic regions of northern Iraq.[126] Undoubtedly sensing Iranian weakness, as well as the seasonal return of Basij volunteers to their villages, Iraq chose April of that year to begin the series of counteroffensives that ultimately forced Iran to the bargaining table.

Despite the ultimate failure of the Guard's war strategy, it must be noted that the Guard, especially in 1986 and 1987, came close to accomplishing key war objectives, the limitations imposed by the unreliable and inconsistent Basij recruitment patterns notwithstanding. Moreover, it can be argued that it was the rivalry and generally poor cooperation between the Guard and regular military—and not the Guard's strategy and tactics—that led to the ultimate loss of the war. For example, the Guard and Basij had successfully cut the crucial Baghdad-Basra highway during the

March 1985 Badr offensive in the Hawizeh Marshes, but the failure of the regular military to commit reinforcements to the Guard and Basij enabled Iraq to encircle and rout the Iranian attack forces.

Although the coincidence of the terrain around southern Iraq, winter, and Basij recruitment patterns was largely fortuitous, it is still worth noting that the Guard was sufficiently flexible operationally to accommodate the constraints imposed by the Basij recruitment patterns. Among other possibilities, the Guard could have opted to conduct smaller but more numerous offensives at many points along the front, in the hopes of surprising the Iraqis and achieving a breakthrough. This strategy, because of its necessarily greater dependence on conventional weapons and tactics, would have conceded a greater war role to the regular military—a consequence that conflicted with the Guard's political objectives and its ideological commitment to a "people's war."

Structure-Functional Resiliency

Structure-functional resiliency refers primarily to the Guard's ability to assume new missions. This analysis, however, is closely related to the evaluation of Guard complexity, to be discussed in the next chapter. The concept does, however, deserve some preliminary treatment here.

It can be argued that the Guard clearly demonstrated its functional adaptability in three key ways: upon the outbreak of war, the Guard made the transition from political militia to armed force capable of fighting interstate war; in 1982, the Guard began operationalizing its commitment to the export of the revolution by sending an expeditionary force to aid Muslim factions in Lebanon;[127] and, in 1988, the Guard's war fighting role ended along with the war, and the Guard's military forces assumed a deterrent role. The Guard also took on increased reconstruction responsibilities.

When Iraqi troops invaded Iran in September 1980, the Guard was a relatively small, factionalized political militia. Nonetheless, largely because of its revolutionary fervor, the Guard rallied to confront the invasion, offering stiff resistance and slowing the Iraqi advance.[128] It was instrumental in eventually driving out the invaders by 1982.[129] In subsequent years, the Guard developed and organized its military component largely along conventional lines, even if it did not adopt conventional tactics and strategies for prosecuting the war. The Guard's military component not only was able to sustain the war effort for eight years against a better organized and equipped enemy, but it was even able to upstage Iran's more highly trained and professional regular military by orchestrating Iran's most successful offensives.[130] Iran's defeat in the war to some extent refutes Adelman's thesis that major social revolutions produce armed forces that are more effective than their prerevolutionary counterparts,[131] but the Iranian military collapse does not suggest that the Guard, as an institution, was unable to adapt to a military role.

The Guard has also demonstrated the organizational flexibility to assume the additional mission of actively exporting the Islamic revolution despite the substantial burden the war placed on the Guard's command structure. The Guard's efforts to violently export the revolution began in earnest in September 1982 when a contingent of Guardsmen was sent to Lebanon ostensibly to help Muslim forces in Lebanon repel the Israeli invasion of that country.[132] Subsequently, the Guard also attempted to subvert the Persian Gulf states, especially Saudi Arabia, and established a network of operatives in Europe.[133]

The Guard pursued export of the revolution despite the substantial organizational requirements posed by the war. For example, Mohsen Rafiq-Dust, who led the original Guard contingent to Lebanon in 1982, continued to oversee Guard forces there even though, as Guard Minister, he had a wide range of war responsibilities.[134] These duties included administration of the Guard's finances, oversight of indigenous weapons production, and weapons procurement.[135] Moreover, the Guard's roughly 2000 fighters in Lebanon, who helped form and train the militant Shia fundamentalist Hizballah (Party of God) militia,[136] were consequently unavailable for training and combat missions at the front with Iraq.

The Guard's activities abroad were opposed or merely tolerated by some political leaders in the regime. Such lack of support for Guard export of the revolution activities included that of Rafsanjani, a major military decisionmaker,[137] and differences between him and the Guard on exporting the revolution undoubtedly spilled over into and complicated the war decisionmaking process. The Guard's ability to consistently pursue major export of the revolution activities in the face of high level political opposition testifies to the Guard's ability to coordinate multiple, unrelated missions; the depth of its ideological fervor and commitment; and its overall political strength in the regime.

The final example of the Guard's functional resiliency is provided by its ability, as an institution, to remain influential and organizationally strong despite the ending of the war—its prime mission, ideological expression, and justification for its claim on national resources. Although its activities are less well publicized than they were during the war, the Guard remains a significant hardline political force. None of the senior Guard commanders who led the Guard during the war have been ousted; to the contrary, several have gained in stature. Ali Shamkhani, the deputy Guard Commander during the war, has taken command of Iran's regular Navy as well as the Guard Navy, and Ali Reza Afshar, Reza'i's chief of staff and

Guard Spokesman, has become Basij Commander.[138] Additional examples of the Guard's continuing political significance will be discussed in Chapter Five.

Notes

1. "Internal Turmoil Roils Iran," *Washington Post;* July 10, 1988; P. A1
2. This criteria of institutional strength was posited by Talcott Parsons. See his *Essays in Sociological Theory* (Glencoe, Illinois: Free Press, 1954) P. 239
3. "Mission, Record of Revolution Guard Corps Reviewed," Iran Press Digest; June 15, 1982 in JPRS July 12, 1982; P. 38
4. John Ellis, *Armies in Revolution* (London: Croon Helm Ltd., 1973)
5. "Khomeini Organizes a New Armed Force," *New York Times;* May 7, 1979; P. A1
6. Ibid
7. "Khomeini Militia Vows to Spread Iran's Revolution," *Washington Post;* May 7, 1979; P. A1
8. "Iran's Islamic Committees Criticized by Premier as 'Rule of Revenge'," New York Times; April 25, 1979
9. "Khomeini Militia Vows to Spread Iran's Revolution," op.cit.
10. "Mission, Record of Revolution Guard Corps Reviewed," op.cit.
11. Jonathan Adelman, *Revolution, Armies, and War: A Political History* (Boulder, Colorado: Lynne Rienner Publishers, Inc., 1985)
12. Ellis, op.cit., Chaps. 7, 8
13. "History and Present Status of IRGC," Iran Press Digest; August 17, 1984; P. 15
14. Nikola Schahgaldian, *The Iranian Military Under the Islamic Republic* (Santa Monica: Rand Corporation, 1987)
15. Ibid
16. Ibid
17. "Background Impressions of New Leaders Discussed," Svenska Dagbladet in Swedish; November 29, 1979; P. 6
18. "Bani-Sadr: Politics vs. the Power of Islam," New York Times; July 24, 1980; P. A3
19. Bani-Sadr's impressions of his relations with the Revolutionary Guard are detailed in his recent book, *My Turn to Speak: Iran, the Revolution,, and Secret Deals With the U.S.* (McLean, Va.: Brassey's [U.S.] Inc., 1991)
20. "Iranian Rightists Assail Bani-Sadr Over Conduct of the War With Iraq," New York Times; January 5, 1981; P. A1
21. "Mission, Record of Revolution Guard Corps Reviewed," op.cit.
22. "History and Present Status of IRGC," op.cit.
23. "Khomeini Bolsters Role of Bani-Sadr," New York Times; May 10, 1980; P. 1

24. "Commander of Iranian Guards Resigns," Washington Post; June 18, 1980
25. Ibid
26. Excerpts from an interview with Kazem Bojnurdi in Jomhuri Islam (The Islamic Republic), reprinted in The Flame; July 1, 1980
27. Shaul Bakhash, *The Reign of the Ayatollahs* (New York: Basic Books, Inc., 1984)
28. Nikola Schahgaldian, op.cit., P. 121
29. "Iranian Rightists Assail Bani-Sadr Over Conduct of the War With Iraq," op.cit.
30. Ibid
31. Ibid
32. Adelman, op.cit.
33. "Khomeini Bolsters Role of Bani-Sadr," op.cit.
34. "Hardline Clerics Undermine Iran's `Moderate' President," Christian Science Monitor; July 24, 1980
35. "Bani-Sadr: Politics vs. Power of Islam," op.cit.
36. "Iranian Rightists Assail Bani-Sadr Over Conduct of the War With Iraq," op.cit.
37. "Khomeini Urges Iranians to Cease Criticizing Bani -Sadr Over the War," New York Times; January 16, 1981; P. A8
38. Bakhash, op.cit.
39. Ronald Perron, "The Iranian Islamic Revolutionary Guard Corps," in *Middle East Insight* (June-July 1985) P. 38
40. "Mission, Record of Revolution Guard Corps Reviewed," op.cit.
41. Roman Kolkowicz and Andrzej Korbonski, eds., *Soldiers, Peasants, and Bureaucrats* (London: George Allen and Unwin Ltd., 1982)
42. Bakhash, op.cit.
43. "Tehran Sees a Rare Sign of War Dissent; Recent Street Protest Suggests Some Tire of Iraq Hostilities," Washington Post; May 17, 1987; P. A31
44. "Politics - Iran-Iraq: Problems at Home Resurface," in *The Middle East*, (October 1988) P. 14
45. "Iran Guard Leaders Slain in Violent Purge," op.cit.; "Khomeini Message to IRGC," Tehran Domestic Service in Persian; 17 September 1988 in FBIS; September 17, 1988
46. "Khomeini Message on Hajj, UN Resolution 598," Tehran Domestic Service in Persian; July 20, 1988 in FBIS July 21, 1988; P. 50
47. "Iranian Commander Takes Blame for War Defeats," United Press International; June 8, 1988
48. Ibid
49. Ibid
50. "Iranian President Quits as Chief of Armed Forces," New York Times; September 3, 1989; P.4

51. "[Khamene'i] Addresses Commanders on Defense Week," Tehran Domestic Service in Persian, September 27, 1989, in FBIS, September 28, 1989

52. Safa Haeri, "Rafsanjani's Costly Blunder," in *Middle East International* (November 4, 1988) P. 10

53. "Majlis Discusses Joint Stock, Merger Bills," Tehran Domestic Service in Persian, September 25, 1988, in FBIS, September 25, 1988

54. "The Present Position of the Revolutionary Guards," Tehran Echo of Iran; October 18, 1988

55. Ibid

56. "Khamene'i Addresses IRGC Commanders," Tehran Domestic Service; September 15, 1988

57. "Guard Corps Official on Defense Readiness," Tehran Domestic Service; September 22, 1988

58. "Three Recent Attempts to Kill Rafsanjani," Kuwait The Kuwait Times; January 11, 1989

59. "IRNA Carries New Ministers' Biographies," IRNA in English in FBIS; September 20, 1988

60. "Majlis Discusses Joint Stock, Merger Bills," op.cit.

61. "Iranian President Quits as Chief of Armed Forces," op.cit.

62. "The Present Position of the Revolutionary Guards," op.cit.

63. "Hashemi-Rafsanjani Speaks on Future of IRGC," Tehran Domestic Service; October 6, 1988

64. Ibid

65. "Khamene'i Addresses IRGC Seminar," IRNA in English; September 15, 1988 in FBIS; September 15, 1988

66. "Iran's Agents of Terror," *U.S. News and World Report;* March 6, 1989; P. 20-25; "Iran Responds in Kind to 'Bullying' by U.S.," New York Times; November 1, 1989; P. A11; "IRGC, Basijis Titles, Ranks Announced," in Tehran Jomhuri Ye-Eslami in Persian; May 7, 1990, P.2

67. Richard Cobb, *The People's Armies* (New Haven and London: Yale University Press, 1987)

68. Kolkowicz and Korbonski, eds., op.cit.; James Hsiung, *Ideology and Practice: The Evolution of Chinese Communism* (New York and London: Praeger Publishers, Inc., 1970) Chaps. 12, 13, 14

69. Adelman, op.cit.

70. Ellis, op.cit., Chap. 7

71. Alexander Werth, *Russia at War: 1941-45* (New York: Carroll and Graf Publishers, Inc., 1964) P. 422

72. "Khamene'i Friday Sermon Address," Tehran Domestic Service in Persian; September 16, 1988 in FBIS; September 16, 1988

73. "Four (Pasdaran) Commanders Become Military Commanders," excerpted from Azadegan in The Flame; July 13, 1980; "IRNA Carries New Ministers' Biographies," op.cit.

74. "Autobiography of Behzad Nabavi," Iran Press Digest; March 13, 1984

75. Bakhash, op.cit., P. 244

76. "Inside Islamic Iran," The Overseas Hindustan Times; April 1, 1982; P. 8

77. "Mission, Record of Revolution Guard Corps Reviewed," op.cit.

78. "Who's Who of Revolution," in *Iran Almanac 1987* (Tehran: Echo of Iran, 1987) P. 369

79. "IRNA Carries New Ministers' Biographies," op.cit.

80. "Iranian Impressions," *Frontline* (January 23 - February 5, 1988) P. 5

81. "Iran's Post-Revolution Development Viewed," in *Sovietskaya Rossiya*, 2nd ed. (February 11, 1989) P. 5 in FBIS; February 14, 1989

82. Robin Wright, "A Reporter at Large - Tehran Summer," *The New Yorker* (September 5, 1988) P. 40

83. "IRGC to Begin Conscription, Deserters to Be Detained," Tehran Domestic in Persian; July 6, 1987

84. Ibid

85. Wright, op.cit.

86. "History and Present Status of IRGC," op.cit.

87. Wright, op.cit., P. 36

88. "Iranian Commander Takes Blame for War Defeats," op.cit.

89. Wright, op.cit., P. 36

90. "U.S. Rejected Proposed Sale of F-5's to Iran," Washington Post; October 20, 1988; P. A1

91. "Iran Guard Leaders Slain in Violent Purge," op.cit.

92. "Tehran Sees a Rare Sign of War Dissent," op.cit.

93. "RafiqDust, Afshar Discuss War," Tehran Television Service in Persian; June 3, 1988

94. "Iran Uses Troops on Domestic Unrest," Christian Science Monitor; June 3, 1988

95. H.H. Gerth and C. Wright Mills, *From Max Weber: Essays in Sociology* (New York: Oxford University Press, 1946)

96. Robin Wright, op.cit., P. 42

97. "Iran's Military Chief Says Gulf War Could Resume," Reuters; December 6, 1988

98. Nader Entessar, "The Military and Politics in the Islamic Republic of Iran," in Hooshang Amirahmadi and Manoucher Parvin, eds., *Post-Revolutionary Iran* (Boulder, Co. and London: Westview Press, 1988) P. 66

99. Ibid.; "Iran Announcement: Offensive is Due," New York Times; November 13, 1987

100. Entessar, op.cit., P. 70

101. D. Fedotoff White, *The Growth of the Red Army* (Princeton: Princeton University Press, 1944)

102. Adelman, op.cit., pp. 102-5

103. Ibid, Chap. 3

104. Ibid

105. Entessar, op.cit.

106. Ibid

107. "IRGC Officials Discuss Postwar Mobilization," FBIS; December 2, 1988

108. Ibid

109. Schahgaldian, op.cit., P. 133

110. "Reza'i Appoints `Meek Mobilization Unit' Chief," Tehran Domestic Service in Persian; February 16, 1984 in FBIS; February 16, 1984

111. "Afshar Appointed Commander of Basij Resistance," Tehran Television Service in Persian; January 2, 1990 in FBIS; January 3, 1990

112. "Iran Announcement: Offensive is Due," op.cit.

113. "Iran Uses Children on Suicide Missions," Moscow Trud in Russian; May 12, 1988 in FBIS; May 12, 1988

114. Ibid

115. Ibid

116. Ibid

117. "RafiqDust, Afshar Discuss War," op.cit.

118. Ibid

119. Chorley, op.cit.

120. "RafiqDust, Afshar Discuss War," op.cit.

121. Ibid

122. Ibid

123. Edgar O'Ballance, *The Gulf War* (London: Brassey's Defence Publishers Ltd., 1988) P. 143

124. Ibid; "Iran Announcement: Offensive is Due," op.cit.

125. Ibid; "Tehran Attempts to Balance Guards' Zeal, Dangers of War," Washington Post; August 23, 1987; P. A1;

126. "Commander Discusses Val Fajr-10 Operations," Tehran Television Service in Persian in FBIS; March 24, 1988

127. Wright, op.cit.

128. "War Becomes Political Boon for Bani-Sadr," Washington Post; October 13, 1980; P. A1

129. "[Khamene'i] Addresses Commanders on Defense Week," op.cit.

130. O'Ballance, op.cit.

131. Adelman, op.cit.

132. Wright, op.cit.
133. "SPA Replies to Besharati's Remarks on Pilgrimage," Saudi Press Agency in Arabic; February 8, 1988; "Iran's Agents of Terror," op.cit.
134. Ibid.; Wright, op.cit.
135. "History and Present Status of IRGC," op.cit., P. 15
136. Wright, op.cit.; Entessar, op.cit., pp. 69-70
137. "Lebanese Battles Demonstrate Syria-Iran Rivalry," Washington Post; January 7, 1990; P. A18
138. "Khamene'i Appoints Shamkani New Naval Chief," IRNA in English; October 30, 1989 in FBIS; October 31, 1989; "New Commander for Guard Corps Navy Named," Tehran Television Service in Persian; December 23, 1990; "Afshar Appointed Commander of Basij Resistance," op.cit.

4

The Guard's
Organizational Complexity

A major hallmark of institutionalization and organizational development of the Guard is the growth in its complexity since its inception. According to Huntington, a key indicator of organizational complexity is the
proliferation and increasing differentiation of its organizational subunits
and its assumption of additional functions.[1] In adapting this framework
to the analysis of a revolutionary armed force, particularly the Revolutionary Guard, it must be shown how the Guard evolved from a patchwork of undisciplined militias and guerrilla groups into an armed force
organized along conventional lines. This is the developmental path which
has generally held true for the Soviet Red Army, the People's Liberation
Army of the People's Republic of China, and the French revolutionary
army—forces forged in major social revolutions.[2]

However, it can be argued that, unlike these revolutionary forces, and
contrary to the expectations of some scholars,[3] the development of the
Guard's organizational complexity has not translated into reduced revolutionary militance, enthusiasm, or willingness to involve itself in politics.
The conventionalization of the Guard's structure did not bring its tactical
and strategic decisionmaking process more in line with those of professional armed forces. Objective military criteria did not replace hardline
revolutionary goals, and conventional organization did not thwart ideological enthusiasm and motivation.

Far from dissipating its revolutionary fervor, the Guard's organizational development helped it operationalize the hardline ideals of Ayatollah
Khomeini and the Islamic revolution. This argument is supported by the
analysis of those Guard subunits that appeared to reflect conventionalization but the missions and activities of which were intended to further
revolutionary ideological goals. Additionally, the Guard's subunit differentiation was not uniform throughout, and, where appropriate and necessary for the fulfillment of its hardline objectives, the Guard was able to
avoid strict specialization and clear chains of command.

The Guard is unique in that the increasing complexity of its organizational structure did not instill military professionalism. At the broadest level, complexity is indicated by the creation of formalized rules and procedures, whereas conventional military professionalism implies a commitment to strict obedience to those rules and procedures at the risk of sanction. Organizationally, increasing specialization of function, the creation and expansion of structures to perform the organization's functions, and compartmentalization of responsibilities are hallmarks of increasing complexity. Military professionalism connotes loyalty to the traditions and procedures of the institution without regard to its policies, decision-making based on objective military criteria, and obedience to the civilian leadership regardless of its policies or ideological direction. In retaining its radical ideology and commitment to enforcing Khomeini's goals, the Guard lacked these criteria of professionalization. For the present, the analysis of Guard complexity will concentrate on the rationalization of the Guard's command, military, and internal security structure, the development of its own Ministry, and its export of the revolution apparatus.

Internal Security Apparatus

At its inception, the Revolutionary Guard's sole function was to ensure internal security. It was the principle armed instrument for consolidating the revolution's hold on power, for eradicating the structures of power that existed under the Shah, and, despite the opposition of the first revolutionary government of Mehdi Bazargan, for administering revolutionary justice to suspected opponents and collaborators and sympathizers of the former regime.[4] Many national and local revolutionary leaders controlled and financed their own Guard contingents, composed largely of Guardsmen these local notables had worked with and recruited during the revolution.[5] The factional nature of the Guard's origins both triggered and complicated efforts by the revolutionary clerical leadership to quickly mold the Guard into a national and more accountable force.

To an even greater degree than the efforts of the political leadership, it was the broad array and strength of the regime's early adversaries—coupled with the Guard's own ideological commitment to destroy these opponents—that catalyzed the Guard's early growth and structural development. To counter the regime's enemies, the Guard needed and justified its numerical expansion and its extension into all regions of Iran. In turn, the Guard's success in crushing the regime's internal adversaries won the trust of the clerics and helped forestall efforts to check its growth, although more moderate leaders did obtain Khomeini's endorsement for curbing the Guard's internal security excesses.[6]

If significant opposition to the revolutionary regime was the prerequisite for the Guard's rapid development as a security militia, then it is not difficult to understand why the Guard grew from an estimated 4,000 fighters at its inception to 25,000 the following year, even before the war with Iraq began in September 1980.[7] During the first four years of the Islamic Republic, armed opposition was omnipresent. The Kurdish rebellion began in 1979, and in December of that year, the Guard was called on to put down serious disturbances in Tabriz (the capital of Iranian Azerbaijan) sponsored by supporters of the eminent Grand Ayatollah Kazem Shariat-Madari.[8] He questioned the basis and form of the new Islamic state envisioned by Khomeini. In major cities, the radical Forqan group conducted sporadic attacks on regime officials; in May 1979 this group apparently was responsible for the wounding of Rafsanjani.[9] During 1980-81, tensions between the clerics and the Mojahedin-e-Khalq grew, resulting in frequent clashes between that group and the Guard as well as MEK-sponsored assassination attempts against officials.[10] The MEK was officially blamed for the bombing of IRP headquarters and the Prime Minister's Office in 1981.[11] In 1983 the Guard led the effort to crush the pro-Moscow Tudeh Party which, like the MEK, had worked with the clerics to overthrow the Shah.[12]

Minor groups also created internal security problems for the regime and the Guard. Other groups that fought against the regime and attacked the Guard in the early years of the revolution included the radical Marxist guerrilla group Fedayeen-e-Khalq, the Communist Paykar organization, and the Kurdish Marxist Komaleh group.[13] In a 1982 interview with the *Tehran Times*, Guard Commander Mohsen Reza'i claimed success in Guard operations against the Toofan group, operating in Kurdistan, and the Sahand organization, which he claimed was comprised of "students and instructors from the University of England and Zionist elements."[14] Anti-regime disturbances were also initiated by Arab nationalist groups in largely Arab Khuzestan Province and by the Qashqai tribe located in the interior.[15]

As the Guard's internal security challenges and corresponding responsibilities grew, its nationwide structure began to take shape. Aside from the positions of Guard Operational Commander and Clerical Supervisor, the first structure to appear publicly was the Supreme Council of the Revolutionary Guard, formally established in October 1979.[16] The Council's membership consisted primarily of early Guard organizers such as Reza'i, Ali Reza Afshar, Ali Shamkhani, Mohsen RafiqDust, Rahim Safavi, Abbas Zamani, and Mehdi Hashemi; they eventually obtained senior command positions as the Guard leadership structure became rationalized.[17]

The composition of the Council reveals its dynamics. That the major Guard organizers were its most powerful members suggests that the Guard's Supreme Council existed de-facto long before October 1979. Moreover, the membership on the Council of Mehdi Hashemi, the radical relative of Ayatollah Montazeri (Khomeini's designated successor until four months before Khomeini's death) who was executed in 1987 for exposing the U.S.-Iran arms deal, indicates that Council membership required a major regional or issue-based constituency.[18] For example, Mehdi Hashemi was the leading spokesman and organizer for those Guards who wanted to accelerate and emphasize export of the revolution activities, even if doing so detracted from the war effort against Iraq.[19] Before the Guard command structure was fully rationalized, the Supreme Council as a whole made Guard decisions and appointed subordinate commanders.[20]

As the Guard leadership structure developed, the Supreme Council's role became more clearly defined. Formally, it was made subordinate to the Guard Clerical Supervisor/Representative of Khomeini and superior to the Commander of the Revolutionary Guard.[21] By 1984, its composition was defined in terms of Guard position instead of individual personalities; it was to include the Guard Commander and his deputy, the Guard Minister, the Commander of the Guard's Central Headquarters and "various other responsible units of the Guard Corps [as required]."[22] After the Corps Ministry was formed in 1982, the Supreme Council was also tasked to act as the principle point of contact between the Guard's operational command and the Ministry.[23]

The Guard's nationwide internal security organization developed in parallel with its national command structure. As at the national level, the local Guard organizations grew directly out of the primordial Guard cells in each locale that secured power during the revolution. Immediately subordinate to the Guard Commander and Supreme Council, the ten Guard administrative regions, each of which roughly corresponds to an Iranian province, were established.[24] Each provincial Guard headquarters was based in the capital of that province.

The Guard's regional command structure mirrored that at the national level. Each Guard region was headed by a regional commander who worked through a broader regional Guard Council composed of leading Guard commanders from the major cities and subordinate jurisdictions in that province.[25] The position of provincial Guard commander was often a stepping-stone to a place in the national Guard leadership; for example, Abbas Mohtaj was Commander of Region 7 (Northwest Border) before gaining a senior position in the Central Headquarters in Tehran.[26]

The district level Guard command is similarly organized, reporting to the regional headquarters above and holding sway over the subordinate base command level. In rural regions of Iran, the district level may have jurisdiction over a substantial geographic area in that province, overseeing many Guard bases located in individual small towns. In more urbanized areas surrounding Iran's provincial capitals, a Guard district command may cover that provincial capital and its environs; base commands are responsible for suburban areas and major sections of the city, and a subordinate headquarters, which may even be a storefront or large house, oversees further subdivisions of the city.[27] The intention and result is that the Guard achieves maximum penetration of the civilian population, in contrast to the regular military, which only has internal security responsibilities in a crisis or emergency and is generally based in garrisons outside densely populated areas.[28]

The Guard's deployment among the population has been partly related to the nature of its adversaries. The Guard's most formidable opponent, the Mojahedin-e-Khalq Organization, like the prerevolutionary Guard itself (the two come from common roots as described in Chapter Two), has operated as an urban guerrilla force, skilled in developing and using clandestine support networks in the major cities.[29] Many Guardsmen on patrol have fallen victim to attacks from the MEK.[30] To weed out support cells of such organized opposition groups, the Guard developed an Intelligence Unit attached to all levels of its command structure.[31] As a testament to the Guard's institutional strength, the Guard's Intelligence Unit was to be merged with the Ministry of Intelligence when that bureau was constituted in 1984, yet the Guard's Intelligence Unit remains separate and active, in part duplicating the efforts of the Intelligence Ministry.[32] In addition to combatting organized opposition, the Guard is also the first line of defense in suppressing significant anti-regime demonstrations.[33]

The Guard's nationwide structure and pervasiveness as an ideological force in society also facilitated its efforts to mobilize popular support and recruits for the war. Immediately after the war began, the Guard was officially charged with mobilizing the "20-million-man army" of Iranians that was to demonstrate the strength of the Islamic revolution by defeating Iraq's well-armed and well-trained forces.[34] This citizens' army was to be recruited and organized through the Guard's network of bases, in conjunction with the formally separate but practically subordinate Basij organization. In the mobilization effort, the Guard established recruitment centers not only at its own garrisons, bases, and urban headquarters but also in local mosques, schools, factories, and government facilities.[35] The Guard's mobilization effort, coupled with its internal security powers, gave the Guard substantial authority at the local level, even over many local civilian government institutions. For example in 1987 the Guard was authorized to draw on the resources of government agencies and universities to provide training facilities, expertise, and recruits for the Guard.[36]

The Guard's pervasive propaganda apparatus helps it mobilize the population and promote the radical political line. The Guard publishes and disseminates a wide range of materials, including books, posters, leaflets, and its own magazine which covers Guard affairs, and it broadcasts a Guard television program.[37] The Guard's major propaganda distribution center is headquartered in the former U.S. Embassy compound in Tehran, which doubles as a Guard school and training center.[38]

To fulfill its ancillary internal role of ensuring popular adherence to Islamic laws regulating social life, the Guard developed additional sub-units. Among these were Sarollah and Jondollah, Guard units that policed the major cities in white Toyota trucks looking for transgressors, such as women who refused to strictly conform to Islamic dress, youths playing Western music, and those eating during the daylight hours of the holy month of Ramadan.[39] These units, which also searched homes for viola-tions of Islamic custom, contributed greatly to the unpopularity of the Guard among the educated, Westernized upper and upper middle classes in Tehran—the social group most opposed to the strict observance of Islamic law and the regime in general.[40]

To a large extent, the Guard's role in maintaining internal order and enforcing Islamic law distinguishes it from other revolutionary armed forces, especially those of Communist regimes, and best exemplifies the Guard's pervasiveness as an institution in revolutionary Iran. In the So-viet Union and the People's Republic of China, the domestic intelligence function is not performed by the Red Army or the People's Liberation Army but by the civilian KGB in the Soviet Union and, in the PRC, the Ministry of State Security.[41] Virtually no other revolutionary armed force has ever played as substantial a role in enforcing adherence to the revolu-tion's social strictures as has the Guard.

Even more distinctive is the Guard's pro-active, rather than reactive, role in suppressing popular unrest. Unlike, for example, the Chinese PLA, which was called into Beijing from outlying garrisons to crush a popular revolt in May 1989, the Guard generally intervenes before demonstrations spread and intensify.[42] There is, moreover, no evidence that the Guard has ever had to await orders from the civilian leadership to disperse or arrest demonstrators, but rather the Guard appears to have assumed the author-ity to suppress demonstrations when they occur.

The Guard has not displayed the hesitation to use force internally that has been shown by its more "professionalized" counterparts among revo-lutionary armed forces. The Soviet Army and the PLA have been widely known to be reluctant to engage protesting civilians. In recent examples, the Soviet Army command is reported to have argued against its January 1990 intervention against popular unrest in Soviet Azerbaijan, leaving the bulk of the fighting to internal security troops under the control of Interior Ministry troops.[43] Some units of the PLA were widely reported to be hes-itant to intervene against the demonstrators in Tiananmen Square in May 1989. The Guard, in contrast, has never hesitated to use force against dem-onstrators, even when those demonstrators were clerics, apparently believing that any opposition to the regime constitutes treason against Islam and against the Guard's father figure (even more so in death) Ayatollah Khomeini.[44] The Guard's ideological commitment to uphold the pure principles of the revolution has clearly not been dampened by its organizational development and specialization.

The Military Structure

Unlike the Guard's internal security structure, which developed as a direct extension of the Guard's prerevolutionary guerrilla network, the Guard's military role grew out of a national emergency (the 1980 Iraqi invasion) for which the Guard was completely unprepared. In a 1985 interview, former Guard Minister Mohsen RafiqDust reviewed both the practical and political factors hindering the Guard's entry into the war:

> When we wanted to send the IRGC to the battlefronts, this force did not have the necessary military formation or organization. The IRGC was not created to defend the country's borders but rather the main aim for the creation of the IRGC was to defend the Islamic revolution. It was at this time that we realized that the imposed war was not against our borders but rather that it was aimed against the Islamic revolution and was bent on its destruction. Therefore, we felt the need to mobilize the IRGC. But when the IRGC wanted to enter the war as a popular force it was faced with problems and obstacles put in its way by the ruling clique [of Bani-Sadr] at that time.[45]

Corroborating the earlier cited assertions of the Guard's unofficial first commander Javad Mansuri, RafiqDust goes on to describe Bani-Sadr's fall as the key turning point that enabled the Guard to assume a more aggressive posture in the war an ultimately, therefore, to drive Iraq out of Iranian territory.[46] The Guard's war successes began with the Guard's first organized offensive of the war, which in late 1981 broke Iraq's seige of Iran's southern city of Abadan.[47] In the same interview, RafiqDust describes how the Abadan battle initiated the process of the Guard's military development along conventional lines:

> When the Iranian forces started widespread operations, it was felt that the IRGC had to be present on the fronts in an organized formation. The organization and reshaping of the IRGC started with the establishment of border companies which took part in the breaking of the Abadan seige. These companies were later expanded into brigades and then armies.[48]

The Guard, paralleling similar directions taken by other revolutionary armies throughout history, began taking on the organizational characteristics of a conventional armed force. However, the Guard's experiences thus far do not support a postulated direct relationship between structural complexity and the diminution of revolutionary ideological commitment. The Guard's ability to organize itself in formations to combat a threat to the survival of the Islamic revolution illustrates its ability to respond organizationally to pressing functional requirements. However, not all of the structures and subunits developed by the Guard were established in response to the objective military threat from Iraq, but rather were created or further differentiated in order to operationalize the Guard's support for the hardline ideology of the Islamic revolution.

During the war, the Guard's military component evolved along the three major criteria of conventional military development—organization, training, and armament. In each of these categories, however, the Guard generally succeeded in melding conventional forms to its revolutionary ideological requirements.

Organization

In military organizational terms, in the course of the war the Guard developed a generally conventional-looking order of battle. The Guard developed separate air, ground and naval services, aside from the Basij foot soldiers it controlled and which have recently been formally incorporated as a formal component of the Guard military.[49] The Guard's ground forces, which required the least technical skill and best reflected the Guard's emphasis on zealous manpower rather than technology, has remained by far its most important and powerful service. Within the Guard's ground forces, conventional formations—organized corps, divisions, brigades, companies, and battalions, with further subdivisions at the divisional and brigade level into separate armor, artillery, infantry, and engineering units—were established.[50] These formations were direct outgrowths of the embryonic "companies" that the Guard organized for its first offensive. By the end of the war, the Guard's fixed ground forces consisted of 21 infantry divisions, 31, including 15 independent brigades, 3 engineering divisions, and 42 brigades specializing in artillery, armor, and, according to the Guard's official spokesman, chemical-biological and "nuclear warfare."[51] Iran is said to have both used and been subjected to chemical weapons in the war with Iraq, and a recent press report claims that the Guard is in control of a nuclear research program, centered at Moalem Kelayeh, northwest of Tehran.[52] This coincides with recent press reports that Iran may be seeking a nuclear capability.[53]

The Guard's mere possession, independent of the strength or effectiveness, of specialized armored and artillery formation demonstrates its ability to improvise. Almost every Guard commander has emphasized the Guard's reliance, at least initially, on captured weaponry for its supply of tanks and heavy artillery. Even as late as 1985, RafiqDust claimed that no heavy weapons were purchased for the IRGC.[54] In the first year of the war Bani-Sadr was the primary obstacle to the Guard's purchases of its own heavy armaments, as discussed previously. After his ouster, the regular military's superior training and experience still entitled it, rather than the Guard, to receipt of most of the heavy weapons acquired abroad.

Nonetheless, the mutual suspicions between the Guard and regular military undoubtedly left the Guard leadership unwilling to rely completely on the regular army for armored and artillery support. Faced with the regular military's reluctance to pursue the war until victory,[55] the Guard hierarchy needed its own source of heavy firepower without which the defeat of Iraq would have been even more difficult and costly. It can therefore be argued that the Guard's establishment of armored and artillery units, although representing conventionalization organizationally, was in reality an example of the Guard's ability to develop organizational structures to further its hardline goals—in this case, ensuring the continuation of the war until victory.

Moreover, that the Guard developed a relatively conventional order of battle does not imply that its unconventional structures were replaced. The Guard's infantry formations consisted of its own fixed forces and the irregular volunteer (Basij) forces which constituted the majority of actual infantry soldiers; Guardsmen essentially served as unit commanders to the young Basij fighters.[56] Thus, a typical Guard division consisted primarily of infantry brigades with its subordinate companies and battalions. Guardsmen held the command and some rank and file positions in each unit, but the majority of the rank and file were Basijis who responded to the periodic national mobilization calls.[57] Armored and artillery units in a given division were primarily manned by the more experienced and better trained Guardsmen, who served continually rather than the limited tours served by the Basij.[58]

The Guard further differs from a strictly conventional military organization in the relationship between its formations at the warfront and its internal structure. Primarily, the Guard's battlefield formations correspond to its territorial organization internally. Corps, divisions, and brigades at the front were composed of Guardsmen and Basijis recruited from corresponding geographic regions in Iran from which these fighters reside. For example, units that comprised the Sarollah Corps were drawn from Guard and Basij fighters recruited and mobilized from Tehran and its surrounding Markazi Province.[59] Kerman Province, which is far less densely populated than Tehran and Markazi, gave rise to the Sarollah Division and the Zolfiqar Brigade, far smaller formations than the Sarollah Corps produced by Tehran and Markazi.[60] This relationship is replicated throughout Iran; the mobilization potential of a given geographic unit largely determines the size of the military formation to which it corresponds. In most professional armies, each unit contains recruits from throughout the country.

To further stress the Guard's Islamic revolutionary nature, many Guard military formations were named for prominent figures in the history of Shia Islam; for example, the Imam Hosein Division is named for the grandson of Muhammad who was killed fighting against overwhelming odds in the Battle of Karbala. It has been argued that, in many ways, the ideology of the Guard—its willingness to fight for Islam no matter the human cost—is intended to emulate the early warriors of Islam who fought with Hosein.[61]

The Guard's territorial military organization, in turn, followed directly from its internal security structure. The Guard militias that emerged from the revolution in the provinces, cities, towns, and villages, were composed of revolutionary recruits from those geographic entities. For example, even after the emergence of the Guard as a national force, the Esfahan Guard has been composed of Esfahanis, not Tehranis, Tabrizis, or Shirazis.[62] Recruits serve in their home districts. When the war began, this territorial structure was simply carried over into the Guard's military organization. The Guard's regional organizations recruited additional Guard fighters and mobilized Basij fighters from their jurisdictions.[63] The Guard headquarters in each geographic subdivision, in addition to housing the administrative and operational apparatus for its Guard contingent, served as the primary war recruitment and mobilization center within its territorial limits.[64]

The advantages of coupling the Guard's battlefield structure with its internal security organization are readily apparent. Within a given geographic area, whether province, city, village, etc., the Guard's role as a pervasive and powerful arm of the government gives the Guard ready access and influence within the prime sources of local manpower, for example local government offices, schools, mosques, factories, and trade and agricultural organizations. Moreover, the Guard's military structure provided each local Guard contingent with substantial incentive to recruit Guard and Basij fighters for the war; the number of frontline troops commanded by a given Guard commander (and therefore the strength of that formation) is directly related to the success of the mobilization effort in that formation's home base.

The key drawback of this system is similarly significant in its impact on the Guard's war fighting ability. Because of the linkage between military formation strength and local mobilization efforts, the overall structure of the Guard's forces at the front depended on consistency and efficiency in the mobilization efforts at the local level. If, for example, a local Guard contingent does not produce the intended number of recruits, its Guard military formation will be severely under strength and unlikely to be able to play its intended role in Guard operations. Such unpredictability complicated war planning and strategy formulation and added to the basic difficulty of the Guard's need to rely on the Basij volunteers.

Despite this linkage between the Guard's military forces and its internal security structure, separate chains of command for the two functions existed. With the exception of the western regions of Iran (which borders Iraq and constituted the warfront), the local Guard internal security commander was a different individual than the Guard military commander of the unit derived from that same locale.[65] A notable example is Tehran. Mehdi Mobaleq has been identified as the Guard commander for Tehran Province, but Hosein Mosleh commands the Sarollah Corps which is the military formation derived from that province.[66] This functional distinction was not present at the rank and file level, however. Individual Guard fighters could be alternately assigned to internal security duty in their home districts or to serve at the front in their corresponding military unit.[67]

The Guard Services

A major indicator of the organizational development of the Revolutionary Guard has been the establishment of separate air and naval services. The formation of these Guard services was officially approved by Khomeini in September 1985, although the Guard Navy had existed unofficially since as early as 1982 as a small marine force, based in the southern port of Bushehr, that prevented smuggling and seaborne infiltration of Iran by regime opponents.[68] Although developed, at least in part, to undercut the regular military's monopoly on air and naval capabilities, these services, especially the Guard Navy, fulfilled key functional requirements—more ideological and political than purely military, it can be argued. The Guard's air and naval services, although giving the Guard the organizational appearance of a conventional armed force, actually helped the Guard implement some of its most militant ideological goals; their military capabilities, however, were marginal.

The Guard Air Force The Revolutionary Guard's Air Force, headed now by Hosein Jalali, has not yet exhibited appreciable tactical or strategic air capabilities.[69] Starting out by taking over the facilities and equipment of the former Shah's Imperial Civil Aviation Club in Tehran,[70] reports suggest that its inventory consists primarily of helicopter and light training aircraft[71] and it did not play a significant combat role in the war. The Guard Air Force did, however, develop 10 missile units that were responsible for air defense against intruding Iraqi aircraft[72] and, according to the Iranian press, fired surface-to-surface SCUD missiles against civilian installations in Iraq.[73] Recent press reports indicate that the Guard Air Force has taken many of the Iraqi jets flown to Iran during the 1991 Persian Gulf war, piloted by Guard air force officers trained in North Korea,[74] and MIG-29s are being acquired. Moreover, the appointment of Jalali in early 1992 (a regular Air Force and former Defense Minister) suggests an attempt to conventionalize and upgrade Guard Air Force capabilities.

Despite the outward appearance of conventionalization represented by the formation of an air force, there were reports during the Iran-Iraq war that the Guard Air Force had been planning to perform Kamikaze missions, presumably against US ships involved in tanker escort operations in the Persian Gulf in the last few years of the war.[75]

The Guard Navy   Formerly headed by the young, radical Hosein Ala'i and now by Ali Shamkhani (who heads Iran's regular Navy as well), the Guard Navy serves as an even better example of Guard militance implemented through conventional military structures. Although it had existed unofficially since 1982 and participated in the capture of Al Faw from Iraq in 1986, the Guard Navy was formally inaugurated in 1987 primarily to retaliate for Iraqi air attacks on Iranian oil shipments and facilities and to intimidate Iraq's Persian Gulf allies, such as Saudi Arabia, Kuwait, Bahrain, and the United Arab Emirates.[76] (The Iranian regular air force suffered from a general lack of spare parts and played a minor role in the war with Iraq.) The Guard Navy was further rationalized through the establishment of three individual Guard naval districts and the formation of its own missile units which controlled several Chinese-supplied surface-to-surface Silkworm missiles.[77]

In 1987-88, the Guard Navy was lavished with resources and publicity not for its role in the Iran-Iraq war but for its challenge to the U.S. naval buildup in the Gulf, which was designed to protect international oil shipping and the Persian Gulf states from Iranian attacks. Even after the U.S. Navy entered the Gulf in force, the Guard Navy harassed international shipping through hit-and-run attacks from its small, fast Swedish built boats manned by RPG-7 toting Guardsmen.[78] The Guard Navy publicly threatened direct attacks against the U.S. fleet itself and US Navy escorted tankers, and its missile unit fired several Silkworm missiles against U.S. ships and U.S.-flagged Kuwaiti tankers and facilities.[79] In 1987 the Guard Navy assembled a large flotilla in preparation for an assault, never followed through to completion, against Saudi oil facilities.[80] Reports also suggest that the Guard Navy was responsible for mining Gulf shipping lanes at the height of the U.S. tanker escort program, apparently in contradiction to the wishes of political leaders in Tehran.[81]

Despite its formation, the rationalization of its structure, and its ability to use the relatively sophisticated Silkworm missile, the Guard Navy's operations, tactics, and goals were highly unconventional. Its place at the vanguard of Iran's efforts to embarrass the U.S. and the anti-U.S. rhetoric of its commanders suggests that promoting the militant ideology of the Guard and the revolution clearly took precedence over achieving pragmatic military objectives over the primary military enemy, Iraq. The Guard Navy's willingness to challenge the U.S. Navy despite its grossly inferior capabilities, thereby provoking U.S. retaliation, indicates that objective military calculations did not drive its decisionmaking.

It has been shown, therefore, that the Guard's movement toward a conventional military structure not only failed to dissipate the Guard's militance but rather provided the Guard greater capabilities to pursue its hardline goals. The rationalization of its ground forces organization and development of separate air and naval services were intended less to enable the Guard to coordinate with Iran's regular military than to help the Guard compete with it for resources and heavy weaponry and to continue the war, if necessary, without the regular military's active participation.

Training and Education

Just as the Guard's conventional military organization masked its underlying unconventionality and hardline ideological goals, the Guard's establishment of a structured training program concealed its adherence to irregular, revolutionary impulses. Moreover, the Guard's institution of its own training programs and facilities, separate from those of the regular military, reinforces the argument that the Guard desired to compete with and supplant the regular military, rather than coordinate with it to fight Iraq. The combination of Guard and regular military training programs would almost certainly have improved the effectivenss of the overall training effort. It can be argued that the Guard built its own training infrastructure to prevent any loss of rank and file ideological commitment that would inevitably have resulted from heavy dependence on the regular military for training.

On the surface, the strides the Guard has made in developing its training programs are impressive. Apparently realizing the military drawbacks inherent in the generally low level of education of its rank and file, in 1982 the Guard inaugurated its first "high school," the Imam Sadegh School, which combined general education, military training, and the teaching of Islamic ideology.[82] The curriculum was set by the Guard, but the school relied on the Ministry of Education to provide general education teachers and on Qom clerics to instruct in Islamic theology.[83] Students at the school, which was set up by the Guard's Training Department, subordinate to the department of Educational Planning, spent part of the two and one half year program at Guard military camps. Over the next two years, the Guard established branches of its high school in all of its administrative districts throughout Iran.[84]

The Guard also moved into higher education. In 1986 it opened its own Imam Hosein University, which has 800 students and graduated its first class in 1988, and offers advanced studies in military sciences, engineering, management, and even medical sciences.[85] After the war, the Guard also founded its own military think tank, the Academy of Multilateral Defense and Strategy of the Revolutionary Guard, headed by Sadeq Haydar Kani.[86] The Guard's advanced education and training institutions are an obvious source of some of the expert and technocratic social segments of the Guard, but only a relatively few Guards participated in these programs.

On a more practical level, the Guard also developed purely military training programs for its rank and file fixed forces in each of its three services. For the Guard's ground forces, its basic training program consisted of a compulsory three months of instruction in Guard tactics and weapons use.[87] This basic training was conducted at Guard bases and garrisons throughout Iran and at the front, and, characteristic of the Guard, was heavily imbued with Islamic ideology and the Guard's militant revolutionary rhetoric.[88] To facilitate its increased use of special commando operations and elite units, the Guard also established a separate Infantry Center of the IRGC Ground Forces, located in Tehran, which offered an intensive infantry training course.[89] Because of the unwillingness of the Guard to train extensively with the regular military, the Guard's armored and artillery training was somewhat less structured, amounting to virtual "on the job training" with the Guard's relatively small inventory of these weapons.

In keeping with the more sophisticated weaponry used by the Guard's other services (Silkworm missiles, air defense systems, helicopters, etc.) the Guard Air Force and Navy established specialized training programs. At its Fajr base, the IRGC Air Force's missile unit underwent specialized training to operate the surface-to-surface SCUD missiles that it fired on targets inside Iraq.[90] The Guard Air Force also trained its own light aircraft and helicopter pilots at its section of Tehran's Mehrabad Airport.[91] The IRGC Navy established its own Marine College as well as specialized courses in seamanship, naval combat, and underwater operations at its Seyyed ol-Shohada base on the southern coast.[92]

In addition to training its own forces in the use of weapons systems and combat tactics, the Guard was responsible for training its Basij fighters. Because the Guard viewed the Basij as essentially expendable soldiers of Islam and the revolution, Basij training by the Guard was, as described previously, militarily inadequate yet rich with ideology. Journalist Youssef

Ibrahim provided a brief picture of Basij "training" by radical young Qom clerics linked to the Guard:

> A common sight at the front are these [Basij] teenagers clustered in prayer groups led by a mullah or sitting quietly listening to religious indoctrination. Their heads wrapped in distinct red bandanas, proclaiming their willingness to become martyrs for Islam, they listen to the same message that is taught at Qom's seminaries: they are the soldiers of Islam, battling blasphemous armies of infidels. This is their destiny. Paradise is their reward.[93]

If the civilian leadership had hoped that the Guard's training programs were sufficient to professionalize the Guard, then these aspirations were unmet. In a major postwar speech to the Guard, then acting Armed Forces Commander-in-Chief Rafsanjani implied that the Guard placed insufficient emphasis on training, referring in particular to the Guard's armored and antitank units.[94] Rafsanjani also criticized the Guard for continuing to rely heavily on crude, unprofessional combat tactics and for continuing to believe that revolutionary fervor was sufficient to counter a better trained and equipped army.[95] According to Rafsanjani, when Iraq invaded Iran in 1980, the Guard:

> had to fight with Molotov cocktails, with stones and sticks, with RPG's and whatever else [it] could get . . . if [Iran is] to rely on the IRGC as an armed force, if the regime is to survive to serve God, the IRGC must not think that when it is attacked it can fight with Molotov cocktails. An armed force must be so prepared that others will not dare to attack. It is the guardian of borders and territory.[96]

More directly than any other civilian political leader, Rafsanjani acknowledged that the Guard's formalized training system was less a vehicle for developing military proficiency than for perpetuating the Guard's revolutionary militance and its institutional independence from the more experienced regular armed forces. The mere existence of a military training program cannot, in itself, transform a revolutionary army into a professional force.

Weapons and Equipment

The Guard was, nonetheless, able to develop capabilities in the use of modern conventional weaponry. Guard units employed air defense systems with at least occasional success against Iraqi warplanes.[97] Guard armored and artillery units, although too few to be decisive, mastered the use of tanks, mechanized vehicles, and heavy artillery, and Guard frogmen and sailors played a role in the seizure of Al Faw and in the capture of an Iraqi militarized oil platform.[98] Guard pilots, even it they did not engage the enemy in sustained aerial combat, flew military helicopters to transport Guard troops into battle.

Highly indicative of the Guard's organizational complexity has been the development of its domestic arms industry. Indigenous arms production enabled Iran to reduce the effects of the Western-led arms embargo while furthering one of the key goals of the Islamic revolution—self-sufficiency and independence. The Guard's indigenous production efforts efforts were controlled by the IRGC Ministry from the ministry's inception in 1982. Although these capabilities were supposedly transferred to the combined Army-Guard Ministry of Defense and Armed Forces Logistics in 1990, press reports suggest the Guard's arms production facilities remain under Guard control.[99] To a greater degree than perhaps any Guard subunit, its weapons research and production apparatus demonstrate the Guard's ability to combine highly educated technocrats and experts and scientific techniques with virtually illiterate, religiously and ideologically motivated warriors under the same organizational umbrella. The character of the Guard, however, continues to lean decidedly more towards that of the latter social grouping.

The Guard's indigenous military production capabilities grew with the Guard itself. According to RafiqDust, these capabilities began in about 1984 with the production of anti-chemical warfare and communications equipment and small arms and ammunition.[100] RafiqDust also confirmed that, in its production efforts, the Guard cooperated not only with the more technically capable Construction Jihad but with the regular military and "industrialists and technocrats" as well.[101]

By 1986-87 the Guard's domestic military production facilities were directing 37 secret weapons development projects, concentrating on light propeller aircraft (the Fajr) for the Guard Air Force and, with Chinese and North Korean help, missile manufacturing capabilities.[102] A "Special Industry Group" within the Guard also was said to produce missile warheads and fuses, as well as a version of the SCUD-B surface-to-surface missile.[103] The Guard claims to have achieved these capabilities by reverse engineering the weaponry supplied abroad.[104] These reports partly corroborate RafiqDust's claims that, by 1988, Iran was nearly self-sufficient in the production of mortars, Katyusha rockets, artillery shells, radios, and attendant scramblers.[105] He also claimed that the Guard's aircraft industries group was mass producing remotely piloted vehicles and that its "self-sufficiency industries' marine group" was producing both small and medium sized naval craft.[106]

The Guard's engineers and experts also apparently succeeded in reverse engineering somewhat more sophisticated weapons and vehicle prototypes. Although difficult to confirm the Iranian contribution to the design and production of these weapons, their possession by the Guard was, in many cases, confirmed by their display on Tehran television. Moreover, although the Guard may have exaggerated its contribution to design and production, it has not been shown that the Guard committed outright falsehood in its claims. Aside from those above, the systems the Guard, and its military production associate, the Construction Jihad, claimed to have produced include an amphibious armored personnel carrier, submarine, tugboat, tanks, hovercraft, and a helicopter.[107]

The Guard's arms production capabilities, like its military organization and training, did not represent a dilution of its revolutionary character in favor of objective scientific principles, but rather provided the Guard with greater capacity with which to attempt to achieve its hardline goals. Moreover, although scientific and technical training almost certainly predisposed the Guard's engineers to question the Guard's unwavering commitment to pursue the war until victory at very high cost in lives, the Guard's technical experts in no way lowered or altered the Guard's war aims. To the contrary, by enabling Iran to circumvent an international arms embargo and compensate for the exorbitant hard currency requirements for purchases from willing sellers, the Guard's war industries experts may have stiffened the Guard leadership's resistance to a negotiated settlement.

The Export of the Revolution Apparatus

In addition to its internal security and military functions, the Guard has assumed the role of vanguard in the effort to export the Islamic revolution. Unlike its other roles, the Guard's export of the revolution activities were proactive, rather that reactive, ie. responses to threats to the revolution. The Guard developed this function to implement Khomeini's vision of a revived Islamic Ummah (unified Islamic nation), headquartered in Tehran and led by Khomeini.[108] If Khomeini were the *Amir al-Mu'minun* (Commander of the Faithful), the Revolutionary Guards were to be his foot soldiers. The Iran-Iraq war itself (after 1982 when Iran drove Iraq off its territory) can be considered a part of the effort to export the revolution. However, because the war was initiated by Iraq—posing a threat to the revolution and Iranian nation itself—the Guard's role in the war will be treated as a military mission rather than an export of the revolution effort. The Guard's anti-Western and anti-U.S. activities, however, are generally included in discussions of export of the revolution.

That the Guard's export of the revolution efforts were not intended to counter a threat to the revolution makes this function particularly significant. The Guard was able to undertake this activity even though engaged in full scale war with Iraq, a conflict that, in itself, could have been expected

to absorb all of the Guard's manpower and command and control resources. Moreover, so strong has been the Guard's commitment to acting
on the militant anti-U.S. tenets of the revolution that the Guard was willing to risk limited armed conflict with the U.S. even though such conflict
would weaken the Guard's ability to perform its more vital military mission against Iraq. Yet another important feature of the Guard's export of
the revolution apparatus is that, in contrast to its military and internal
security structure, differentiation and comparmentalization was not in
evidence. The non-specificity and fluidity of the Guard's export of the
revolution apparatus reflected the nature of the mission—the need to prevent the targets of this activity from positively identifying the Guard's
responsibility for it.

The Guard's export of the revolution efforts fall into several, often
overlapping, categories: overt military or political intervention in support
of Islamic revolutionaries in other states, except Lebanon;[109] violent activities directed against the U.S. and other Western governments;[110] and
covert action against conservative Arab governments and regime opponents.[111] Although under the control of the Guard's national command
structure, the Guard agents and units that undertook the above missions
worked with a fluid network of hardliners within the Iranian regime and
outside Iran.[112] Mission objectives were often linked to internal Iranian
developments; this internal political aspect of the Guard's export of the
revolution activities will be addressed in a subsequent chapter.

Political/Military Intervention

The primary example of the Guard's export of the revolution is its presence in Lebanon since 1982. The Guard's Lebanon contingent both helped
form and subsequently trained and backed the militant Lebanese Shia
fundamentalist organization Hizballah, with the intention of establishing
an Islamic republic in Lebanon.[113] The Guard's Lebanon contingent, which
has numbered about 2000 fighters, has generally been led and manned by
the most ideologically radical Guardsmen.[114] Aside from direct military
support and training for Hizballah, the Guard has played a highly ideological and political role in Lebanon's Bekaa Valley, proselytizing among
the local population and establishing schools, hospitals, mosques and
welfare organizations, creating support for the Islamic revolution and
generating recruits for Hizballah.[115]

Although under the command of the Reza'i and the Guard's military
leadership, RafiqDust and Iranian clerics and political leaders often exer-
cised influence over the Guard's Lebanon contingent. However, it can be
argued that an unclear chain of command can be expected in this situation
in which (1) substantial disagreements existed in Tehran over the opti-

mum level and methods of Guard activity in Lebanon; (2) the Guard had an interest in concealing responsibility for some of its activities there; and, (3) many different Iranian leaders had personal and political ties to various Lebanese Shia militants.[116] For example, former Guard Minister RafiqDust made frequent trips to Lebanon and played a key role in Guard activities in Lebanon because he had established extensive ties there during his prerevolution guerrilla training in Lebanon and because he was formally responsible for providing logistics and supplies for the Guard.[117] During his visits, RafiqDust generally met with Syrian President Hafez al-Asad to diffuse any Syrian-Iranian tensions (Syria supported Iran in the war, largely due to longstanding enmity with neighboring Iraq) caused by the frequent clashes between the Syrian backed, secular Shia group Amal and Iran's fundamentalist client, Hizballah.[118]

Below RafiqDust and the national Guard leadership level, the commander of the Guard's Lebanon contingent served on the broader council of Iranians and Lebanese Shia religious and militia leaders that formulates overall policy for militant Shia groups in Lebanon, according to a credible press report.[119] Former Iranian Ambassador to Syria and Interior Minister Ali Akbar Mohtashemi-Pur, a prominent hardliner, was also instrumental, along with the Guard, in forming Hizballah and he apparently continues to have considerable influence in Lebanon.[120] In addition, the Iranian embassies in Syria and Lebanon, Iran's Foreign Ministry, and individual Iranian leaders all attempt to exert influence over the Guard's activities and Iranian policy in Lebanon.[121]

There were press reports, however, that Iranian political leaders had decided to withdraw the Guard from Lebanon.[122] Reza'i's November 1991 statement that the Guard's military role was winding down, and the release of the remaining U.S. hostages in Lebanon by December 1991 appeared to support these reports.[123] However, in other comments, Reza'i denied that the Guard would withdraw,[124] suggesting that an internal Iranian debate was taking place in which the Guard was resisting a withdrawal of its forces. Nonetheless, the intensified activities of Hizballah against Israeli troops in Southern Lebanon in 1992 suggest that, for now, the Guard is winning this debate, even if it lost the debate over releasing the U.S. hostages there.

Activities Directed Against the United States

The Guard's Lebanon contingent was also a base from which the Guard implemented its militant anti-American ideology. By attacking U.S. interests, the Guard hoped to create greater appeal for the Islamic revolution among those in the Arab, Muslim, and Third World who resented Western domination. According to press reports, the Guard's Sheikh Abdullah

Barracks in the Bekaa Valley served as the center at which the Guard trained Lebanese Shia militants, including those of Hizballah and Islamic Amal (a more militant breakaway faction of the Syrian supported Amal group led by Nabih Berri), which may have been responsible for such anti-U.S. acts as the 1983 bombings of the U.S. Marine barracks and the U.S. Embassy in Beirut.[125] The Sheikh Abdullah Barracks also reportedly housed some of the U.S. hostages at various times in their captivity in Lebanon.[126] Lebanon also served as the apparent venue for the Guard's reported plans to bomb Pan Am Flight 103 in December 1988, the political causes and implications of which will be discussed later.[127]

Because of its role as the father and protector of Hizballah, umbrella group for the hostage holders, it is likely that the Guard contingent in Lebanon was involved in the decisions to release all remaining U.S. hostages in Lebanon. Lebanese security officials say they believe the Guard actually initiated the hostage taking in Beirut, by capturing David Dodge, an American, in 1982.[128] Former hostages have said that their guards sometimes brought them food from a nearby Revolutionary Guard base and that they could sometimes see Revolutionary Guards marching near their places of captivity.[129] The Guard was involved in and received weapons from the 1985-86 U.S.-Iran arms deal, probably partly in exchange for the Guard's cooperation in arranging for the release of some U.S. hostages in connection with the deal.[130] For both the Guard and its Lebanese allies, any apparent ideological compromise in that affair was probably erased by the capture of additional hostages to replace those released in the U.S.-Iran arms deal.[131]

Covert Action Against Arab Governments

Aside from its activities in Lebanon, the Guard has carried its export of the revolution activities to the Arab states, primarily Iraq's Persian Gulf allies. Unlike the Guard's Lebanon activity, this took the form of covert action rather than direct intervention. As is the case with its Lebanon involvement, however, the Guard has been the most powerful and capable operational component but by no means the only organization or group involved in the effort; it has shared authority on this issue with a wide variety of Iranian political leaders and foreign allies.[132] The organizational structure by which the Guard carried out this activity has been, consistent with all its export of the revolution missions, fluid and non-specialized. Again, however, the Guard held sway over the training and arming of militant foreign proxies at many locations throughout Iran, using many of the same training and indoctrination techniques it employed on its Basij soldiers in the war with Iraq.[133]

The Guard's covert action apparatus represents the only example in which the Guard's mission-specific organizational structure actually became less specialized over time. During about 1981-83, the Guard's efforts to subvert the conservative Arab states were run by its Office of Liberation Movements, headed by the radical member of the Guard's Supreme Council, Mehdi Hashemi.[134] Hashemi was a relative of Ayatollah Montazeri and a friend of Montazeri's son, Mohammad, an extreme supporter and early organizer of the Guard's export of the revolution efforts.[135] In about 1983 Hashemi and the Office of Liberation Movements were formally separated from the Guard, possibly as part of a power struggle with Reza'i and other commanders who wanted to focus primarily on the war with Iraq and to centralize the Guard's export of the revolution activities under their command.[136] The Guard continued its export of the revolution activities, albeit without a separate organizational subunit formally responsible for the activity. In 1986, Hashemi was arrested for helping his patron Montazeri leak news of the U.S.-Iran arms deal and he was executed the following year.[137]

Press reports in the mid 1980s described a "War on Satan Committee" as the Guard's special apparatus for coordinating covert activities throughout the Arab world.[138] However, there is substantially more evidence that the Guard worked closely with the Supreme Assembly for the Islamic Revolution in Iraq (SAIRI), an umbrella group of Islamic militants operating in most states of the Persian Gulf including, as its name implies, Iraq.[139] SAIRI, led by mid-ranking cleric Muhammad Baqr Hakim, (son of a revered Iraqi Shia cleric, Ayatollah Muhsin al-Hakim) was formed in late 1981 to centralize control over several different militant groups including the Islamic Da'wa (Call) Party, an Iraqi fundamentalist opposition group; Islamic Amal (Action), another militant fundamentalist group active in Iraq and the Persian Gulf states; and the Islamic Front for the Liberation of Bahrain which, with Iranian backing, was accused of sponsoring an attempted coup in Bahrain in 1981.[140] Tehran-based SAIRI, apparently with the help of the Guard, was also the leading force in the Shia uprising against Saddam Husayn in southern Iraq in the wake of the 1991 Gulf War.[141]

Iran's official media has confirmed the close links between SAIRI and the Guard. In the last days of the Iran-Iraq war, the Guard publicly called for a mobilization of SAIRI volunteers (Iraqis who had defected to Iran) to the warfront with Iraq.[142] In 1984 the Iranian press reported that SAIRI publicly thanked the Guard for allowing SAIRI forces to participate in Guard maneuvers.[143]

In addition to working through proxies, the Guard's own agents have been highly active in the Arab world. Most notable have been the Guard's efforts to foment unrest in Saudi Arabia, particularly surrounding the annual Hajj, or Islamic pilgrimage season. Iranian leaders have publicly admitted that the Guard smuggled explosives into the Kingdom in the 1986

Hajj.[144] The Guard was reportedly heavily involved in planning and provoking the rioting in Mecca by Iranian pilgrims during the 1987 Hajj, which resulted in approximately 400 deaths at the hands of Saudi security forces.[145] Guard agents, primarily in Europe, have also been responsible for recruiting Shia militants to carry out Guard sponsored operations in targeted Arab states.[146] There are also recent press reports the Guard is becoming active in Sudan, training Islamic militants there to help spread revolution throughout Muslim parts of Africa.[147]

To support its covert mission, the Guard has tapped its network of allies within Iran. In particular, Iran's deputy Foreign Minister for Arab Affairs Hosein Sheikh-ol-Eslam, a key leader of the "Students" that held the U.S. hostages in Tehran during 1979-81, has helped his ideological and political allies in the Guard by helping to place Guardsmen in positions at Iran's embassies in Europe, Africa, and Asia.[148] Under diplomatic cover, Guard agents are reported to orchestrate and recruit for Guard operations worldwide, and assassinate Tehran's opponents abroad.[149] These assassinations may also be sponsored by the ministry of intelligence.

The varied means and organizations through which the Guard has pursued its efforts to export the revolution clearly demonstrates its ability to avoid formal organizational specialization and differentiation when doing so furthers the performance of a specific mission. That the Guard was able to aggressively pursue efforts to export the revolution while simultaneously engaged in a major war further demonstrates the Guard's flexibility and the depth of its ideological commitment. However, the Guard's involvement in export of the revolution does not, in itself, distinguish the Guard from other revolutionary armed forces. Almost all revolutionary militaries have performed some similar mission at the behest of their respective leaders. The French revolutionary army fought full scale wars as much to export the French revolution as to protect France's national security; the Cuban military, for example, has was ordered into Angola in the 1970s to bolster a Marxist regime there; and the Red Army invaded Afghanistan in 1979 to prop up the faltering Communist regime led by the People's Democratic Party of Afghanistan.

Nonethless, as exemplified above, in most revolutionary societies the role of the military in export of the revolution has generally been confined to direct intervention; covert action has been reserved primarily for separate civilian dominated intelligence services such as the Soviet KGB. In the USSR, the KGB, not the military intelligence organization, the GRU, has had primary responsibility for "active measures,"—the effort to promote or bring to power local Communist parties.[150] In the People's Republic of China, similar active measures operations have been performed by the International Liaison Department and the United Front Work Department, intelligence organs which are distinctly separate from the PLA.[151]

By contrast, in revolutionary Iran the Guard has been dominant in most forms of export of the revolution—covert and overt. Moreover, unlike its counterparts in other revolutionary societies, the Guard has initiated and vigorously asserted its leading role in export of the revolution activities rather than merely implement the initiatives of the civilian leadership.[152] Even more significantly, it will be shown later that the Guard has vigorously pursued export of the revolution activities despite apparent opposition, or, at best, ambivalence, from its civilian superiors.[153] Moreover, to a degree unknown among other revolutionary armed forces, the Guard's support for export of the revolution has merged with its role as a bulwark of hardline politicians and policies.[154]

Administrative Bureaucracy

A major indicator of the increase in the Guard's complexity and its transition from a chaotic revolutionary militia to a more conventional organizational structure was the establishment of an independent Ministry of the Revolutionary Guard in November 1982. Shortly after its formation, the Ministry functions were publicly defined as providing for the Guard's logistics, procurement, finances, legal, and personnel services and serving as the Guard's liaison with the Majles and the executive branch.[155] As an extension of its procurement function, the Ministry also managed the Guard's indigenous military production efforts, which began on a large scale in 1985-86.[156] Particularly significant was the Ministry's assumption and regularization of the Guard's budgetary and financial administration; initially the Guard was funded largely through donations from key clerics and regime supporters.[157] Clerical contributions continued on a symbolic basis, however.[158]

The Guard Ministry's role in weapons acquisition was also instrumental in molding the Guard into a truly national armed force. In the Guard's first few years, each Guard provided his own weaponry, most of the available weapons were originally captured from the Shah's arsenals during the revolution, or, after the war broke out, captured from Iraq.[159] The Ministry centralized the allocation and acquisition of weapons, fulfilling another key requirements for the creation of a national rather than private or local force.[160] According to Weber, this transition from private to national control over the legitimate use of force in society is a major indicator of nation building.[161] In a revolutionary society, the centralization of armed force is an indicator of the consolidation of the revolutionary regime.

In addition to the manifest functions of the Guard Ministry in helping impose structure on the Guard, the Ministry fulfilled a latent function for the civilian leadership. By assigning the Guard a Cabinet level ministry, the political leadership had hoped to increase their control over the Guard; the Guard Minister, like other Iranian ministers, was accountable to the Majles and the Prime Minister.[162] This measure of control was displayed in September 1988 when the Majles voted to remove RafiqDust, making him a scapegoat for the Guard's battlefield collapse and the loss of the war.[163] Although RafiqDust, because of his role in weapons procurement since the Guard's inception, was a logical candidate to become the first Guard Minister, his appointment also furthered the clerics' political objectives. RafiqDust, the reported brother-in-law of Rafsanjani,[164] has been a generally conservative element within the Guard leadership and more amenable to civilian government control than his colleagues in the Guard military structure.[165]

RafiqDust himself mirrors the ambivalence with which the Guard viewed the formation of the Ministry. On the one hand, RafiqDust has been a longtime Guard stalwart and one of its early organizers. On the other, he is more conservative than the majority of the Guard leadership and rank and file. Similarly, the Guard welcomed the formation of its own Ministry to lobby for its interests in Cabinet debates, but resented the measure of control the formation of the Ministry would presumably give civilian leaders over its affairs.[166]

Unlike the other components of the Guard, the Ministry, as a subunit, was unable to resist the conservative influences of specialization and bureaucratization. This is because the Ministry did not provide Guard radicals sufficient opportunity to express their ideological commitment, for example, in battle against Iraq. Because of its administrative functions, the Ministry contained a cadre of administrators, experts, and managers as well as some non-Guard personnel, social elements unlike the militants that formed and still dominate the Guard.[167] It built a national military production infrastructure and a worldwide, if inefficient and allegedly corrupt, procurement network, and it developed the infrastructure to oversee the Guard's nationwide network of cooperatives and social service programs for Guard families.[168] To perform its several missions the Ministry created several specialized executive departments, including an inspectorate, a logistics department, industrial research and personnel directorates, and offices of the economic, planning, and social advisors, functions not conducive to providing an outlet for Guard militance.[169]

If political leaders expected that the Guard Ministry and RafiqDust would impose a measure of moderation on the Guard, then these leaders underestimated the Guard military leadership's ability to circumvent or impose their will on the Ministry rather than vice versa. The Guard Ministry was the least radical component of the Guard, but, precisely for that reason, it was the least powerful Guard component. For example, according to the Iranian exile press, Guard Commander Reza'i successfully prevented RafiqDust from bringing the Guard's internal security apparatus under Ministry authority.[170] Although the Ministry was chartered to control Guard personnel policy, in practice the Guard's longtime Spokesman and Chief of Staff Ali Reza Afshar (now Basij commander) almost invariably announced Guard personnel shifts and major mobilizations. It was Afshar, not a Guard Ministry official, who ultimately became deputy for Manpower in the combined General Headquarters established by Rafsanjani in June 1988.[171]

Additional evidence for the weakness of the Guard Ministry as a power base within the IRGC is provided by the ouster of RafiqDust in 1988. His ouster for the Ministry's alleged mismanagement (failure to properly store munitions, jeopardizing public safety, overpaying for weapons purchased abroad, and failure to keep troops adequately supplied) was ironic in that RafiqDust was the most politically responsive to the wishes of the political leadership of any of the Guard leaders.[172] Moreover, he was made a scapegoat for the loss of the war even though, among the Guard leaders, he was probably the least responsible for the battlefield setbacks because he did not command forces or prominently figure in strategy formulation. As acting Armed Forces chief, Rafsanjani should probably have dismissed Reza'i for alleged battlefield incompetence rather than allow the Majles, which he dominated as Speaker and as Iran's most clever politician, to vote out RafiqDust.[173] It can be argued that Rafsanjani clearly calculated that the dismissal of RafiqDust posed far less danger of a Guard backlash than would the firing of the far more powerful Commander Mohsen Reza'i.

Perhaps the best evidence for the organizational weakness of the Ministry within the overall Guard structure was its abolition as an independent Ministry after the death of Ayatollah Khomeini. When Rafsanjani formed a new government in 1989, the Ministry was combined with the regular military's Defense Ministry into a Ministry of Defense and Armed Foces Logistics, headed by a non-Guard, civilian technocrat, Akbar Torkan.[174] However, in contrast to past incidents of Guard resistance to civilian efforts to weaken it, the Guard did not vigorously protest the abolition of its Ministry, almost certainly in part because the Guard Ministry was out of step with the Guard command ideologically and politically. Instead, the Guard leaders have continued to run most of their affairs independently of the new combined Ministry; they have retained control of Guard military production facilities, the major function formally assigned the combined Ministry,[175] and the Guard has even engineered the appointment of an experienced, former deputy Guard Minister, Mahmud Pakravan, into the number two slot at the combined Defense Ministry.[176]

The relative weakness of the Guard Ministry within the Guard exemplifies the Guard's ability to resist the conservative forces of organizational complexity. The Guard Ministry itself could not resist the conservative influences of its own internal structure, but the Ministry did not, as political leaders expected, extend that conservatism and bureaucratic rationality to the Guard military and internal security structure. Although the abolition of the Guard Ministry was an important organizational loss for the Guard, it can be argued that the Ministry's integration with that of the regular military actually strengthened the Guard's ideological purity by removing from the Guard its least ideological component. Moreover, the Guard command, both before and after the abolition of the Guard Ministry, had demonstrated its ability to usurp or dominate the operations of the Guard Ministry virtually at will. These factors may help explain why the Guard leaders, radicals all, did not vigorously oppose the Ministry's integration into the new combined Ministry of Defense and Armed Forces Logistics.

Military Command Structure

Additional evidence for the Guard's ability to resist the effects of organizational complexity can be found at the level of the top military leadership. The current Guard leaders (who have dominated the organization since the fall of Bani-Sadr) have remained among the regime's most radical advocates, despite the demands of their positions and the war, their need to work within the overall regime decisionmaking structure, and their experience with the limits to which ideological zeal can affect objective military outcomes. Their radicalism has persisted even though, like the military and internal security structure they have commanded, they have developed a top echelon command structure similar in appearance, if not in actual leadership dynamics, to that of conventional armed forces worldwide and to that of Iran's regular military.

As described earlier in this chapter, the current Guard leadership structure developed from the collegial Supreme Council of the Revolutionary Guard. In September 1981 Reza'i ascended to supreme Guard leadership because of his large following in the Guard (derived from his leadership of the MIR), his opposition to Bani-Sadr, his aggressive efforts to crush the Mojahedin-e-Khalq, and his willingess and ability to take the Guard on the offensive against Iraq.[177] Shortly after assuming leadership, Reza'i appointed Ali Shamkhani as his deputy when Shamkhani's predecessor, Mohsen Koladuz, died in an air crash.[178] RafiqDust's appointment as first Guard Minister in November 1982 was the next major development of the Guard leadership structure. As the Guard accelerated its efforts in the mid-1980s to undermine the regular military, in part, by demonstrating equivalent organization, the Guard leaders established formal Staffs.

The Joint Staff, which was set up in 1986 as the Guard's separate ground, air, and naval services were becoming established, was composed of Reza'i, his deputy Shamkhani, and the commanders of the three

Guard military services.[179] In 1986, Reza'i appointed Shamkhani to the concurrent post of Commander of the IRGC Ground Forces which, because of the overwhelming dominance of the Ground Forces in the Guard, dominated the Joint Staff.[180] In 1987, Guard Navy and Air Force Commanders Hosein Ala'i and Musa Refan, respectively, were named, thus rounding out the composition of the Joint Staff.[181] The Joint Staff was formally integrated into Rafsanjani's combined Army-Guard General Headquarters when that body was set up in 1988. However, in 1989, perhaps in an effort to curry the Guard's favor, Iran's new supreme leader Ali Khamene'i approved the formal reconstitution of a separate Guard command staff and the Guard's new Central Headquarters Staff was formed, headed by Mohammad Baqr Zolqadr, an anti-Shah guerrilla and original Guard member.[182] The combined regular military and Guard Headquarters was retained, however, even if in a weakened form.

The original version of the Central Headquarters Staff (before the formation of the General Armed Forces Headquarters) was essentially Reza'i's staff when it was formed in late 1984 to help Reza'i and the other Guard leaders cope with the demands of the war and the attendant expansion of the Guard.[183] It was also formerly a separate entity from the Joint Staff (the two bodies are now essentially one). The Central Staff was first headed by Reza'i's longtime ally Ali Reza Afshar, who doubled as the Guard's official Spokesman. In 1987, Mohammad Foruzandeh headed Central Headquarters; he was named a deputy in the General Armed Forces Headquarters Staff in 1989.[184] Abbas Mohtaj, former Commander of Guard region 7 (Kurdestan) served as Foruzandeh's deputy until Mohtaj's recent appointments as deputy commander of the Guard's Ground Forces, and then deputy commander of the regular Navy.[185]

In completing the development of the Guard leadership structure, each of the three Guard armed services developed organized staffs. Rahim Safavi, longtime Chief of Operations on the southern front, became deputy Guard Ground Forces Commander when that service was organized in 1986; he has since become Reza'i's deputy Commander of the overall Guard.[186] In 1987, Hosein Dehqan, a former Guard commander in Lebanon, became deputy commander of the Guard Air Force,[187] (he served briefly as commander) and Ali Akbar Ahmadiyan became Chief of Staff of the IRGC Navy under Hosein Ala'i.[188]

In establishing a conventional command structure, the Guard leaders appeared to compartmentalize their responsibilities to best cope with the demands of the war, for which the Guard was not only unprepared but was not even yet organized as a military force. Although the development of a formal command structure partially accomplished this objective, it can be argued that the Guard command structure also masked the informal and collegial nature of the Guard leadership and broadened its base among the rank and file. As has been shown, all of the Guard leaders were guerrillas before the revolution; they were allies and early organizers of the Guard; and all, in the course of their Guard service, have, either in statements or actions, expressed unwavering support for the radical principles of the revolution. As examples, among the lesser known commanders, Dehqan served in Lebanon, the prime expression of Guard radicalism,[189] and Mohtaj was cited in an opposition press report as playing a role in the rioting by Iranian pilgrims in Mecca during the 1987 Hajj.[190]

With the exception of RafiqDust, none of the major Guard leaders possessed specific expertise that uniquely qualified him for a specific position in the command structure. In part because of the young chronological age of the Guard, none had risen through the ranks of a specific Guard military service or component, and none had significant conventional military experience before the revolution. All of them owed their positions to their roles in the struggle against the Shah and to their common bonds as builders of the Guard.

In addition, the collegial and professionally non-specific nature of the Guard leadership is exemplified by the frequency and extent to which they switched positions or replaced each other, as outlined above, as well as the apparent lack of rivalry among them. With the exception of the more conservative RafiqDust, and in contrast with the public differences within the regime as a whole, none of the Guard leaders ever publicly disagreed with another or deviated from radical positions on major issues. The Guard leadership structure, therefore, serves as yet another example in which the Guard's organizational complexity did not represent professionalization of the Guard; neither did their command responsibilities transform the Guard leaders from radical ideologues into professional officers.

Notes

1. Samuel P. Huntington, *Political Order in Changing Societies* (New Haven and London: Yale University Press, 1968)
2. Katharine Chorley, *Armies and the Art of Revolution* (Boston: Beacon Press, 1973) Chaps. 11,12
3. Ibid.; Morris Janowitz, *The Military in the Political Development of New Nations* (Chicago: University of Chicago Press, 1964); Amos Perlmutter, "Civil-Military Relations in Socialist Authoritarian and Praetorian States: Prospects and Retrospects" in Roman Kolkowicz and Andrzej Korbonski eds., *Soldiers, Peasants, and Bureaucrats* (London: George Allen and Unwin Ltd., 1982) David Rappoport, "The Praetorian Army" in Kolkowicz and Korbonski, op.cit.
4. Shaul Bakhash, *The Reign of the Ayatollahs* (New York: Basic Books, Inc., 1984) pp. 227-30

5. Nikola Schahgaldian, *The Iranian Military Under the Islamic Republic* (Santa Monica: Rand Corp., 1987) P. 66
6. Bakhash, op.cit., pp. 225-9
7. Schahgaldian, op.cit., P. 69
8. Bakhash, op.cit., P. 89
9. "Ayatollah, Aide of Khomeini, Shot," Washington Post; May 26, 1979
10. Bakhash, op.cit., pp. 219-20
11. Ibid
12. Ronald Perron, "The Iranian Islamic Revolutionary Guard Corps," in *Middle East Insight*; June-July, 1985, P. 39
13. Bakhash, op.cit., pp. 220-4
14. "IRGC Commander on Internal Security of Country," Tehran Times; December 30, 1982
15. Schahgaldian, op.cit., pp. 122,143
16. Ibid, P. 69
17. "Biographies Cited," Tehran IRNA in English; November 9, 1982; "Armed Forces Mark War Week in Tehran," IRNA in English September 25, 1984; *Pars Daily News;* March 7, 1981; and *Tehran Akbar* (News); Vol. IX, No. 40; May 14, 1983
18. "Mehdi Hashemi's Confessions," excerpted from Tehran The Islamic Republic in Akhbar (News); Vol. VII, No. 205, December 10, 1986; "Why Khomeini's Designated Heir Quit," Washington Post; April 10, 1989, P. D8
19. "Lebanese Weekly on Hashemi, McFarlane," in FBIS; November 5, 1986
20. "New Tehran Guards Commander," Tehran Domestic Service in Persian; July 12, 1981
21. "History and Present Status of IRGC," in Tehran Iran Press Digest; August 7, 1984
22. "Duties, Aims, Policies of Guard Corps Elaborated," Tehran Kayhan in Persian; February 14, 1984, P. 167
23. Ibid, P. 170
24. "History and Present Status of IRGC," op.cit., P. 16 For example, Region Ten is headquartered in Tehran; Region 2 in Esfahan; Region 5 in Tabriz; Region 7 in Bakhtaran; and Region 9 in Bushehr.
25. Ibid, P. 15
26. "Bakhtaran Mopping Up Operation Successful," Pars Daily News; August 29, 1984
27. "Duties, Aims, Policies of Guard Corps Elaborated," op.cit.; "IRGC's Afshar on Beyt ol-Moqaddas, Guards Day," Tehran Domestic Service in Persian; March 15, 1988
28. "Iran" in *Defense and Foreign Affairs Handbook 1989* (Alexandria, Va.: International Media Corp., 1989) P. 514
29. Bakhash, op.cit., pp. 219-20

30. "100 Are Executed for Opposition to Iranian Regime," Washington Post; October 6, 1981
31. "Rafsanjani Addresses Intelligence Seminar," Tehran IRNA in English; December 31, 1988
32. Duties, Aims, Policies of Guard Corps Elaborated," op.cit.
33. Perron, op.cit., pp. 35-9
34. "History and Present Status of IRGC," op.cit.
35. "Tehran Announces Dates for Dispatch of Troops," Tehran Domestic Service in Persian; February 25, 1988
36. "IRGC Spokesman Outlines Civil Defense, Support Programs," Tehran Kayhan; November 7, 1987, P. 2
37. Schahgaldian, op.cit., P. 75
38. "Slow Day at the Spy Shop in Tehran," New York Times; June 29, 1990, P. A3
39. "The Bombs Knock Holes in Morale," The Economist; June 22, 1985
40. Ibid
41. Jeffrey Richelson, *Foreign Intelligence Organizations* (Cambridge, Mass.: Ballinger Publishing Co., 1988) P. 277
42. "The Bombs Knock Holes in Morale," op.cit.
43. "Gorbachev's Unwinnable War," The Economist; January 27, 1990, P. 47
44. "Khomeini's Remarks Sparked Riot," United Press International; March 8, 1989
45. "Interview With Mohsen RafiqDust," Tehran Ettelaat; September 22, 1985, P. 4
46. Ibid
47. Edgar O'Ballance, *The Gulf War* (London: Brassey's Defence Publishers, 1988) pp. 67-8
48. "Interview With Mohsen RafiqDust," op.cit.
49. "IRGC Commander Reza'i Interviewed," in FBIS; March 2, 1990
50. Nader Entessar, "The Military and Politics in the Islamic Republic of Iran," in Hooshang Amirahmadi and Manoucher Parvin eds., *Post-Revolution Iran* (Boulder, Co. and London: Westview Press, 1988) P. 66
51. Akhbar, Vol. IX, No. 141; September 17, 1988 Press reports have indicated a possible Guard chemical weapons production program. See New York Times "Shipment of US Chemical Seized on Way to Iran," March 23, 1989, P. A13
52. "Iranian Bomb," Washington Post, January 12, 1992 p. C7
53. "U.S. Move To Halt Nuclear Technology Sale Angers Iranians," Washington Post, November 22, 1991, p. A35
54. "Interview with Mohsen RafiqDust," op.cit.
55. Robin Wright, "Iran's Armed Forces: the Battle Within," The Christian Science Monitor; August 26, 1987, P. 1
56. "History and Present Status of IRGC," op.cit.

57. "Iran" in *Defense and Foreign Affairs Handbook 1989*, op.cit. P. 514
58. "IRGC Officials Discuss Postwar Mobilization," in FBIS; December 2, 1988
59. "I Sarallah Corps Commander on Volunteer Training," Tehran Domestic Service; November 15, 1987
60. "Musavi Addresses Kerman Residents," Tehran Domestic Service in Persian; November 12, 1987
61. Entessar, op.cit., P. 66
62. "Karaj Mobilization Units to Hold Maneuvers 26 November," Tehran Domestic Service in Persian; November 16, 1987
63. Ibid
64. "I Sarallah Corps Commander on Volunteer Training," op.cit.
65. Schahgaldian, op.cit., P. 78
66. "In Brief" in Tehran Akhbar, Vol. IX, No. 151; September 29, 1983; Tehran Kayhan; March 30, 1988
67. "Iran Uses Troops on Domestic Unrest," Christian Science Monitor; June 3, 1988
68. "New Marine Forces to Combat Smugglers, Rebels," Tehran Kayhan in Persian; October 31, 1982, P. 15
69. "Iran" in *Defense and Foreign Affairs Handbook 1989*, op. cit.
70. "History and Present Status of IRGC," op.cit., P. 14
71. "Iran" in *Defense and Foreign Affairs Handbook 1989*, op.cit.
72. Tehran Akhbar; Vol. IX, No. 141; September 17, 1988
73. "Guards Fire Missile at al-Mawsil," IRNA in English; March 7, 1988
74. "Iran Adds Iraqi 'Asylum' Aircraft to Its Air Force," London Al-Sharq al-Awsat, December 2, 1991. p. 1
75. "Iran" in *Defense and Foreign Affairs Handbook 1989*, op.cit.
76. "IRGC Navy Commander on US `Declaration of War'," Tehran Domestic Service in Persian; June 28, 1987
77. Robin Wright, "Iran's Armed Forces: the Battle Within," op.cit.
78. "Signs of Split in Leadership Seen in Iran's Counterattack on US Navy," Christian Science Monitor; April 20, 1988, P. 7
79. Ibid.; "Iranians Celebrate Missile Attack as Much Needed Morale Booster," Washington Post; October 18, 1987
80. "Saudis Negotiate for Gulf Barge Base," Washington Post; August 1, 1989, P. A22
81. "Signs of Split in Leadership Seen in Iran's Counterattack on US Navy," op.cit.
82. "IRGC to Get Own High School With Special Courses," Iran Press Digest; August 18, 1982, P. 10
83. Ibid
84. "Khamene'i Attends IRGC University Graduation," Tehran IRNA in English; March 7, 1988

85. Ibid
86. "Kim Chong-Il Receives Gift From Iranian Group," Pyongyang KCNA in English; April 5, 1989
87. "History and Present Status of IRGC," op.cit.
88. "IRGC Minister Addresses Infantry Training Center," Tehran IRNA in English; February 28, 1988
89. Ibid
90. "IRGC Air Force Begins Missile Training," Tehran Domestic Service; February 25, 1988
91. "Rafsanjani Attends IRGC Graduation Ceremony," Tehran IRNA in English; October 12, 1988
92. "Reza'i Presides Over IRGC Graduation Ceremonies," Tehran Domestic Service in Persian; September 4, 1988
93. Youssef Ibrahim, "Holy City Teaches, Exports Revolution," The Wall Street Journal; April 12, 1984, P. 34
94. "Hashemi-Rafsanjani Speaks on Future of IRGC," Tehran Domestic Service in Persian; October 6, 1988
95. Ibid
96. Ibid
97. Tehran Akhbar, Vol. IX, No. 141; September 17, 1988
98. Ibid
99. "IRGC Exhibits Achievements at Tehran Trade Fair," Tehran Domestic Service in Persian; September 20, 1989
100. "A Perspective From IRGC Ministry: Interview With IRGC Minister Mohsen RafiqDust," Iran Press Digest; November 20, 1984, P. 14
101. Ibid
102. "Anoushiravan Ehteshami, "Iran's Domestic Arms Industry," paper presented at Chatham House conference entitled "The Iranian Revolution, Ten Years Later," January 19-20, 1989, reprinted in Tehran Echo of Iran, No. 16; February 23, 1989, pp. 20-4
103. Ibid
104. "RafiqDust, Kharrazi on War of Cities," Tehran Television in Persian; March 10, 1988
105. "Guards Minister on Arms Production," Tehran Domestic Service in Persian; January 27, 1988
106. Ibid
107. "Amphibious Personnel Carrier Manufactured," Tehran Television; February 1, 1988; "Guard Corps Minister on Military Self-Sufficiency," Tehran Domestic Service; November 8, 1987; "IRGC Minister Announces Launching of New Tugboat," Tehran IRNA in English; November 24, 1987; "Reza'i: New Tank Under Manufacture; 3 New Planes Tested," IRNA in English; November 7, 1987; "First Hovercraft Manufactured by IRGC," Tehran Domestic Service in Persian; Febru-

ary 6, 1989; "Musavi Hears Report on New Helicopter," Tehran Domestic Service in Persian; April 11, 1989

108. "Khomeini Militia Vows to Spread Iran's Revolution," Washington Post; May 7, 1989, P. A1
109. Robin Wright, "A Reporter at Large," The New Yorker; September 5, 1988, pp. 41-2
110. Perron, op.cit., pp. 38-9
111. "Iran's Armed Forces: the Battle Within, op.cit.
112. "Iran's Agents of Terror," US News and World Report; March 6, 1989, pp. 20-5
113. Robin Wright, "A Reporter at Large," op.cit.
114. "U.S. Journalist Kidnapped on Iranian Orders," London The Independent; July 1, 1987, P. 1
115. Robin Wright, "A Reporter at Large," op.cit.
116. "Iran's Agents of Terror," op.cit.; "Rafsanjani Losing Influence Over Shiite Militants," Washington Post; January 8, 1990, P. A17
117. "Iran's Besharati, RafiqDust in Syria for Talks," Paris AFP in English; May 12, 1988
118. Ibid
119. Mohammed Selhami, "I Met the Suicide Men," *Paris Jeune Afrique;* January 25, 1984, pp. 41-51
120. "Rafsanjani Losing Influence Over Shiite Militants," op.cit.
121. "Iran's Agents of Terror," op.cit., P. 23
122. "Pullout Won't Lessen Iran's Sway in Lebanon," New York Times, October 16, 1991. p. A5
123. "Shift by Shiites Seen Speeding Release of Western Hostages," Washington Post, November 21, 1991. p. A44
124. "Pullout Won't Lessen Iran's Sway in Lebanon," op,cit.; Interview with Mohsen Reza'i in Jane's Defence Weekly, November 16, 1991. p. 980
125. "Iran's Agents of Terror, op.cit., P. 24
126. Ibid
127. "Closing in on the Pan Am Bombers," *US News and World Report;* May 22, 1989, pp. 23-4
128. "Iranians to Withdraw Troops From Lebanon," New York Times, October 13, 1991. p. 19
129. "Iran Paid for Release of Hostages," Washington Post, January 19, 1992. p. A1
130. *Report of the President's Special Review Board* (The Tower Commission Report) February 26, 1987, see especially pp. B-31, 48, 57, 88; Michael Ledeen, *Perilous Statecraft* (New York: McMillan, 1988) see especially pp. 131-3, 234-5, 241, 256
131. "Bush Took Bogus Call On Hostages," Washington Post; March 9, 1990, P. A1

132. Robin Wright, *Sacred Rage, The Wrath of Militant Islam* (New York: Simon and Schuster, 1985) see pp. 26-9, 33-7

133. Robin Wright, "A Reporter at Large," op.cit.

134. "Mehdi Hashemi's Confessions," excerpted from Tehran The Islamic Republic in Akhbar, Vol. VII, No. 205; December 10, 1986

135. "Lebanese Weekly on Hashemi, McFarlane," op.cit.

136. Ibid

137. "Why Khomeini's Designated Heir Quit," op.cit.

138. Amos Perlmutter, "Containment Strategy for the Islamic Holy War," Wall Street Journal; October 4, 1983

139. "Iranian-Based Al Dawa Terrorist Group Expands Its Activities," Washinton Post; November 8, 1985, P. E4

140. Ibid.; "Conservative Arabs Still Hostile Toward Iran," New York Times; February 22, 1990, P. A5

141. "Anti-Saddam Uprising Spreads in South Iraq," Washington Post; March 5, 1991, P. A1; "Iraq and the Ayatollahs," Washington Post; March 15, 1991 P. A23

142. "IRGC Announces SAIRI Recruitment Drive," Tehran Domestic Service in Persian; July 14, 1988

143. "Iraqi Mujahidin to Join Jerusalem Maneuvers," Tehran IRNA in English; February 8, 1984

144. "Iran Admits Smuggling Explosives," Riyadh Domestic Service in Arabic; May 17, 1989

145. "Iran's Armed Forces: the Battle Within," op.cit.

146. "Iran's Agents of Terror," op.cit.

147. "Iran Shifting Its Attention From Lebanon to Sudan," New York Times, December 13, 1991. p. A7; "U.S. Aide Calls Muslim Militants Big Concern in World," New York Times, January 1, 1992. p.3

148. "Iran's Agents of Terror," op.cit.

149. "Killings in Austria, Emirates Laid to Iran," Washington Post; August 3, 1989, P. A1

150. Jeffrey Richelson, *Sword and Shield: Soviet Intelligence and Security Apparatus* (Cambridge, Mass.: Ballinger Publishing Co., 1986) Chapter 7

151. Jeffrey Richelson, *Foreign Intelligence Organizations*, op.cit., pp. 278-81

152. Robin Wright, "A Reporter at Large," op.cit.

153. "Closing in on the Pan Am Bombers," op.cit.

154. Ibid

155. "A Perspective From IRGC Ministry: Interview With IRGC Minister Mohsen RafiqDust," Tehran Iran Press Digest; November 20, 1984; "History and Present Status of IRGC," op.cit.

156. "Interview With Mohsen RafiqDust," Tehran Iran Press Digest; August 22, 1984

157. Schahgaldian, op.cit., P. 66

158. "Montazeri Meets With IRGC Minister," Tehran Television Service in Persian; November 11, 1988

159. "A Perspective From IRGC Ministry," op.cit.

160. "History and Present Status of IRGC," op.cit.

161. H.H. Gerth and C. Wright Mills, *From Max Weber: Essays in Sociology* (New York: Oxford University Press, 1946) pp. 47-9

162. "History and Present Status of IRGC," op.cit.

163. "3 Ministers Get No-Confidence Vote," Tehran Domestic Service in English; September 12, 1988

164. "Personalities Vying for Succession in Iran," London Al-Dustur in Arabic, No. 261; November 22, 1982, P. 84

165. "Tehran Attempts to Balance Guards' Zeal, Dangers of War," Washington Post; August 23, 1987, P. A1

166. "Personalities Vying for Succession in Iran," op.cit.; "Opposition to Ministry of Guards," Free Voice of Iran in Persian; May 19, 1982 in JPRS 80975; June 3, 1982

167. "Minister Outlines Duties of Revolution Guard Corps," Tehran Sobh-E-Azadegan in Persian; November 13, 1982, P. 2

168. "Moderation Emerges as Iran Edges into New Era," Washington Post; October 24, 1988, P. A1; "A Perspective From IRGC Ministry: Interview With IRGC Minister Mohsen RafiqDust," op.cit.

169. "New IRGC Officials Appointed," Tehran IRNA in English; February 1, 1989

170. "Reza'i Wins Battle for Control of Guards," London Iran Press Service; May 12, 1983, pp. 6-7

171. "General Command Deputy Calls for Volunteers," Tehran IRNA in English; August 31, 1988

172. "Tehran Attempts to Balance Guards' Zeal, Dangers of War," op.cit.

173. Robin Wright, "Wily Speaker Excels at Iran's Political Game," Christian Science Monitor; August 27, 1987, P. 1; "Voice of Moderation Emerges as Iran Edges into New Era," Washington Post; October 24, 1988, P. A1; "Iran-Iraq: Problems at Home Resurface," *The Middle East*; October 1988, P. 14

174. "Biographies of New Cabinet Summarized," Kayhan al -Arabi; August 26, 1989, pp. 2,6; "Iran After Arms," The Middle East Today, No. 194, February 6, 1992.

175. "IRGC Exhibits Achievements at Tehran Trade Fair," op.cit.

176. "New Appointments to Various Ministries Announced," London Kayhan in Persian; January 2, 1990, P. 2

177. "Guard Commander on New Programs, Strategy," Tehran Domestic Service in Persian; September 15, 1981

178. Tehran Akhbar; January 18, 1982

179. "Readiness Exercises Announced," Tehran Domestic Service in Persian; November 15, 1987

180. "Shamkhani Appointed IRGC Ground Forces Commander," Tehran IRNA in English; May 11, 1986

181. "IRGC Air Forces Commander on Retaliatory Capabilities," Tehran Domestic Service; March 2, 1988; "IRGC Navy Commander on US `Declaration of War'," Tehran Domestic Service in Persian; June 28, 1987

182. "Reza'i on Establishment of New IRGC Staff Command," Tehran Domestic Service in Persian; September 28, 1989; "Revolution Guards Corps Chief of Staff Interviewed," Tehran Times in English; February 13, 1990, pp. 2,7

183. Schahgaldian, op.cit., P. 118

184. "Khamene'i Announces New Appointments," Tehran Television Service in Persian, October 1, 1989

185. "Officials on France, Saudi Arabia, Gulf," Tehran Domestic Service; May 5, 1988; "Bakhtaran Mopping Up Operations Successful," Paris Daily News; August 29, 1984

186. Khamene'i Appoints 3 Military Commanders," Tehran Domestic Service in Persian; September 24, 1989

187. "Tehran Phone-In Program With IRGC Officers," Tehran Domestic Service in Persian; September 24, 1987

188. "Army, Navy Battle Against US Fleet," Tehran IRNA in English; April 19, 1989, p. 189. Mohammed Selhami, "I Met the Suicide Men," op.cit. pp. 41-51

190. "Opposition Statement Cited on Mecca Incidents," Baghdad Iraqi News Agency; August 6, 1987

5

The Guard's Political Autonomy

Another criteria of an institution's strength is its autonomy. Autonomy represents the degree to which an organization has "its own identity and values distinguishable from those of other institutions and social forces," and is free of the control by a particular social group, such as a family, ethnic group, tribe, class, or political faction.[1] The Syrian military serves as an example of a military institution that can be considered lacking in autonomy, because it is dominated by the minority Alawites, a formerly underprivileged, religiously heterodox group of families that comprises about 10% of the Syrian population.[2]

Although it is not difficult to show that the Revolutionary Guard is relatively autonomous, it will be useful to broaden the measurement somewhat in analyzing the Guard. In particular, as a military and security institution, the measurement of autonomy is appropriately applied to the analysis of civilian political control over the Guard—the degree to which the Guard ran its own affairs and resisted political interference.

The question of civilian political control also facilitates comparisons between the Guard and other revolutionary armed forces. The Guard, because of its depth of ideological commitment and role in helping the revolution triumph, resisted civilian political control to a greater extent than it counterparts in other societies. Because the Guard appropriated for itself the role of guardian of the revolution and its values, the Guard, as an institution, viewed civilian political control as an unnecessary affront. This attitude on the part of the Guard flowed directly from the Guard's role as a major independent element in the revolutionary coalition that brought Khomeini to power. The precursors of the Guard, unlike the precursors of the Chinese People's Liberation Army or Soviet Red Army, were not creatures of the civilian grouping that ultimately came to power—the prerevolutionary Guard was an associate and partner, working in parallel with these revolutionary clerics.[3]

Another criterion which properly falls within the scope of the analysis of autonomy is the ability of the Guard to place and maintain its members, former members, and allies in key positions outside the Guard. Whereas in some cases former Guards used their service as a springboard to government, there are several major examples in which Guard associates and former members who entered government continued to work closely with the Guard even when doing so may have jeopardized their careers in the government. Most significantly, the Guard was even able to strongly influence appointments in Iran's regular military. In contrast, at no time did the regular military determine or influence personnel shifts in the Revolutionary Guard.

The final component of Guard autonomy is its policymaking influence and operational independence. The Guard was able to largely determine war strategy even though its strategic and tactical recommendations were far from optimal from a professional military standpoint. The Guard's strategy, doctrine, and tactics incurred opposition from the regular military and even some of the Guard's civilian superiors. The Guard's strong ideological commitment even led it to undertake operations that appeared to conflict with the overall policy goals of some clerical leaders.

Mastership of Its Own House

The key to demonstrating Guard autonomy is to show that the Guard, not the civilian leadership of Iran, controlled the Guard's internal affairs. This is not to say that the Guard refused to work within the overall governmental system or that it openly challenged civilian authority—to do so would have been to challenge Khomeini himself. It is to argue, however, that the Guard was able to resist the imposition of or circumvent many of the types of political controls placed on other revolutionary armed forces throughout history. The key indicators of the Guard's organizational sovereignty would include: the ability of the Guard, rather than civilian politicians, to determine the composition and personnel in its top command; the authority of the Guard leadership, rather than political leaders or clerical overseers, to appoint lower level Guard commanders; and, the general weakness of the political oversight apparatus and its inability to influence internal Guard decisions.

A strong indicator of the Guard's organizational sovereignty has been its ability to determine its own leadership. It has previously been shown that Reza'i's predecessors as Guard Commander, all tools of various political leaders vying for influence, were ousted due to the lack or the withdrawal of support among the rank and file Guardsmen. Reza'i did not gain his position as Commander through the patronage of high ranking clerics but because he controlled the core of the early Guard, the Mojahedin of the Islamic Revolution, from which he helped construct the Guard after the triumph of the revolution.[4] He has maintained his position, despite his political differences with such powerful politicians as Rafsanjani, because of his popularity among the Guard rank and file.[5] Reza'i personifies the Guard itself. His lower middle class roots, strong record of armed struggle against the Shah, and unwavering support for the hardline ideology of the revolution have apparently made him an ideal role model to the fighters and subordinate commanders he leads.

The political leadership did not impose Reza'i's subordinate commanders on him. As discussed previously, the current Guard leadership grew out of the collegial Supreme Council of the Revolutionary Guard, the composition of which reflected the comradeship among the Guard leaders before the revolution. It was Reza'i, not the political leadership, who tapped Shamkhani as deputy Guard commander in 1982 and as the Guard's first Ground Forces commander in 1986, and who appointed or promoted the other Guard leaders to top positions.[6]

Even though at various times over the past two years Rafsanjani, Khamene'i and former Representative to the IRGC Abdollah Nuri have assumed or been granted the authority to appoint or remove Guard commanders, in practice Reza'i has continued to determine top Guard leadership changes. In early 1990 he, in fact if not name, appointed longtime ally and deputy Ground Forces commander Rahim Safavi to be his new deputy Guard Commmander (Shamkhani became commander of Iran's regular Navy in late 1989); named Guard stalwarts and prerevolutionary guerrillas Mostafa Izadi and Mohammad Baqr Zolqadr to head the Guard Ground Forces and Central Headquarters, respectively; and moved Abbas Mohtaj from Central Headquarters to deputy Ground Forces Command.[7] Shamkhani subsequently brought Mohtaj in as his deputy of the regular Navy.[8] It was also Reza'i who orchestrated Shamkhani's appointment to head the Guard Navy in 1990 as well as the regular Navy.[9] These men all owe their positions to Reza'i and to their common bonds as ideological hardliners and former guerrillas who helped topple the Shah.

It cannot be argued that the ouster of the less radical former Guard Minister Mohsen RafiqDust, an ally of Rafsanjani, by the Majles in 1988 contradicts the assertion that the Guard chooses its own leaders. He did have substantial legitimacy in the Guard as an organizer of violent anti-Shah demonstrations and in helping construct the Guard from its constituent prerevolutionary militias.[10] His prominence also derived from his role as head of the "welcoming committee" that received Khomeini upon his triumphant return to Tehran in 1979.[11] However, his political weakness relative to the other Guard leaders—coupled with his accountability to the Majles as a Cabinet Minister—led him, not the other Guard leaders, to become a scapegoat for the loss of the war. Moreover, Rafsanjani subsequently had to allay the backlash from RafiqDust's supporters in the Guard by appointing him to be his personal military adviser.[12] Perhaps most important, political leaders were unable to replace RafiqDust with a pragmatic Guard outsider; political leaders instead had to concede the Guard Ministry post to the hardline Reza'i ally Ali Shamkhani, thus solidifying the control of the radical core Guard leadership over all Guard components.[13]

The Guard itself clearly controls advancement and appointments within its ranks. The Iranian press has noted occasions on which the Guard leaders have visited individual provinces to inaugurate new provincial Guard commanders.[14] To take the case of Tehran as an example, the Iranian press has reported that the Supreme Council of the Guard appoints the Tehran Guard commander and that he, in turn, appoints the commanders of individual Guard garrisons in the city.[15] This system generally holds throughout Iran and in the Guard's military structure at the front. Since the Guard began to consolidate its organizational structure, (about 1982), there have been no known cases in which political leaders or clerical overseers have inserted Guard outsiders into the command structure or overruled Guard appointments. There have been cases in which local Guard commanders have been removed; however, those instances are linked primarily to factional infighting within the Guard or possible renegade action by individual commanders which conflicted with the orders or policies of Guard superiors.[16]

There have been very few, if any, concrete criteria for advancement in the Guard, but political connections to civilian leaders do not appear to have figured prominently in the selection process since the early 1980s. A journalist who was allowed to visit the front during the war reported that Guard commanders often simply "emerge"—their aggressiveness and ability to improvise earns them the respect of their colleagues and thus, recognition as a commander.[17] This informal recognition is then affirmed by command superiors in a formal appointment.

Because traditional military system of ranks did not exist during the war, unit sizes varied widely, and formal military education was both relatively unavailable and shunned by the unorthodox Guard, professional military criteria for advancement could not be set, even if the Guard leaders had wanted to institute such criteria. The Guard leaders thus had broad leeway to promote the most aggressive and inherently talented recruits.[18] For example, the Guard leaders have noted that, on occasion, even Basijis who have proven their mettle on the battlefield have risen to command Guard units.[19] Mostafa Izadi and Mohammad Baqr Zolqadr, both guerrillas under the Shah, were little known but highly successful frontline commanders during the war, and were rewarded with top commands in 1990, according to the Iranian press.[20]

Demonstrated ability to crush internal opposition, in addition to pre-revolutionary guerrilla leadership, were prerequisites for advancement as well. For example, Abbas Mohtaj commanded Guard security units in Fars Province and then helped crush Kurdish unrest as Guard commander in Northwest Iran before his assignment at Central Headquarters. The radical Ahmad Kanani was Guard Commander of Khorasan Province before becoming the first commander of the Guard's Lebanon contingent, a high profile assignment.[21] As Khuzestan Province commander in 1980, Ali Shamkhani helped put down a local regular army coup that year as well as Arab nationalist disturbances there.[22] His success undoubtedly supplemented his personal ties to Reza'i in accelerating his rise to national prominence.

As shown above, a variety of factors influence advancement—performance, personal ties to other Guard leaders (though not necessarily Guard outsiders), the respect of one's colleagues, and aggressiveness against the regime's internal and foreign opponents. The importance of personal ties to other Guard leaders and the respect of Guard colleagues might appear to contradict the more objective performance criteria. Further examination, however, reveals ideological commitment to the hardline principles of the revolution as the common thread among all these factors.

To Guard decisionmakers, competent performance was not defined in terms of such professional military criteria as tactical brilliance, optimal use of available weaponry, or the ability to seize tactical objectives with acceptable human or materiel losses. "Competence" was represented by the ability of a Guard commander to gain ground and continue on the offensive, no matter the disproportionate cost in Iranian lives or the tactical and strategic drawbacks to pressing an attack.[23] Competence in internal security matters similarly meant rooting out the regime's opponents thoroughly, no matter the reaction from the local population. It did not imply the ability to defuse opposition with the least violence possible through compromise. This aggressiveness represented the manifestation of the Guard's ideology—to demonstrate the power of the Islamic revolution by toppling Iraqi President Saddam Husayn at all costs and by defeating regime enemies internally. In turn, the stronger the commitment of an individual commander to those hardline objectives, the more respect gained among his similarly fervent colleagues and the more likely was that commander to attract the attention and the patronage of like minded superiors in the chain of command.

The criteria of advancement were clearly the Guard's own. The strong ideological component to the Guard's advancement criteria differed strongly from the more traditional, professional measures of the regular military. It was precisely the differences between the two forces in defining "competence" or "success" that placed them at loggerheads in debates over strategy and tactics. Moreover, statements made by the

Guard's civilian superiors (except Ayatollah Khomeini) both before and after the war, suggest that they, too, sharply disagreed with the Guard's ideologically motivated criteria of success. This was reflected best in a major speech by Rafsanjani shortly after the war, in which he called for a major overhaul of the Guard's method of operations to approximate that of a more professional military organization.[24]

The Clerical Oversight Apparatus

Another strong indicator of the Guard's institutional autonomy is the weakness of the clerics' oversight apparatus, the Iranian equivalent of the political commissariat structure found in many authoritarian regimes of both the right and the left. In Iran this system is represented by the Office of the Representative of the Imam to the IRGC, a position held by Mohammad Araqi, a mid-ranking cleric, until March 1992.[25] The Representative to the IRGC also formally serves on the Supreme Council of the Guard. According to a Tehran newsletter, since the formulation of the position in 1979, the Representative of the Imam's formal powers have included the ability to countermand orders and decisions of the Guard Commander and Supreme Council; ensure that Guard decisions conform ideologically, politically, and religiously, to the guideline set down by the supreme Leader (first Khomeini, now Ali Khamene'i); appoint and supervise the network of clerical overseers below; and approve the appointment of senior Guard commanders below the Commander-in-Chief level.[26]

When the previous IRGC Representative, Abdollah Nuri, (who is now Iran's Interior Minister) was appointed in 1989, he was granted additional powers to both approve and dismiss all Guard commanders, including Reza'i.[27] The sweeping formal powers prompted justified speculation that the appointment of Nuri, a radical who had undergone guerrilla training in Lebanon before the revolution with many future Guards,[28] was intended to partially weaken Rafsanjani, to whom Khomeini had delegated similar powers when he appointed Rafsanjani acting Commander-in-Chief of the Armed Forces in June 1988.[29]

Despite these formal powers, the clerical oversight apparatus has, in reality, been ineffective in imposing the intended degree of clerical control over the Revolutionary Guard. The position itself was originally IRGC Superviser and reflected an attempt by the clerics to directly command the Guard. It was downgraded to that of Representative of the Imam to the IRGC after the first few clerical supervisers, unable to impose control over the Guard, were taken out of that position or resigned.[30] Following former IRGC Representative Fazlollah Mahallati's death in a 1986 plane crash, the position was formally vacant until Nuri's appointment in

1989.[31] Mahallati's deputy, mid ranking cleric Araqi, took over the post in an acting capacity but, because he was not formally promoted to the full Representative position, he therefore lacked the full powers of the office.[32] This guaranteed the weakness of the whole clerical oversight apparatus under Araqi during those three years. (In 1990, when he replaced Nuri, Araqi was given the full title of IRGC representative.) Moreover, even though a clerical overseer was to be attached to all major Guard formations, there were no clerical officials posted to the Guard Air Force, Ground Forces staff, and Central Headquarters staff until early 1990, according to a Tehran newspaper.[33] The Guard Air and Ground Forces were both constituted in about 1986. The appointment of a clerical representative to the Guard Air Force was outweighed shortly thereafter by the ascension of Hosein Dehqan to commander of that Guard service. A former commander of the Guard's Lebanon contingent, Dehqan is one of the most radical and least pliable (to civilian authority) of the Guard leaders.[34]

Even Nuri, with all the formal powers granted him and his own personal stature in the regime, did not improve clerical control over the Guard during nearly two years as Representative to the Guard. Nuri's radical background (in addition to his prerevolutionary guerrilla training, in 1980 he served as superviser of the Iranian media along with one of Iran's most radical clerics, Ali Akbar Mohtashemi[35]) and the warm public praise he was given by Reza'i upon his appointment,[36] suggest that Nuri's appointment was engineered or approved by the Guard. He could have been considered more the Guard's agent within the leadership rather than the clerics' overseer of the Guard. Moreover, despite Nuri's formal powers, he played no apparent role in the several major Guard appointments during his tenure as Representative, or the reconstitution of the Guard's independent command staff, all of which were engineered by the Guard leaders.[37] In addition, in 1990 Nuri was appointed to head an internal National Security Council, which, combined with his position as Interior Minister (which he held concurrent with his Representative post in 1990), was designed to centralize control over all internal security forces.[38] Nonetheless, the Guard's internal security forces remained outside Nuri's purview, again demonstrating the Guard's ability to resist civilian control.

The weakness of the formal civilian oversight apparatus in the Guard stands in contrast to that imposed on the Guard's counterparts in other revolutionary societies. Although the Chinese PLA's political involvement and influence has fluctuated throughout the history of the Chinese Communist revolution, the Communist Party's penetration of the PLA has been extensive. During the initial formation of the PLA in the late 1920s and early 1930's (before the Communists took power in 1949, the PLA was called the Red Army), Mao Zedong, as organizer of the Red Army, instituted a dual command system. In the system, military unit commanders shared authority with party political officers attached to those units; military orders needed the commissar's countersignatures.[39] With the possible exception of the Cultural Revolution period (1966-76), the party has maintained strict control over and a significant presence within the PLA. The party's Military Commission, headed by senior party leaders, has been a primary instrument of that control, as a supplement to the commissariat system.[40]

Soviet Communist Party control of the Soviet Red Army was similar and just as comprehensive as that rendered over the PLA by the Chinese Communist Party. In the early years of the Red Army, like those of the PLA, command was similarly shared between commissars and military officers, although the emphasis on professionalism ultimately led to the command supremacy of Red Army officers over political commissars.[41] Although Timothy Colton, in contrast to other observers, argues that the political commissars in the Red Army rarely acted counter to the interests or arguments of Red Army military officers, even he acknowledged a significant political presence throughout the Soviet Army structure which was be used to firmly assert party policies when strong Party-Army differences emerged.[42]

In addition to the party commissariat, additional civilian oversight of the Red Army was conducted by the KGB, which is authorized to investigate and weed out dissent or espionage in the Army.[43] It was the KGB that implemented Stalin's Great Purge in the Red Army, which victimized 3 of 5 Marshals, all 8 Admirals, 60 of 67 Corps Commanders, half of all brigade commanders, and even 11 Vice-Commissars of Defense.[44] The lack of Red Army resistance to the purge itself serves as an example of party control over the Red Army. A decade earlier, the Stalin-dominated party apparatus easily outmaneuvered Trotsky supporters in the Red Army, leading to the fall of Trotsky and the solidification of party control of the Army.[45]

This degree of civilian penetration and control that existed over the Red Army and PLA has never existed in Iran's Revolutionary Guard. There is no evidence that any of the clerics assigned to oversee Guard units have ever held veto power over military decisions or actions made by Guard unit commanders. Despite the clear dissatisfaction of the Guard command with the decision to abandon the war effort in 1988,[46] not only were major purges not instituted, but, with the exception of RafiqDust—who was not in the military command structure—no senior Guard leader was even dismissed. Although the Guard's radical policy influence has declined following the death of Khomeini and the Guard Ministry has been combined with that of the regular military, the Guard has made some notable and significant organizational gains since Khomeini's death, such as gaining de-facto control over Iran's regular Navy. Moreover, aside from the Office of the Imam's Representative to the IRGC, no other Iranian government institution, most notably the Ministry of Intelligence or Interior, has oversight or investigative powers in the Guard and the Guard has its own court system to try abuses.[47]

A possible explanation for the relative weakness of the civilian oversight apparatus in the Guard as compared to those in the Red Army and PLA can be found in the historical roots of these armed forces and the structure of their political systems. Both the Soviet Red Army and the PLA were formed by their respective Communist Party organizations—in the case of the PLA to help bring the party to power militarily, and in that of the Soviet Red Army to help consolidate the victorious Bolshevik revolution. These two forces were therefore subordinate to civilian authority from their inception.

The Guard, on the other hand, developed out of revolutionary precursors which worked in parallel with, rather than subordinate to, Khomeini and his revolutionary clerical lieutenants. In addition, Iran's cleric-dominated political leadership never organized itself into a cohesive, disciplined, party structure comparable to Communist parties in the Soviet Union and PRC. The only attempt at such organization, the Islamic Republican Party, was highly factionalized, inflexible, and insufficiently autonomous to become institutionalized; it was formally disbanded in 1987 after several years of virtual inactivity.[48]

The Chinese Communist Party and, before its collapse, the Communist Party in the Soviet Union, have served as the authoritative custodian of revolutionary values and ideology in China and the former Soviet Union, and they set down criteria of loyalty for their respective militaries. In revolutionary Iran, only Ayatollah Khomeini's pronouncements, both in life and in death, define revolutionary orthodoxy. Because the Guard views itself as the institutional vanguard of Khomeini's ideals (a Guard self-perception reinforced by the numerous instances in which Khomeini's clerical lieutenants have attempted to temper his hardline policies)[49]—the clerics and their Guard oversight officials have been poorly positioned to define for the Guard the criteria of loyalty. Paradoxically, statements by some of the Guard leaders have occasionally stopped just short of accusing some of the leading clerics of disloyalty to the principles of the revolution.[50] To the Guard commanders, therefore, the presence of clerical overseers monitoring the loyalty of the most ideologically pure revolutionary institution is illegitimate.

Political Network

It is not only the Guard's ability to resist civilian interference in its internal affairs that indicates its institutional autonomy. More positively, the Guard was able to determine or influence personnel assignments and the activities of other institutions in Iran, including the regular military, and place current and former Guards in important government positions. In some cases, although direct Guard pressure cannot be established, the Guard's political and ideological support for its allies in government may have indirectly helped these officials survive political challenges. Moreover, some of the Guard's governmental allies helped it and other radicals undertake activities that were opposed by Iranian government leaders.

The Cabinet

The most appropriate institution with which to begin illustrating the Guard's institutional network is the Cabinet, which, until 1989, was run primarily by a Prime Minister, but is now directly subordinate to the Presidency (the prime ministership was abolished in the new constitution approved in 1989). At the time of Ayatollah Khomeini's death, the Guard or former Guard organizers, associates, and members held 5 out the 25 Cabinet positions. These included the Ministry of the Revolutionary Guard, held by Ali Shamkhani; Posts, Telephones, and Telegraphs, held by former Oil Minister Mohammad Qarazi, who formed a militia during the revolution which was incorporated into the early Guard in 1979;[51] Labor and Social Affairs, held by the radical Abol Qasem Sarhadizadeh, a former member of Abbas Zamani's Islamic Nations Party who joined the Guard after the revolution;[52] Construction Jihad, headed by Qolam Reza Foruzesh, a student holder of the U.S. Embassy hostages (a group closely related to the Guard, as shown earlier) and organizer of the Jihad, the Guard's sister organization, in Khuzestan Province;[53] and Heavy Industries, headed by MIR founder Behzad Nabavi. In addition, the Interior Ministry was, at the time, headed by Ali Akbar Mohtashemi-Pur, the hardline former Ambassador to Syria who, with the Guard, helped organize the extremist Hizballah organization.[54] Until 1988, a former member of the Guard's Supreme Council, Hasan Abedi-Jafari, was Minister of Commerce.[55] A former commander of the Guard's Imam Hosein garrison, Reza Harandi, a civil engineer, was deputy Minister of Culture and Higher Education.[56]

The strong presence of former Guards and Guard allies in the Cabinet does not automatically imply that the Guard had a significant measure of control over the policies of these officials, or that the Guard was consistently able to sustain this level of representation in the Cabinet. For example, the first Cabinet formed after the war and Khomeini's death, which produced a general weakening of regime radicals vis-a-vis more pragmatic elements, witnessed the loss of Sarhadizadeh, Nabavi, and Mohtashemi-Pur, the ministers most sympathetic to and closely associated with the Guard and its radical ideology.[57] The Guard also lost its most direct Cabinet representation when the Guard Ministry was combined with that of the regular military. Mohammad Qarazi, who has remained in the Cabinet, has not been a consistent advocate for radical policies.

Nonetheless, the significant Cabinet presence of Guard allies and former members demonstrates the civilian leadership's recognition of the Guard as a powerful constituency, the sidelining of which may entail political costs. Perhaps even more significant, despite the presence of pragmatic conservatives in all of the Islamic Republic cabinets thus far, former regular military officers have headed few, if any, ministries besides the exception of the Ministry of Defense. Behzad Nabavi's association with the Guard almost certainly contributed to his surviving several past challenges and accusations of corruption,[58] even if the Guard and other radicals were unwilling to cause additional turmoil in the wake of Khomeini's death by demanding that Nabavi and other Guard allies remain in the Cabinet. According to some press reports, these radicals voluntarily withdrew in protest from the first post-Khomeini Cabinet after realizing that President Rafsanjani intended to moderate Iran's domestic and foreign policies.[59] In 1992, Ali Larijani, a former adviser to the Guard, was appointed Minister of Islamic Guidance.

Although no former Guard has ever held the position of Foreign Minister, some of the Guard's closest government allies and several former Guards have held senior positions at the Foreign Ministry. Javad Mansuri, the Guard's unofficial first commander, and Hosein Sheikh-ol-Eslam, a leader of the "Students" who held the U.S. Embassy hostages, were appointed Foreign Ministry Undersecretaries for Cultural and Consular Affairs, and for Political Affairs, respectively, in 1981.[60] In the same set of appointments, which were made by the radical Prime Minister and MIR co-founder Ali Rajai in 1981, Abdollah Nuri was made Foreign Ministry Representative to the Majles.[61] Hamid Mo'ayyer, another student hostage holder, has served as chief of the Foreign Ministry's African Affairs Department.[62] In 1984, Ali Mohammad Besharati, an anti-Shah guerrilla, former director of the Guard's Intelligence Unit, and former member of the Guard's Supreme Council, became Deputy Foreign Minister.[63]

The Foreign Ministry official most supportive of the Guard has been Director for Arab Affairs Hosein Sheikh-ol-Eslam, a former Student hostage holder. As discussed previously, he has worked with the Guard in placing its members in Iranian embassies abroad.[64] He has also been a vocal and active supporter of the Guard's policy positions and activities, even when those stances and actions differed with those advocated by Sheikh-ol-Eslam's superior, the pragmatic Foreign Minister Ali Akbar Velayati. For example, Sheikh ol-Eslam is reported to have authorized the 1987 kidnapping of American journalist Charles Glass by the Guard's militant associates in Lebanon[65] and to have used the Guard/Komiteh abduction of British diplomat Edward Chaplin to sabotage efforts by pragmatic Iranian leaders to improve relations with the UK.[66] The same year, he played a prominent role in criticizing France for the alleged beating of Iran's attache in Paris.[67] The episode escalated into a major Iranian-French dispute and diplomatic relations were broken, a result which pragmatic Iranian leaders almost certainly did not want.

Both Sheikh-ol Eslam and Mansuri have suffered from the general weakening of the radicals, including the Guard, in the wake of Khomeini's death. Although Sheikh-ol-Eslam has been less active since Khomeini's death, it is highly likely that without the backing of the Guard and other radicals, Velayati might have, by now, succeeded in ousting him from the Foreign Ministry entirely. Javad Mansuri, who was a less active if no less radical supporter of the Guard in the Ministry, was appointed Ambassador to Pakistan. This is a key assignment as military ties between the Guard and the Pakistani military have broadened over the past few years, but the appointment removed Mansuri from political influence in Tehran.[68]

Besharati, a former teacher from a middle class religious family,[69] has retained his position at the ministry, but he has not been as supportive of the Guard's agenda as would be expected for a former Guard Supreme Council member. He no longer displays the radicalism he did as an early Guard leader. He frequently mediated ceasefires in the 1988-90 clashes between Iranian-backed Hizballah and Syrian-supported Amal in Lebanon, even as the Guard was arming, training, and fighting alongside Hizballah.[70] Moreover, Besharati publicly advocated the release of foreign hostages held by Hizballah in Lebanon, a position opposed to that taken by the Guard.[71]

Several other former Guards and Guard associates have been appointed to ambassadorships, though not to reduce their influence in Tehran but to extend the influence of the Guard abroad. Mehdi Ahari-Mostafavi, appointed Iran's Ambassador to Bonn in 1987, reportedly was associated with the Revolutionary Guards who protected the U.S. Embassy in Tehran while the U.S. hostages were held there in 1979-81 and he also was involved in the Embassy takeover.[72] Hosein Malaek also reportedly was a U.S. Embassy hostage holder and was appointed Iran's Charge d'Affaires in London in 1987 but he was denied accreditation by Britain because of his involvement in the Embassy seizure.[73] Ahmad Kanani, the first commander of the Guard's Lebanon contingent, became Ambassador to Tunisia, presumably because the Guard viewed Tunisia's growing fundamentalist movement as an opportunity for influence there, and Kanani's experience in export of the revolution activities made him well suited for that post.[74] The Guard's first formal commander Abbas Zamani was posted to Pakistan in the early 80s, and he may have been at least partly responsible for the burgeoning military relationship between Iran and Pakistan—a relationship that has included several visits to Pakistan by Reza'i and Shamkhani.[75]

Other Institutions

The cabinet is not the only governmental arena in which membership or association with the Guard has served as a key qualification for office. Several anti-Shah guerrilla leaders who became Guard commanders, as well as some local clerics around whom Guard units organized during the revolution, achieved election to the Majles, riding on hardline credentials. One of the most prominent Guard allies in the Majles was one of its early organizers and, briefly its commander—Abbas Duzduzani, who became chairman of the Majles Defense Committee in the mid 1980s.[76] In that position Duzduzani, who has continued to advocate radical positions and trumpet his relationship with the Guard, was able to help the Guard lobby for its budgetary requests.[77] Duzduzani's Defense Committee successor, Hojjat ol-Eslam Rasul Montaja-Nia, similarly was radical who headed the Guards and Komitehs in Khomein, Ayatollah Khomeini's home town.[78] The Majles Defense Committee chair was next held by Ali Akbar Mohtashemi-Pur, perhaps the Guard's most prominent patron.

Recent examples of less prominent local Guard leaders-turned-Majles deputies represent diverse constituencies throughout Iran. These Majles representatives include Mohammad Ali Arabi, former commander of the Kashmar Guard contingent; Kamel Abedinezad, a former teacher and commander of a Guard unit in Kurdestan; Hojjat-ol Eslam Ansari, who headed the Guards in Kerman Province; Marzieh Hadidchi, a Tehran Majles deputy who trained in Lebanon and helped organize the Guard in Hamadan; Mohammad Ali Karimi, a Guard official in Bojnurd; Ahmad Molazadeh, who organized the Guard, Komiteh, and Construction Jihad in Gonabad; Hojjat-ol Eslam Movahedipur, organizer of Guard and Komiteh forces in Saveh; Hojjat ol-Eslam Shushtari, who organized the Guards in Nayshahpur; and Mohammad Subhan Allahi, a Majles representative from Tabriz and former math teacher, who worked in the Guard's Public Relations Office.[79]

Naturally, the popularity and authority of these local leaders may have accounted for their election to the Majles as well as their ability to organize Guard units; their association with the Guard coinciding with but not necessarily causing election. Nonetheless, because of the Guard's ability to mobilize the population at the local level, its support has been a benefit to candidates (particularly radicals) seeking election to the Majles. On several occasions, political leaders, primarily the pragmatic ones, have warned the Guard not to interfere in Majles elections[80] and, in 1987, the government admonished Majles candidates not to use the Revolutionary Guard insignia in campaign material, an acknowledgement that radical Majles candidates sought close association with the Guard to garner electoral support.[81]

The Guard's former members also have served in local government, the Foundations, and in other revolutionary institutions. After his ouster as Guard Minister, Mohsen RafiqDust became head of the Foundation of the Oppressed, which uses the Shah's confiscated assets to help poor families and war veterans.[82] Mohsen Mirdamadi, a civil engineer, was an architect of the U.S. Embassy takeover, a deputy Prosecutor-General, and then head of the International Relations Department of the Guard's Propaganda and Publishing Unit before becoming Governor General of Khuzestan Province, a key battleground and staging area for Iranian forces during the war; he was replaced in early 1990.[83] Mohammad Asgarzadeh, a student hostage holder, served as a Guard district commander before becoming a deputy Minister of Islamic Guidance and then deputy Prosecutor-General for cultural affairs.[84] Habib Bitaraf, also a former hostage holder, also became a top official in the Prosecutor-General's office after service in the Guard.[85]

Nonetheless, the Guard's influence in government—and the willingness and ability of its allies to advocate radical positions—has not been uniformly strong throughout the revolution thus far. Since the death of the Guard's father figure and ultimate patron, Khomeini, several of the Guard's allies in government have been weakened (Mansuri, Mohtashemi-Pur), or been forced out of government (Nabavi, Sarhadizadeh, Mirdamadi). Others have been coopted by the system and have distanced themselves from the Guard on some issues (Qarazi, Besharati).

The ebb and flow of the Guard's influence with the political climate in Tehran is to be expected. Whereas their associations with the Guard and radical issue positions once helped political leaders rise to prominence, these factors became a liability after the chief radical policy initiatives— working towards the defeat of Iraq and violent export of the revolution— had led Iran into international isolation and economic disaster. The death of Ayatollah Khomeini left the radicals exposed. What is significant is that the Guard and its political allies, both those that have retained their positions and those that have not, have generally refused to compromise their ideological principles in order to retain positions of influence. Mohtashemi has continued to forcefully advocate radical positions despite losing his seat in the Majles in April-May 1992.[86] Nabavi and Sarhadizadeh also ran for seats with radical backing in 1989 mid-term Majles elections but lost.[87] It is in this sense that the Guard is autonomous rather than subordinate. It has demonstrated that its views, its former members, and its associates can permeate the government under conducive political circumstances;

the Guard's opponents have not shown a similar capacity to infiltrate the Guard when pragmatic political winds prevail.

Regular Military Assignments

Even stronger evidence of Guard autonomy can be found in its relationship with the Iranian regular military. As a revolutionary institution, it is to be expected that the Guard would have political allies in a revolutionary government and that service in or association with the Guard would help officials rise in the regime power structure. However, the Guard was also able to affect personnel assignments in the regular military, the Guard's primary institutional rival. That the regular military suffered the Guard's influence in its affairs indicates a significant measure of regular military subordination vis-a-vis the Guard.

The precedent for Guard influence in regular military personnel assignments was set in the early 1980s. In March 1981, the Guard joined junior regular officers in achieving the reinstatement of then Col. Ali Sayyid-Shirazi, who was removed by senior officers as commander of the regular military's 28th Division in Kurdistan for alleged killing of Kurdish villagers.[88] At the time, Shirazi was the Guard's closest and most influential ally in the regular military; he shared the Guard's ideological fervor and supported the integration of the regular military into the Guard.[89] The Guard's support was undoubtedly a crucial factor in Shirazi's retention and subsequent promotion to commander of the regular military's Ground Forces.

Paradoxically, the same influence the Guard brought to bear in propping up Shirazi in 1981 was used against him five years later. Despite Shirazi's efforts to increase the regular military's ideological character, he fundamentally was a professional officer who based military decisionmaking on the objective principles of military science rather than ideology.[90] Iran's loss of the town of Mehran in the spring of 1986, which the Guard blamed on the regular military's overall lack of enthusiasm for the war effort and refusal to coordinate with the Guard, aggravated personal and substantive differences between Shirazi and Reza'i.[91] The outcome of the ensuing power struggle was clearly resolved in favor of Reza'i and the Guard; Shirazi was removed from command of the regular military Ground Forces and, to assuage the regular military, he was assigned a seat on the Supreme Defense Council, Iran's highest military body.[92] To balance out Shirazi's vote on the Council, then Guard Minister RafiqDust was also given a seat but, unlike Shirazi, he retained his existing position as Guard Minister.[93] Shirazi's removal from the chain of command represented, by far, a net reduction in Shirazi's prestige and overall influence in the regime.

Appointment to the Supreme Defense Council was a similar consolation prize for another senior regular military officer who disagreed vociferously with the Guard's strategy and tactics. As Ground Forces Commander when the war broke out and then Chief of the regular military's Joint Staff, then Brig. Gen. Qasem Ali Zahir-Nejad cultivated a reputation as a thorough military professional and Iranian nationalist, loyal to whatever regime was in power.[94] His professional judgment consistently compelled him to argue against high casualty human wave offensives used by the Guard and Basij and against prosecution of the war until victory at all costs.[95] In 1984 Zahir-Nejad, like Shirazi two years later, was "promoted" to a relatively powerless seat on the Guard/radical dominated Supreme Defense Council and was succeeded by the more pliable Esma'il Sohrabi as Chief of the Joint Staff.[96]

Zahir-Nejad's successor, Sohrabi, befell a similar fate, albeit under different circumstances, at the hands of the Guard. In May 1988, three weeks after Iraq's unexpected recapture of its southern Al Faw peninsula, Sohrabi was dismissed, evidently a scapegoat for the defeat for which the Guard shared at least equal responsibility militarily.[97] Moreover, Sohrabi was replaced by Brig. Gen Ali Shahbazi, who reportedly has close links to and the support of the Guard by virtue of his service in the Guard's guerrilla warfare headquarters in the southern city of Ahvaz.[98] Even in military defeat, therefore, the Guard's institutional strength was in evidence. From an objective military standpoint, the defeat at Al Faw should probably have precipitated greater, not less, emphasis on regular military experience and decisionmaking criteria to the exclusion of the Guard's unorthodox and high casualty tactics and strategies.

Evidence that the Guard's institutional strength vis-a-vis the regular military has survived the loss of the war and Khomeini's death came in 1989 and early 1990. The regular Navy's respected and professional commander, Admiral Hosein Malekzadegan, was replaced in October 1989 by Ali Shamkhani, the Guard's most prominent figure after Reza'i.[99] Although Shamkhani was granted the Navy title of Rear Admiral to placate the regular Navy, it is well known that Shamkhani has no professional naval experience and that he is clearly identified with the Guard and his longtime ally and superior, Reza'i.[100] In late April 1990, Shamkhani brought longtime senior Guard commander Abbas Mohtaj to serve as his deputy in the regular Navy, essentially giving the Guard control of the top echelon of that regular military service.[101] Their appointments represented the first time that Guardsmen had ever taken over the top command of a regular military service, almost certainly weakening regular military morale severely and reiterating the durability and consistent strength of the Guard as an institution.

Policymaking

Another measure of Guard autonomy is its degree of influence in the formulation and implementation of war, security, and export of the revolution policy. It is in this arena that the Guard has operationalized its unwavering hardline ideology when possible, despite professional and rational arguments to the contrary and despite more pragmatic policy goals of some of its civilian superiors. This is not to say that the Guard openly defied civilian authority or that it formulated and implemented major military, internal security, and export of the revolution policies independently of political leaders. However, it can be argued that the Guard was able to drive most aspects of war strategy throughout the conflict, and that, without necessarily countermanding specific orders, it undertook hardline actions and operations that sometimes conflicted with the goals of its civilian superiors. The Guard never hesitated to exploit differences among civilian leaders—made easier by the vagueness and generally radical direction of Khomeini's guidelines—to steer policy in a radical direction.[102] Moreover, the Guard demonstrated a willingness to risk alienating or embarrassing its civilian superiors, who could retaliate against the Guard by curtailing its budget, recruitment authority, and weapons allocations. It also has undertaken high risk military operations rich in ideological content but militarily ill advised and potentially detrimental to the Guard's own military posture and prestige.

After Iran had driven the invading Iraqi troops from Iranian territory in 1982, the firm consensus among all military and civilian elements to continue prosecuting the war essentially ended. Only Khomeini's unwavering determination to continue the war until the overthrow of the Iraqi regime muted differences between the Guard and other pro-war radicals on one side, and the regular military and its conservative political allies on the other.[103] However, the aging revolutionary was rarely if ever involved in the details of the planning and implementation of his overall policy guidelines, leaving ample room for constant and acrimonious debate among his government and military subordinates over how best and at what level to prosecute the war.[104]

Despite the opposition of the regular military and its conservative allies, the Guard ensured that Khomeini's commitment to prosecution of the war until victory was fully implemented, at least until Iran's military collapse caused even Khomeini, if not the Guard, to abandon the pro-war stand.[105] In almost every year of the war, the regular military vehemently argued that the war be prosecuted more conservatively—that continuous but smaller, well planned attacks relying on heavy artillery and armor replace the Guard-driven, lightly-armed, manpower-intensive, mass offensives.[106] In 1985, after a failed major offensive in the Hawizeh Marshes in March, the regular military and its pragmatic allies (primarily President and SDC Chairman Khamene'i) apparently succeeded in persuading Khomeini to, at least temporarily, prosecute the war at a lower level; the shift was even announced by then Guard Chief of Staff Ali Reza Afshar.[107] However, even that year the Guard ultimately prevailed, obtaining approval not only to organize and launch a major offensive, but gaining more cooperation from the regular military than in any past or subsequent offensive.[108]

The Guard's war policy influence can be only partly attributed to its civilian allies on the Supreme Defense Council, where most war strategy debates were fought.[109] This is because its civilian allies were not consistently supportive of the Guard's war policy recommendations. For example, until 1987 Rafsanjani, as Khomeini's first Representative to the SDC had been a Guard ally. Following Iran's high casualty offensive that year, he publicly questioned the continued use of mass offensives and appeared to favor the more conservative, professional approach advocated by the regular military.[110] The Guard nonetheless continued to mobilize volunteers for a mass offensive and launched its Val Fajr 10 offensive in northern Iraq in March 1988.[111]

Civilian Leadership

The argument for Guard autonomy can be carried a step further than the assertion that the Guard was able to prevail in war strategy debates despite opposition from some political leaders. Strategy debates were a legitimate, accepted forum for airing and resolving professional, ideological, and political differences. The case for Guard autonomy can be strengthened significantly by demonstrating that the Guard was politically independent of specific factions within the leadership and that, on certain selected occasions, it undertook military actions which were apparently in opposition to the policy directions and goals of its civilian superiors.

Exemplifying the Guard's political independence, it threw its support to those leaders who advanced hardline policies, and withdrew that support if and when those political leaders adopted more conservative positions. For example, for the first seven years of the war, Rafsanjani advocated war until victory and the use of mass offensives to achieve that objective.[112] In part because of these positions, he had the Guard's support—support which helped him rise to prominence within the leadership.[113] In 1984 the Guard even reportedly colluded with Rafsanjani to undermine then President and Supreme Defense Council Chairman Ali Khamene'i by purposely violating a U.N.—brokered moratorium on the shelling of civilian targets.[114] Rafsanjani challenged Khamene'i's revolutionary credentials for accepting the moratorium and Khamene'i even reportedly offered to resign.[115] When Rafsanjani shifted against continuation of the war in 1988, he lost the Guard's support; a respected Arab newspaper even reported several assassination attempts against him by Guards vehemently opposed to his role in ending the war.[116]

This is not to argue that the Guard is a kingmaker in Iranian politics. The rift between Rafsanjani and the Guard since 1988 has not prevented Rafsanjani from emerging as a dominant figure in post-Khomeini politics. Similarly, although the Guard is most enthusiastically supportive of hard-liners Mohtashemi and Ayatollah Khomeini's son, Ahmad,[117] neither of these leaders has succeeded in upstaging Rafsanjani politically and the Guard's support did not prevent Rafsanjani from dropping Mohtashemi and Nabavi as Ministers of Interior and Heavy Industries, respectively, in 1989. These examples support the argument that the Guard has held fast to its ideologically hardline character even when doing so distances the Guard from the dominant political faction at any given time.

Some of the military operations undertaken by the Guard perhaps best exemplify its autonomy. As the war dragged on, it expanded in scope, giving the Guard greater opportunity to assert its independent role. This particularly held true for fast-breaking, crisis situations in which extended debate was not possible and the Guard's internal opponents were less able to constrain the Guard. Such opportunities were afforded the Guard by the deepening involvement of foreign (particularly the U.S.) and Arab parties in the war. The Guard Navy was the optimum instrument for striking at some of these outside parties. (Iran's Air Force was insufficiently capable of effectively striking international shipping from the air.) International and Arab adversaries of Iran were brought more directly into the war by the "tanker war" (attacks by both sides against each others' oil shipments); the Iranian capture of Al Faw, which brought Kuwait within striking range of invasion and Saudi Arabia and other Gulf states into closer cooperation with Iraq; and the U.S. Navy buildup in the Gulf to protect the Gulf Arab states and international shipping.[118] Moreover, growth in the operational capabilities of the Guard Navy coincided with the increasing international and Arab involvement in the war.

The U.S. buildup in the Gulf was intended, in part, to counter the Guard Navy's harrassment of international oil shipments.[119] Not intimidated, but rather energized by the U.S. naval buildup and its oil tanker reflagging and escort program, the Guard, with the cooperation of some regular Navy elements, began mining the international shipping lanes of the Persian Gulf.[120] In August 1987, during the passage of the very first convoy escorted by the U.S. Navy, a reflagged Kuwaiti tanker, the Bridgeton, struck one of these mines a few miles from a major Guard Navy base off the Iranian coast.[121] After U.S. retaliation against Iranian offshore oil platforms and the capture of an Iranian mine laying craft, the Iran Ajr, the Guard briefly discontinued the mine laying activity. It resumed the mining in early 1988, however, despite the reported efforts of Rafsanjani to avoid further confrontation and Iranian Foreign Ministry efforts at the United Nations to begin exploring the possibility of ending the Iran-Iraq war.[122] Moreover, the 1987 capture of the Iran Ajr was virtually simultaneous with the conservative President and SDC Chairman Ali Khamene'i's speech at the U.N., in which he presumably wanted to partially temper Iran's radical image and paint Iraq as the aggressive party in the war.[123] The Iran Ajr incident therefore undercut Khamene'i's intended message and diplomatic efforts, raising questions as to whether the Guard had engineered the Iran Ajr incident primarily to undermine Khamene'i's speech.

That the Guard was willing to challenge the U.S. directly, despite the objective military drawbacks and despite the reluctance of civilian leaders to sanction such ideologically motivated and impulsive actions, was illustrated again in April 1988. About a month earlier, the Guard had resumed mining the shipping lanes of the Gulf. These mines laid by the Guard were subsequently swept by the Iranian regular Navy, apparently on orders from Rafsanjani—another illustration of the extreme differences between the Guard and more pragmatic elements on this issue.[124] One of the mines laid (and not successfully swept) hit the USS Samuel B. Roberts, prompting U.S. retaliation on April 18th. Guard Commander Reza'i reportedly was the driving force behind a direct Iranian naval counterstrike against the attacking U.S. Gulf fleet.[125] Because the Guard Navy consisted of small speedboats, the attack was conducted by the heavier but still vastly mismatched regular Navy vessels; the battle resulted in the destruction by the United States of about 20% of the regular Navy's active warship fleet. The Guard's organization of the attack—coupled with the participation of the regular Navy despite its professional opposition to such a mismatched engagement—demonstrates that the Guard was in de-facto command of the regular Navy as well as Iran's naval policy during that engagement.[126]

The United States was not the only object of the Guard's ideologically motivated military assertiveness. In 1987, after a U.S. retaliatory strike against Iranian offshore installations, the Guard fired a Chinese-supplied Silkworm missile against Kuwaiti oil facilities.[127] After the seizure of Al Faw brought Iran within easy reach of Kuwaiti territory, the Guard declared that the overthrow of the conservative monarchy in Kuwait was an additional Iranian objective in the war; the statement was not reiterated by, and almost certainly was issued without consulting, senior political leaders.[128] In July 1987, the Guard Navy seized the crews of three small Kuwaiti boats, calling them "Kuwait spy boats."[129] In October of that year, a large flotilla of Guard Navy speedboats assembled for an attack on Saudi Arabian offshore oil facilities.[130] The flotilla never actually reached the oil platforms because the fleet was detected and deterred by the Saudis.[131] Although civilian political leaders may have supported some of the above Guard actions after they occurred, (to do otherwise would jeopardize any Iranian leader's revolutionary credentials) these actions clearly contradicted the efforts by pragmatic civilian leaders to improve relations with both Saudi Arabia and Kuwait in an effort to blunt their support for Iraq.[132]

Export of the Revolution Policy

The Guard has also demonstrated its assertiveness on non-military issues, primarily export of the revolution. As is the case with the Guard's military activities, it cannot be definitively shown that the Guard ever purposely disobeyed specific orders from its civilian superiors, but several export of the revolution actions by the Guard appear to have run counter to the policy directions of these civilian leaders.

The primary arena for Iran's efforts to export the Islamic revolution has been Lebanon, and it is there that the Guard operationalized its hardline views. Most notably, the Guard provided training and, according to some reports, direct military support[133] to Hizballah in that militia's repeated clashes during 1987-90 with its rival, Syrian-backed Amal.[134] (Amal is similarly Shia but, unlike Hizballah, non-fundamentalist.) This aid to Hizballah was provided even as Iranian civilian leaders were trying to broker a permanent end to the clashes in order to preserve the relationship with Syria.[135] (Syria, Amal's patron, was the only Arab state that backed Iran throughout the entire war and its support was crucial in alleviating Iran's sense of isolation during the war. Libya backed Iran until about mid-1986, when it adopted a balanced position between Iran and Iraq.) Iran's mediation efforts were conducted primarily by its relatively moderate Foreign Minister Velayati, former Guard and now pragmatic Deputy Foreign Minister Besharati, and, until his ouster in 1988, the only non-radical Guard leader—former Guard Minister RafiqDust.[136] RafiqDust was probably representing the Guard's position in the mediation and talks; however, that the Amal-Hizballah clashes continued during the talks illustrates that RafiqDust was insufficiently powerful or popular among the Guard rank and file to restrain Guard forces in Lebanon.

The strains imposed on the Syria-Iran relationship by the feud between Iran's client, Hizballah and Syrian-supported Amal naturally impacted on the issue of the the release of Western hostages held by Hizballah. On this issue, there were common interests between pragmatic Iranian leaders who need to attract Western investment to improve Iran's devastated economy and Syria, which needs to improve relations with the U.S. to compensate for its loss of Soviet support. This common agenda led Iranian pragmatists and Syria (supporters of the hostage release) to cooperate against the Guard, other Iranian radicals, and Hizballah, which opposed the hostage release.[137]

In early 1990, at the same time Iranian pragmatist were working to persuade Hizballah to release its American hostages, a policy the Guard opposed,[138] it was reported that Syria prevented additional or replacement Guard forces from transitting into Lebanon.[139] Syria's attempts to limit Guard forces in Lebanon were essentially confirmed by a leading militant cleric in Lebanon, Shaykh Shaban, leader of the Tawhid (Unity) movement, who publicly reiterated that the Guard's presence in Lebanon was "legitimate."[140] For his part, Rafsanjani was seeking to directly blunt Guard influence in Lebanon, and thus the chances that the Guard could block a hostage release. He reportedly attempted to assign a more loyal or at least more pliable Guard unit to the Guard contingent in Lebanon.[141] By May 1990, two U.S. hostages—Robert Polhill and Frank Reed were released, and by December 1991 all American hostages had been freed. However, reports in early 1990 that Hizballah was given new heavy weapons by Iran,[142] which it needed to fight against Amal, suggest that the cooperation of Hizballah, the Guard, and other Iranian radicals was purchased, rather than compelled, by Iranian pragmatists and the Syrians. U.S. officials have also reportedly said that the Iranian government paid the hostage holders $1–2 million for each hostage released (as well as funded their captivity).[143] In addition, many believe that the U.S. decision in November 1991 to release to Iran $278 million in compensation for Iranian military equipment, arbitrated through the U.S.-Iran Claims Tribunal at the Hague, was at least tacitly linked to Iran's cooperation in the release of the hostages.[144]

Despite any financial benefits to the hostage holders or to Iran, the release of the hostages represented a political victory for Rafsanjani over the Guard and the hostage holders in Lebanon. Rafsanjani's maneuvering to strengthen his hand over hostage events in Lebanon was undoubtedly helped by the Iraqi invasion of Kuwait, which resulted in the release from Kuwaiti prisons of relatives of a leader of the hostage holders, Imad Mugniyah. The release of these Da'wa Party prisoners had been a key demand of the hostage holders in Lebanon.[145] Moreover, Rafsanjani was able to use the continued deterioration of Iran's economy—coupled with the apparent financial and political benefits which Iran would accrue if it helped release the hostages—in his debate with the Guard and the hostage holders. Rafsanjani undoubtedly made the case that the deterioration of Iran's economy threatened the clerical regime itself, and with it, the Khomeini legacy the Guard had consistently fought to preserve.

There are other examples in which the Guard has undertaken covert actions as an expression of the hardline ideological principles of the revolution even though such actions conflicted with the goals and policies of its civilian superiors. The Guard was involved in inciting the late July 1987 riots by Iranian pilgrims in the Saudi holy city of Mecca. This action clearly ran counter to efforts by Rafsanjani to improve relations with the Gulf monarchies, including Saudi Arabia, and blunt Arab support for Iraq.[146]

The Guard has trained foreign proteges in the hijacking of commercial jetliners[147] and, in one such incident, the hijacking of a TWA passenger jet in 1985, Rafsanjani reportedly played a role in ending the jet seizure.[148] Despite Rafsanjani's efforts in 1989-90, as Iran's new President, to improve Iran's image abroad (Iran even invited U.N. officials to conduct a human rights inspection in 1990), the Guard and its political allies have continued to assassinate regime opponents abroad. The same week former U.S. hostage Robert Polhill was released by Hizballah in Lebanon, a result of Rafsanjani's efforts, Mojahedin-e-Khalq leader Masud Rajavi's brother was assassinated in Geneva, probably by Guard operatives.[149] Iran's Ambassador to Switzerland Hosein Malaek, a former "Student" hostage holder and ally of the Guard, reportedly helped coordinate the assassination.[150] The assassination of former Iranian Prime Minister Shahpur Bakhtiar in late 1991—at a time when Rafsanjani was trying to facilitate the release of the last of the American hostages in Lebanon—may also have been a Guard operation.[151] The killing also caused French president Francois Mitterand to cancel a planned visit to Iran.

The U.S.-Iran Arms Deal

Autonomy is represented not only by the difficulty of civilian leaders in restraining the Guard's radical impulses, but also by the Guard's ability to assert its political and institutional interests in controversial civilian policy decisions. A useful example of this ability on the part of the Guard is provided by the U.S.-Iran arms deal in 1985-86. Apparently recognizing that the ideologically motivated Guard would oppose direct dealings with the U.S., civilian leaders involved in the affair at first attempted to conceal the negotiations from the Guard, according to an Israeli arms dealer involved in an initial phase of the deal.[152] This same participant reports that the Guard, once it became aware of and then involved in the affair, took control of a 1985 shipment of U.S. weapons, which landed in Iran.[153] Accounts by participants in the affair confirm that the Guard indeed received the shipment.[154] In subsequent phases of the affair, the Guard apparently became even more deeply involved, negotiating directly with some of the American participants and continuing to take possession of the weapons shipped to Iran.[155]

Although the Guard appeared to have compromised its ideology somewhat by dealing with the U.S. and undoubtedly cooperating in arranging the release of U.S. hostages by Hizballah, the Guard viewed the weapons it received as a vehicle for achieving the ultimate ideological goal of defeating Iraq in the war.[156] This reasoning may account for Ayatollah Khomeini's eventual support or acquiescence in the exchange; as the Guard's infallible father figure, Khomeini's support for a policy decision virtually ensured Guard support as well.[157] Moreover, that three hostages were subsequently captured to replace those released in the deal further alleviated the sense of ideological compromise on the part of the Guard and Hizballah.[158] The Guard, by obtaining the weapons it desperately needed for major offensives in 1986 and 1987, (both of which brought Iranian forces to the outskirts of the Iraqi city of Basra), actually furthered its primary ideological and military objective. Moreover, that the Guard ultimately received most of the weapons shipped by the U.S. demonstrated that, if the regime had intended to allocate the weapons shipments to the more conservative regular military, the Guard was sufficiently influential to redirect the weapons shipments to itself.[159] If reports that the political leadership initially intended to conceal the dealings from the Guard are true, then the Guard's substantial role in the affair demonstrates its pervasiveness and permeation of the whole civilian government structure.

Conclusion

There is strong evidence to support the conclusion that the Guard is an autonomous, and not subordinate institution, and that its autonomy was driven largely by its tenacious hold on its radical ideology. Because of its independent roots in the revolution and its self-defined role as a bastion of hardline revolutionary values, the Guard has resisted the civilian penetration and control of its affairs that characterized Communist Party control over the Guard's counterparts, the Soviet Red Army and China's People's Liberation Army. The Guard not only has served as a springboard for its members, former members, and ideological allies to attain high positions throughout the governing structure, but it also has had significant influence in determining the composition of the top command of its chief institutional rival, the regular military. Some of the Guard's allies in government have worked with the Guard in support of hardline policies even when doing so may have blocked their own career prospects or risked angering other senior political leaders. Moreover, the Guard has frequently undertaken actions that clearly conflicted with the policy goals of several of its civilian superiors and, during the war, generally succeeded in winning adoption of its zealous and irregular strategies and tactics over strong opposition from the regular military and conservative politicians.

The common thread among the several facets of Guard autonomy has been its zealous commitment to the ideological principles of the revolution. For example, the Guard has resisted significant clerical control not because its leaders seek ultimate power in Iran but because the Guard, viewing itself as the protector of the revolution and its values, does not recognize any organization as more revolutionary or loyal to the revolution than it is. In those instances in which the Guard has engineered the ouster of regular army officers and the appointment of those more pliable, it has generally done so to ensure full regular military support and cooperation in fulfilling its maximalist goals. Since the war with Iraq ended, the Guard has achieved direct control over a regular military service, the Navy. (However, in 1992, the Guard accepted the appointment of a regular military officer, Hosein Jalali, to head its Air Force, its most technologically dependent service.) The Guard's assertiveness in military and export of the revolution policy has clearly been ideologically motivated; many of its actions have jeopardized the Guard's institutional interests by risking a backlash from pragmatic civilian leaders who have been in a position to cut the Guard's budget, weapons allotments, and recruitment authority.

The strength of the Guard's ideological commitment is its most distinctive characteristic when it is compared to other major revolutionary armed forces. Neither the Soviet Red Army or PLA has established itself as a bastion of revolutionary orthodoxy to the degree the Guard has in Iran. These armies also have not resisted civilian control to the same degree as the Guard, even though some of them, especially the PLA, have intervened in politics at the behest of civilian factions.

The primary factor that accounts for the Guard's autonomy is undoubtedly its independent roots in the revolution. Unlike the PLA, Soviet Army, French revolutionary army, and other revolutionary forces, the Guard was not created by the civilian revolutionary leadership. It developed from a pre-existing structure of underground guerrilla groups and militias that battled the Shah alongside, not subordinate to, the revolutionary clerics. The Guard, therefore, has an independent legitimacy which it continues to assert, even when doing so may conflict with the policies and goals of its civilian superiors.

Notes

1. Samuel P. Huntington, *Political Order in Changing Societies* (New Haven and London: Yale University Press, 1968) P. 20
2. Martha Kessler, *Syria: Fragile Mosaic of Power* (Washington, D.C.: National Defense University, 1987)
3. "Islamic Revolutionary Guard Corps" in *Iran Almanac 1987* (Tehran: Echo of Iran, 1987) P. 124
4. Ibid.; "Organization of Mujahedin of Islamic Revolution" in Tehran Iran Press Digest; March 5, 1985, P. 4; "BBC Report on Dissolution of the MIR" in Tehran Akhbar (News); Vol. VII, No. 154; October 7, 1986
5. "Iranian Emigre Opposition on Commanders' Deaths," Paris Iran-e Azad in Persian; April 16, 1983, P. 4
6. Nikola Schahgaldian, *The Iranian Military Under the Islamic Republic* (Santa Monica, Calif.: Rand Corporation, 1987) P. 119

7. "Khamene'i Appoints Three Military Commanders," Tehran Domestic Service in Persian, September 24, 1989; "[Khamene'i] Appoints 2 More Military Commanders," Tehran Television Service in Persian, September 22, 1989 in FBIS, September 25, 1989

8. "Deputy Commander of the Navy Appointed," Tehran Domestic Service in Persian; April 18, 1990

9. "New Commander for Guard Corps Navy Named," Tehran Television Service in Persian; December 23, 1990 in FBIS NES; December 24, 1990, P. 45

10. "Islamic Revolutionary Guard Corps" in *Iran Almanac 1987*, op.cit.

11. "Mohsen RafiqDust" in Tehran Sourush; January 1983, P. 41

12. "Iran: Rafsanjani's Costly Blunder" in *Middle East International*; November 4, 1988, P. 10

13. "IRNA Carries New Ministers' Biographies," Tehran IRNA in English; September 20, 1988

14. "IRGC Spokesman Warns Saudi Arabia," Tehran IRNA in English; May 6, 1988

15. "New Tehran Guards Commander," Tehran Domestic Service in Persian; July 12, 1981

16. "Iran Guard Leaders Slain in Violent Purge," Washington Times; March 23, 1989, P. A7; "Khalkhali, Others, Discuss Yazdi, Cooper, U.S.," Tehran Resalat in Persian; September 28, 1989, pp. 3,4,7

17. John Simpson, *Inside Iran* (New York: St. Martin's Press, 1988) P. 288

18. Ibid

19. "IRGC Officials Discuss Postwar Mobilization" in FBIS; December 2, 1988

20. "Khamene'i Appoints Three Military Commanders," op.cit.; "[Khamene'i] Appoints 2 More," op.cit.

21. "In Brief" in Tehran Akhbar (News); December 21, 1981

22. "Four (Pasdaran) Corps Commanders Become Military Commanders," Tehran Azadegan excerpted in Tehran The Flame in English; July 13, 1980

23. "Clandestine Radio Discusses Iran-Iraq War Flare Up," Voice of Iran in Persian; March 25, 1982 in JPRS 80522; April 8, 1982 P. 45

24. "Hashemi-Rafsanjani Speaks on Future of IRGC," Tehran Domestic Service in Persian; October 6, 1988

25. "Khamene'i Appoints New IRGC Representative," Tehran IRNA in English; June 26, 1990

26. "History and Present Status of IRGC," Tehran Iran Press Digest; August 7, 1984, P. 16

27. "Khomeini Appoints Nuri His IRGC Representative," Tehran Domestic Service in Persian; March 9, 1989

28. "Article Recounts 10 Years of Khomeini Terrorism," Paris Lettre Persane in French, No. 46; June 1986, pp. 6-10
29. "Iran Guard Leaders Slain in Violent Purge," op.cit.
30. Schahgaldian, op.cit., pp. 120-1
31. "Rafsanjani Friday Prayer Sermon," Tehran IRNA in English; March 10, 1989
32. Ibid
33. "Revolution Guard Corps Representatives Named," Tehran Jomhuri-Ye Eslami in Persian; March 1, 1990, P. 2
34. "Khamene'i Appoints New Air Force Commander," Tehran Domestic Service in Persian; April 24, 1990; "Iran: Pan-Islamic Revolution - The Men and Machinery Behind Exporting the Revolution," The Middle East Reporter; September 1, 1984, P. 12; Mohammed Selhami, "I Met the Suicide Men," Paris Jeune Afrique in French; January 25, 1984, P. 57
35. "Temporary Radio, TV Supervisors Appointed," Tehran Domestic Service in Persian; November 7, 1980
36. "IRGC Commander Cables Khomeini on Corps' Fidelity," Tehran Domestic Service in Persian; March 10, 1989
37. "Khamene'i Appoints Three Military Commanders," op.cit.; "[Khamene'i] Appoints 2 More Military Commanders," op.cit.; "Reza'i on Establishment of New IRGC Staff Command," Tehran Domestic Service in Persian; September 28, 1989
38. "Interior Minister Named Security Council Head," Tehran Domestic Service in Persian; September 10, 1989; "Powers of Security Forces Chief," Tehran Domestic Service in Persian; September 10, 1989
39. William Pang-Yu Ting, "The Chinese Army" in Jonathan Adelman, ed., *Communist Armies in Politics* (Boulder, Co.: Westview Press, 1982) pp. 32-3
40. "Chinese Army Gains Political Power But Loses Support of the People," Washington Post; October 1, 1989, P. A22
41. Jonathan Adelman, "The Soviet Army" in Adelman; ed., op.cit.
42. Timothy Colton, *Commissars, Commanders, and Civilian Authority* Cambridge, Mass. and London: Harvard University Press, 1979) Chapter 9
43. Ibid. pp. 225-6
44. Adelman, "The Soviet Army," op.cit., P. 19
45. Ibid
46. "Iran-Iraq: Problems at Home Resurface," The Middle East; October 1988, P. 14
47. "Iran and Iraq: In Brief; Ruling on Jurisdiction of Iran's Revolutionary Guard Courts," Tehran Domestic Service; March 7, 1985
48. "Wily Speaker Excels at Iran's Political Game," Christian Science Monitor; August 27, 1987, P. 1

49. "Iran's Presidential Contender Wants Post of Premier Abolished," Reuters; April 18, 1989; INA (Iraqi News Agency) on Background to Accepting 598," Baghdad INA in English; July 30, 1988

50. "Guard Corps Official on Defense Readiness," Tehran Domestic Service; September 22, 1988

51. "Islamic Revolutionary Guard Corps (IRGC)," op.cit.

52. "Who's Who of Revolution" in *Iran Almanac 1987*, op.cit., pp. 460-1

53. "IRNA Carries New Ministers' Biographies," Tehran IRNA in English in FBIS; September 20, 1988

54. "U.S. Calls Iranian Cleric Leading Backer of Terror," New York Times; August 27, 1989, P. 16

55. "Who's Who of Revolution," op.cit., P. 302

56. Ibid, P. 300

57. "Ministers' Biographies Detailed," Tehran IRNA in English; August 29, 1989

58. "Cabinet Debate Postponed: Motion on Nabavi," Tehran IRNA in English; August 20, 1989

59. "Rafsanjani Sweeps Out Hardliners," Washington Post; August 20, 1989, P. A1

60. Tehran Pars Daily News; April 18, 1981

61. Ibid

62. Asahi News Service; May 20,, 1986

63. "Who's Who of Revolution," op.cit., P. 24

64. "Iran's Agents of Terror," US News and World Report; March 6, 1989, pp. 20-5

65. "Tehran Said to `Order' Glass Kidnapping," London The Independent; July 1, 1987

66. "Absent Minister Holds Key," London the Times; June 2, 1987, P. 6

67. "Iran Threatens to Break Relations with France," Reuters; July 16, 1987

68. "Borujerdi Appointed Deputy Foreign Minister," Tehran Tehran Times in English; December 3, 1989, P. 2; "IRGC Minister Returns from Pakistan," Tehran IRNA in English; January 27, 1989

69. "Who's Who of Revolution," op.cit., P. 24

70. "Iranian Official Says All Hostages May Be Freed Within 10 Months," New York Times; March 19, 1990, P. A2; "Iran, Fearing Loss of Syria Tie, Widens Aid to Lebanon Shiites, New York Times; December 29, 1989, P. A3

71. "Iranian Official Says All Hostages May Be Freed Within 10 Months," op.cit.

72. "Washington Dateline," Associated Press; October 9, 1987

73. "Britain Blocks Appointment of Militant to Iranian Embassy," Reuters North European Service; February 20, 1986

74. "Briefs: Iran" in FBIS; July 2, 1986; "Dossier of a 'Moderate'Iranian," Washington Post; July 8, 1987
75. "Abu Sharif to Be New Iranian Envoy," Pakistan the Muslim in English; December 3, 1981
76. "Autobiography: Abbas Duzduzani, Former Minister of Islamic Guidance," Tehran Iran Press Digest; March 6, 1983, P. 14
77. "Report on Proceedings of 31 December Majles Session," Tehran Resalat in Persian; January 1, 1990, pp. 5,9; "Iran Buys New Weapons, Rebuilds Battered Military," Associated Press; April 26, 1989
78. "Who's Who of the Revolution," op.cit., P. 431
79. Ibid
80. "Voice of Moderation Emerges as Iran Edges into New Era," Washington Post; October 24, 1988, P. A1
81. "Majlis Candidates Warned On Use of Insignia for Publicity," Tehran Domestic Service in Persian; April 2, 1988
82. "RafiqDust Named Chairman of Oppressed Foundation," Tehran Domestic Service in Persian; September 6, 1989
83. "Who's of the Revolution, op.cit.; Asahi News Service; May 20, 1986; "Tavalla'i Appointed Khuzestan Governor-General," Tehran Domestic Service in Persian; January 30, 1990
84. Asahi News Service; May 20, 1986
85. Ibid
86. "Leading Hard-Line Politician is Elected to Iran's Parliament," New York Times; December 19, 1989
87. "Tehran Times On Mid-Term Majles Elections," Tehran Tehran Times in English; November 28, 1989, P. 2
88. Schahgaldian, op.cit., P. 113
89. "Shah Provided Arms for Iran's Victories," Washington Post; April 8, 1982, P. A28
90. "On Changes in Military Command," Tehran Iran Press Digest; August 12, 1986, pp. 1-4
91. Ibid
92. Ibid
93. "Khomeini Appoints New Members of Supreme Defense Council," Xinhua General News Service; July 14, 1986
94. Schahgaldian, op.cit., P. 115
95. "Internal Political Struggle, War Condition Examined," London Al-Dustur in Arabic; No. 335; August 13, 1984, pp. 9-10
96. "On Changes in Military Command," op.cit., P. 2
97. "Hardliner Gets Top Military Command in Iran," Associated Press; May 12, 1988
98. Ibid

99. "Khamene'i Appoints Shamkhani New Naval Chief," Tehran IRNA in English; October 30, 1989

100. "Iran Notes Anniversary of Fall of U.S. Embassy," New York Times; November 4, 1989, P. A3

101. "Deputy Commander of the Navy Appointed," op.cit.

102. "Which Official Determines Iran's Foreign Policy?," Tehran Echo of Iran, No.9; January 5, 1989, P. 7

103. "Tehran Sees a Rare Sign of War Dissent; Recent Street Protest Suggests Some Tire of Iraq Hostilities," Washington Post; May 17, 1989, P. A31

104. "Which Official Determines Iran's Foreign Policy?," op.cit.

105. "U.S. Rejected Proposed Sale of F-5's to Iran," Washington Post; October 20, 1988, P. A1

106. "Iran's Armed Forces: the Battle Within," Christian Science Monitor; August 26, 1987, P.1

107. "Khomeini Shifts Tactics, Says Official in Tehran," Washington Post; June 23, 1985, P. A18

108. Shahram Chubin and Charles Tripp, *Iran and Iraq at War* (Boulder, Co.: Westview Press, 1988) pp. 76-7; Anthony Cordesman, *The Iran-Iraq War and Western Security 1984-87* (London: Janes Publications, Inc., 1987) P. 92

109. "Tehran Attempts to Balance Guards' Zeal, Dangers of War," Washington Post; August 23, 1987, P. A1

110. "Human Wave Raid Loses Iran's Favor," New York Times; July 5, 1987

111. "Iran: Commander Discusses Val Fajr-10 Operations," in FBIS; March 24, 1988

112. Edgar O'Ballance, *The Gulf War* (London: Brassey's Defence Publishers, Inc., 1988) pp. 161, 164, 187-8

113. "Power Struggle Between Montazeri, Rafsanjani Groups Cited," London Keyhan in Persian; February 12, 1987, P. 16

114. "Divisions in Iran Said to Thwart an Offensive," Washington Post; June 21, 1984, P. A25

115. Ibid

116. "Three Recent Attempts to Kill Rafsanjani," Kuwait Times; January 11, 1989

117. "Divided Iranians Seem Unable to Settle on Firm Policy Course," New York Times; October 10, 1989, P. A1; "Son of Khomeini Gains in Authority," New York Times; May 22, 1989, P. A1

118. "Iran" in *Defense and Foreign Affairs Handbook 1989* (Alexandria, Va.: International Media Corp., 1989) P. 508; "Iran: Guards Chiefs Outline Arms Programs," Tehran Keyhan in Persian; November 8, 1987 in FBIS; November 17, 1987

119. "Iran Threatens to Attack Arab States That Back Iraq," Associated Press; July 24, 1987; "Iran" in *Defense and Foreign Affairs Handbook 1989*, op.cit.

120. "Iran's Navy Gets Ready for Guerrilla War Against U.S.," Associated Press; June 30, 1987
121. "Iran Threatens to Attack Arab States That Back Iraq," op.cit.
122. "Signs of Split Seen in Iran's Counterattack on US Navy," Christian Science Monitor; April 20, 1988
123. "Gulf Awaits Iranian Retaliation After US Gunship Attack," Reuters; September 23, 1987
124. "Iran's Armed Forces: the Battle Within," op.cit.
125. "Hardliner Gets Top Military Command in Iran," op.cit.
126. "Signs of Split Seen in Iran's Counterattack on US Navy," op.cit.
127. "Iranians Celebrate Missile Attack as Much-Needed Morale Booster," Washington Post; October 18, 1987
128. "Iran: Guards Chiefs Outline Arms Programs," op.cit.
129. "Iran Says Three Kuwaiti Boats Seized in Gulf," Reuters; July 21, 1987
130. "Iranian Speedboats Reportedly Chased From Kuwaiti -Saudi Port, Associated Press; October 3, 1987
131. Ibid
132. "Tehran Attempts to Balance Guards' Zeal, Dangers of War," op.cit.
133. "Hizballah, Revolutionary Guards Set Up Joint Command," Beirut Voice of Lebanon in Arabic; April 18, 1988
134. "Lebanese Battles Demonstrate Syria-Iran Rivalry," Washington Post; January 7, 1990
135. Ibid
136. "Beirut Sources on US Hostage Release Moves," London Al-Sharq Al-Awsat in Arabic; April 18, 1989, pp.1-2; "Iran's Besharati, RafiqDust in Syria for Talks," Paris Agence France Presse in English; May 16, 1988
137. "Iran and Syria Discuss Efforts to Free Hostages," New York Times; March 5, 1990, P. A7
138. "More Iranian Guards Reported Off to Beirut," London Al-Majallah in Arabic; April 19-25 1989, P. 8
139. "Fighting Between Muslim Factions Flares in Beirut," New York Times; January 23, 1990, P. A3
140. "Lebanese Islamic Leader Comments on Hostages," Tehran IRNA in English; March 6, 1990
141. "Rafsanjani Losing Influence Over Shiite Militants," Washington Post; January 8, 1990, P. A17
142. "Iran Reportedly Gave Weapons to Obtain U.S. Hostage Release," New York Times; April 23, 1990, P. A8
143. "Iran Paid For Release of Hostages," Washington Post, January 19, 1992. p. A1
144. Ibid.
145. Ibid.

146. "Saudi Envoy Gives Indonesian President Video of Mecca Riots,"
     Reuters; August 12, 1987
147. "Iran Helped to Free Hostages, US Says," Washington Post; July 5,
     1985, P. A1
148. Ibid
149. "Iranian Exiles Accuse Rafsanjani of Directing Terrorism, Killings
     Abroad," Washington Post; April 27, 1990, P. A35
150. Ibid
151. "Iran: People's Mojahedin Accuse Pasdaran of Bakhtiar Murder,"
     FBIS, August 12, 1991.
152. "Israel, Nimrodi Gives Details of Iran Deals," in Tel Aviv Yedi'ot
     Aharonot in FBIS; February 18, 1987
153. Ibid
154. Michael Ledeen, *Perilous Statecraft* (New York: McMillan Publishing
     Co., 1988) P. 131
155. Ledeen, op.cit., pp. 234-6
156. "The Other Side of the Hill," The Economist; December 6, 1986
157. Ibid
158. "U.S. Was Preoccupied With Secret Arms Deal at the Time of '86
     Kidnappings," Washington Post; May 1, 1990, p. A19
159. *Report of the President's Special Review Board;* February 26, 1987 P. B-48;
     Ledeen, op.cit., P. 133

6

Guard Factionalism

The final major measure of institutionalization against which the Revolutionary Guard must be evaluated, is the degree of coherence versus fractionalization, where greater coherence corresponds to a higher degree of institutionalization.[1] Although this is an important criteria for assessing any institution, it is particularly significant for analyzing a military institution in which the need to act as a unit is imperative. This is especially crucial for a military force engaged in a major war as was the Revolutionary Guard during 1980-88. On yet another level, the coherence measurement especially applies to analyzing a revolutionary organization such as the Guard which, at its inception, was virtually defined by its high degree of factionalism. It was a product of the many disparate primordial revolutionary elements which formed it. In turn, the purpose of assessing cohesiveness in a revolutionary military institution is to help judge its transition from a revolutionary to a professional military organization. According to Chorley, professionalization is the last stage in the development of a revolutionary armed forces.[2]

In the case of the Guard, increased organizational cohesiveness (ability to act as a unit and the relative absence of factionalism within its ranks) has not translated into an equal degree of professionalism. Coherence is a necessary but not sufficient ingredient of professionalism. Professionalism is a broader measure which implies that military decisionmaking and procedures are based on objective, rationally derived criteria designed to maximize military effectiveness and that the military institution is loyal to and faithfully obeys whatever civilian regime is in power, regardless of the leadership's policies or ideology. As a component of professionalism, coherence represents the degree to which a clear chain of command within the institution is obeyed.

The Guard has made significant strides toward cohesiveness, developing from a patchwork of individual militias into a relatively organized force capable of acting as a unit. However, the Guard has not become a professional force. Consistent with the findings for all the analytic measures used thus far, the Guard's increasing cohesiveness has contributed only to an outward appearance of a professional military organization. However, the Guard fails to meet the substantive criteria of professionalization—unquestioned obedience to civilian authority, absence of political involvement, and a scientifically based decisionmaking process. The Guard's resistance to professionalization, in turn, reflects the depth and strength of the Guard's continuing commitment to the hardline ideological principles of the revolution, which are incompatible with the scientific and politically neutral foundations of military professionalism. To this extent, therefore, the Guard does not display a key characteristic in the generic framework of revolutionary armed force development postulated by Chorley.[3]

Several Guard actions have been improperly attributed to factionalism, and actually represented a manifestation of the Guard's ideological commitment and resistance to professionalization. These specific political expressions of Guard ideology can be distinguished from the military operations and decisions cited as evidence of Guard autonomy in the preceding chapter. The military and export of the revolution actions cited previously were those which appeared to conflict with the goals and policy directions of its civilian superiors but did not violate specific civilian orders. By contrast, the events and actions which will be discussed in this chapter represent deliberate interference in the political process and overt expressions of the Guard's radical ideology with the definitive intention of embarassing or undermining conservative or pragmatic political leaders and institutions.

The Guard, even under the pressures of full scale war against Iraq, has been unwilling to abandon its ideological character in favor of professionalization. Moreover, although some of the Guard's more overtly political acts may have been committed by small groups of Guards, the actions themselves represented the desire, and probably the specific commands, of the senior Guard leadership. The actions and operations represented the will of the entire Guard, not merely rogue factions within it. In the preceding chapter, it was shown that the Guard has resisted professionalization on the key aspect of wardecisionmaking; the present discussion will primarily focus on the Guard's interference in the political process.

The Decline of Guard Factionalism

Contrary to the assertions of a number of press reports on the Guard,[4] factionalism within the organization has declined dramatically since the early days of the revolution. Factionalism can be defined as the existence within an organization of two or more groups, each working to protect its own interests (ideological, political, ethnic, familial, or regional) or to make its goals the goals of the organization as a whole. According to this definition, it can be argued that factionalism within the Guard has become virtually insignificant.

As explained previously, the Guard formed from two major elements— revolutionary guerrilla groups (most notably the Mujahedin of the Islamic Revolution) that had been fighting the Shah for many years, and militia groups that organized around key revolutionary clerics and non-clerical militants during the revolution. It is self evident that the latter militias, because they formed independently around local leaders, each initially constituted separate factions loyal to the militia organizer. However, even the first major Guard component—the organized guerrilla core of the early Guard—was highly factionalized. An unofficial Tehran paper reports that before the revolution, Reza'i, RafiqDust, and Minister of Posts, Telephones, and Telegraphs Mohammad Qarazi each led individual clandestine guerrilla groups under the overall banner of the Mujahedin of the Islamic Revolution.[5] Each incorporated his forces into the newly forming Revolutionary Guard when the revolution triumphed.[6] The Iran Press Digest similarly reports that the MIR itself was a coalition of seven smaller groups: Towhidi Badr, Towhidi Saf, Fallah, Khalq, Mansooron, and Omat Vahedeh.[7] That these groups within the MIR were willing to put aside their parochial interests and work together after the revolution undoubtedly contributed to the strength of the MIR within the early Guard.

A major group which competed with the MIR was led by Abbas Zamani, who, with Bani-Sadr's patronage, eventually became the Guard's first official operational commander. Zamani's militia was centered around the former Islamic Nations party which he helped found in the 1960s and its successor group, the Party of God (Hizballah).[8] Zamani was ousted as Guard commander in July 1980 as his patron, Bani-Sadr, began losing power to the clerics and the MIR faction within the Guard, which had been instrumental in helping radical clerics bring Bani-Sadr down, became the undisputedly dominant element within the Revolutionary Guard.[9] The dominance of the MIR explains how Reza'i, a major figure in the MIR, became Guard Commander in September 1981.

The organized guerrilla element of the early Guard also encompassed a faction centered around Ayatollah Montazeri and his relative by marriage, Mehdi Hashemi. Mehdi, the brother of Ayatollah Montazeri's son-in-law Hadi Hashemi, was a political ally of Montazeri's late son Mohammad Montazeri, and an original member of the Supreme Council of the Revolutionary Guard.[10] The faction was held together by the personal relationships among these figures and their overriding belief that the Guard should devote more of its resources to the violent export of the

Islamic revolution even at the expense of the war effort.[11] Mohammad Montazeri and Mehdi Hashemi underwent guerrilla training in Lebanon before the revolution and were both heavily involved in promoting the Guard's presence in that country.[12]

This faction also eventually lost out to the MIR in the internal struggle for control of the Guard and the direction of the Guard's radical activities and the faction has been severely weakened. Mohammad Montazeri was killed in one of the major bombings in Tehran in 1981.[13] In 1982, Mehdi Hashemi was ousted from the Guard and formed a separate Office of Liberation Movements, although the Office apparently still organized some export of the revolution activities in cooperation with the Guard.[14] In 1986 Hashemi was arrested for leaking news of the U.S.-Iran arms deal and he was subsequently executed.[15] In early 1989, largely because of his earlier efforts to protect Mehdi Hashemi as well as such advocates for domestic freedoms as former Prime Minister Bazargan, Ayatollah Montazeri himself was dismissed by Ayatollah Khomeini as designated successor.[16]

Because of the Guard's early factionalism and the sucess of its constituent components in incorporating the militant supporters of the revolution into its ranks, political leaders of every stripe competed for influence within the Guard as a means of bolstering their own political futures. Among the less successful efforts, Bani Sadr spoke before the first open organizational meeting of the MIR after the triumph of the revolution (April 5, 1979) in an effort to attract its, and by extension, the nascent Guard's, support.[17] His failure to gain its favor was starkly evident in the key role played by the MIR/Guard in helping Bani-Sadr's clerical opponents remove him from power. Shortly after the revolution then Prime Minister Bazargan's liberal-nationalist allies Ibrahim Yazdi, whose ideology was certainly unlikely to attract most Guards, failed to attract broad Guard support even though he controlled a small revolutionary militia in Tehran.[18] Mostafa Chamran, a pragmatic ally of the clerics who was appointed Defense Minister to help solidify regime control of the military, as well as the more radical theoretician Jalaledin Farsi, were similarly unable to gain significant followings in the Guard.[19] In the early 1980s, Hojjat ol-Eslam Mohamad Reza Mahdavi Kani, leader of the Tehran Militant Clergy Association, a rival of the Islamic Republican Party, unsuccessfully attempted to gain formal authority over the Guard in addition to the security powers he then held as Interior Minister.[20]

Only Ayatollah Khomeini had the charismatic presence to appeal directly to rank and file Guardsmen. In order to gain support within the Guard, his subordinates, therefore, had to build ties to the Guard's local leaders and organizers, or alternately, to gain positions of authority in organizing the overall national structure of the Guard as it coalesced. By using a combination of both approaches, the IRP clerics succeeded, at least initially, where their political rivals had failed.[21] As noted previously, the IRP built an effective alliance with the MIR. The IRP also positioned two of members, Rafsanjani and Khamene'i, as Guard Supervisers, even though the Guard opposed and was able to limit such direct IRP control over its affairs.[22] Once the IRP clerics had effectively outflanked their political rivals within the Islamic regime, competition for the Guard's support was centered within the IRP, with Rafsanjani generally gaining the upper hand until 1988, when he lost the Guard's support by playing a key role in Iran's decision to end the war with Iraq.[23] (The IRP was officially abolished in 1987 but the ties among its organizers generally remained.) Currently, although the Guard follows the orders of Khamene'i as supreme leader and Rafsanjani, as President, its emotional support is widely believed to lie with such radical leaders as former Interior Minister Ali Akbar Mohtashemi and Ayatollah Khomeini's son, Ahmad.[24]

It can be shown that the factionalism which characterized the Guard's early existence has been significantly reduced, if not eliminated. In part because of the war, which helped the Guard leaders bring all elements of the organization under a centralized command structure, almost all of the individually, personally, and regionally based Guard factions have been subordinated and integrated into the national command structure. Although some local clerics and provincial authorities retain influence over local Guard contingents, many of these local authority figures undoubtedly now identify with the national or local institutions, such as the Majles or local government structure, which they have joined.[25] There is little evidence of local Guard units violating the orders of the national Guard leadership once clear Guard policy positions have been articulated or specific orders transmitted. Moreover, since the expulsion of Mehdi Hashemi from the Guard in the early 1980s, no Guard commander has developed a major following independent of Reza'i and the other core Guard leaders. As discussed in Chapter 5, the Guard's ability to gain and maintain control over its own affairs has limited the ability of civilian leaders to cultivate factional support within the organization.

This is not to argue that political factionalism within the Guard has been completely eliminated. For example, during his three and a half years as designated successor to Khomeini, Ayatollah Montazeri attracted a following among Guards based primarily in his home town of Najafabad and the nearby major city of Esfahan.[26] When Montazeri was dismissed by Khomeini as designated successor in early 1989, some pro-Montazeri Guards reportedly protested the dismissal of their patron and were subsequently purged from the organization.[27] Three years earlier, a small number of Guard loyalists of Mehdi Hashemi allegedly returned from the warfront to protest Hashemi's arrest, a similarly clear display of lingering political factionalism within the Guard.[28]

Even Rafsanjani has apparently been able to retain the support of some in the Guard, despite his shift since 1988 to more pragmatic, non-ideological positions generally rejected by the overwhelming bulk of the Guard. In late 1989, Rafsanjani reportedly was able to transfer some Guard's more amenable to his authority to the Guard's Lebanon contingent, presumably to help him in subsequent maneuvering to persuade Hizballah, which the Guard armed and trained to release some of the U.S. hostages it held.[29] The Guard's Lebanon force has been the cornerstone of its export of the revolution effort and therefore, by its very existence, has exemplified the Guard's most radical impulses. The Lebanon contingent, like the rest of the Guard, considered a unilateral release of U.S. hostages as a deviation from the anti-U.S. ideology of Khomeini and the revolution.[30] The more moderate Guard contingent Rafsanjani was able to assign to Lebanon, therefore, provides some evidence for the existence of a more moderate faction within the Guard unit.

That the Guard's top leadership was unwilling or unable to block the assignment of some moderate Guards to Lebanon and the early 1990 release of two U.S. hostages may indicate that Rafsanjani and Khamene'i reached an understanding with the top Guard commanders. Khamene'i's permission that the Guard reconstitute its full Central Headquarters staff and that Shamkhani and Mohtaj become Commander and deputy Commander, respectively, of the Iranian regular Navy, may have been offered in exchange for the Guard's silence or cooperation in the release of Western hostages in Lebanon.[31] The Guard leaders likely were also promised a major share of the weapons purchased by the Shah but held by the U.S. which presumably would be released to Iran following a release of all U.S. hostages. As demonstrated in the U.S.-Iran arms transactions during 1985-6, the Guard has shown a willingness to temporarily compromise its militance in exchange for weapons or authority it needs to further more important hardline objectives.[32] In this case, gaining control of the regular Navy, which the Guard views as a bastion of prerevolutionary values and which has valuable military assets with which the Guard can strike at Iraq, conservative Gulf states, or even the U.S., was seen by the Guard as worth some compromise on the hostage issue. Indeed, in June 1990 Shamkhani announced that the Iranian Navy may block Iraqi warships transitting the Strait of Hormuz, a statement which weakened Rafsanjani's attempt to arrange direct talks with Iraq toward a final peace settlement—a settlement which, to the Guard, represents capitulation.[33] The acquisition of additional weapons would also be seen by the Guard as advancing its efforts to strengthen the Islamic revolution and spread it to other countries.

Another example of factionalism in the Guard occurred in 1987, following Iran's high casualty, unsuccessful battle to seize Iraq's southern port city of Basra. In clear contrast to the commitment of the Guard leaders, as well as Khomeini, to war until victory, a group of Guards reportedly demonstrated on a major Tehran thoroughfare calling on Khomeini to "forgive" Iraq's President Saddam Husayn, essentially a request that Khomeini end the war.[34] The absence to that point of any overt support within the political leadership—let alone the Guard—for a negotiated settlement of the war prompted informed speculation that more pragmatic elements within the leadership, possibly Khamene'i or Rafsanjani, had organized their loyalists in the Guard to participate in the demonstration.[35] Those Guards who constitute a base of support for more pragmatic political leaders are probably drawn from the "opportunistic" social elements within the Guard, described in Chapter Two. As in this anti-war demonstration, the opportunists can disrupt the Guard's radical solidity, but they are not a sufficiently strong element to shift the Guard in a more pragmatic, professional direction.

The examples above show that there is some remaining factionalism in the Guard, but these relatively discreet events and actions contrast sharply with the clear presence of several major and distinct factions that characterized the Guard's early years. Although troublesome to the radical Guard leadership, the remaining presence of some minor factions within the Guard are far less serious than the major power struggles for control of the organization itself that occurred during and shortly after the Guard's formation. That political leaders must manipulate minor factions within the Guard as an alternative to exercising firm control over the organization as a whole represents the lack of success of the political leadership in professionalizing the Guard. The Guard has become relatively cohesive, but not professional, and the two concepts must not be perceived as coterminus.

That ideology takes clear precedence over professionalization in the Guard is revealed by even a cursory examination of Guard press statements. The Guard leaders and newspapers catering to the Guard (such as Pasdar-e-Islam) continue to stress the need to adhere to the values of the revolution, such as helping Islamic movements worldwide and ensuring that national economic policies primarily focus on helping the *Mustazafin*—the dispossessed or oppressed.[36] It should also be noted that the Guard displays none of the hesitancy to suppress internal dissent by force exhibited by its more professionalized counterparts among revolutionary armed forces, especially the Soviet Army and PLA. The assertion of Iranian political leaders that the demands of the Iran-Iraq war accounts for the failure of the Guard to professionalize is inconsistent with the experiences of these other revolutionary armed forces. In the cases of the Soviet Red Army and the PLA, the need for objective military success in war, including civil war, accelerated rather than hindered professionalization.[37] Engaged in all out war for eight years, the Guard had the same need for military efficiency yet, uniquely in the case of the Guard, this need did not overcome the Guard's ideological fervor and ideologically based decisionmaking.

Politically Motivated Actions

In the previous chapter, several military actions and decisions undertaken by the Guard were used to demonstrate Guard autonomy. In those cases, the Guard's activities were directed primarily against foreign adversaries of the revolution and it cannot be definitively shown that these actions directly violated civilian orders to the contrary. But there have also been cases of the Guard's direct and deliberate interference in the political process within Iran and clear violations of or challenges to civilian authority. Moreover, the events and actions presented here represent not Guard factionalism, but rather the ideological fervor and unprofessionalism of a military/security organization in which political involvement to further the hardline goals of Khomeini and the revolution have been consistently encouraged from the very top of the organization. Therefore they reflect rather than contradict the priorities and political and ideological goals of the senior Guard leadership, they clearly do not represent evidence for continuing Guard factionalism.

The first and a particularly useful example of the Guard's indiscipline and ideologically motivated willingness to interfere in politics is commonly referred to as the "Chaplin affair." In 1987 an Iranian diplomat in London, Majid Qassemi, was arrested there on minor criminal charges. Qassemi reportedly was a relative of a senior Guard commander;[38] upon hearing of his arrest, a group of Guards, possibly with the cooperation of a Tehran Komiteh, retaliated by abducting, interrogating, and beating British diplomat Edward Chaplin at a Guard location in Tehran.[39] The Guards' action was a clear violation of not only international law but also of Iranian civilian authority, especially that of the judiciary and the Foreign Ministry.

What began as an apparent impulsive act of revenge by Tehran Guards quickly escalated into a broader challenge to pragmatic elements within the Foreign Ministry and the leadership in general. The Guard's chief ally in the Foreign Ministry, undersecretary Hosein Sheikh-ol Eslam took advantage of pragmatic Foreign Minister Velayati's absence from Iran to precipitate a major row with the UK by arguing that Chaplin should be tried for spying.[40] This was a clear attempt by the Guard and Sheikh-ol Eslam to undermine Velayati and his pragmatic foreign policy efforts to improve ties with the West—policies which ran counter to the viscerally anti-Western tenets of the revolution and the Guard. Although the detention of Chaplin may have been conducted by a small group of Guards, the subsequent effort to parlay the action into a radicalization of Iranian foreign demonstrates that the abduction had the support of the Guard hierarchy.

Another example of Guard interference in the foreign policy process occurred in the wake of the death, at the hands of Saudi security forces, of 400 Iranian pilgrims who rioted in Mecca in late July 1987. As discussed previously, the rioting itself was probably inspired by the Guard and other Iranian radicals in the Iranian pilgrimage delegation. A few days after the Mecca incident, Western diplomats recognized several Revolutionary Guard members orchestrating the sacking of the Saudi and Kuwaiti embassies in Tehran.[41] Of particular significance, these diplomats reported that Iranian Foreign Ministry officials warned their Saudi and Kuwaiti counterparts of the impending attack and that they (the Iranian Foreign Ministry officials) were powerless to prevent it.[42] That the assault on the two embassies was planned sufficiently in advance for other Iranian officials to learn of it suggests that the whole Guard leadership structure was involved in the action and that it was not the work of an individual Guard faction. The attempt by Foreign Ministry officials to prevent the embassy sacking is a clear indicator of a political power struggle on this issue. This retaliatory attack on the embassies supports the assertion that the Guard is far from a professional armed force, aloof from domestic politics.

In 1988-89, in the wake of its military unraveling in the war, the Guard's unauthorized interference in domestic political affairs became more direct and more violent. As stated previously, the rift between the Guard and Rafsanjani over the decision to accept a ceasefire with Iraq apparently precipitated several attempts on Rafsanjani's life by Guards who believed that Rafsanjani, in engineering acceptance of the ceasefire, had sold out the revolution.[43] In at least one case in early 1989, some southern front Guard formations were purged for allegedly plotting against some members of the clerical leadership, presumably including Rafsanjani.[44] As recently as June 1990, a group of Guards allegedly sabotaged a jet Rafsanjani was to use to return to Tehran after viewing damage from a major earthquake; Rafsanjani had elected to travel by car, thus escaping the attempt on his life.[45]

It must be noted that rank and file Guardsmen were receiving ample signals of the Guard leadership's displeasure with Rafsanjani's moderate policies, and therefore perceived sanction for these anti-Rafsanjani actions. For example, Reza'i himself set such a tone just days after Iran's official acceptance of the ceasefire in July 1988. While announcing the Guard's intention to comply with the political decision to end the war, he said that the Guard "will not be like the peace seekers of yesterday who, today, during a time of peace, turn into revolutionaries and warmongers."[46] Reza'i was undoubtedly referring to Rafsanjani, who attempted to appear bellicose in public statements after privately helping engineer Iran's acceptance of the ceasefire. Moreover, some of the above cited assassination attempts by Guard groups occurred around the time of the September 1988 post-war gathering of Guard commanders in Tehran in which the Guard leaders expressed open opposition to any attempts to abandon the principles of the revolution or weaken the Guard as the institutional protector of those principles.[47]

Late 1988 witnessed yet another highly violent effect of the Guard's continued politicization, even if the activity itself was directed outside Iran's borders and carried out by surrogate groups. It has been widely reported that the Revolutionary Guard, in collaboration with its radical political allies in Iran, authorized the Popular Front for the Liberation of Palestine—General Command (PFLP-GC) to sabotage an American commercial jet in retaliation for the mistaken U.S. downing of an Iranian passenger jet over the Persian Gulf in July 1988.[48] (The PFLP-GC is a radical Palestinian nationalist group based in Lebanon, with which the Guard's Lebanon contingent had forged close links prior to the Pan Am bombing.[49] According to international investigators, the actual bombing of Pan Am 103 in December 1988 was accomplished by Libyan agents after the PFLP-GC's bombing plot was discovered and derailed by German investigators.[50] However, some believe the Libyan bombing of Pan Am 103 was a continuation of the PFLP-GC plot rather than a separate operation.[51])

Whether or not the PFLP-GC, acting on behalf of the Guard and other Iranian radicals, actually placed the bomb aboard Pan Am 103, the bombing of a U.S. passenger jet served the PFLP-GC's agenda by embarrassing the mainstream PLO (which had accepted the concept of a negotiated settlement with Israel and renounced terrorism), and setting back the Arab-Israeli peace process. For the Guard and other Iranian radicals, the bombing fulfilled an ideologically motivated commitment to avenge the U.S. shootdown of the Iranian airbus in July and to undercut the efforts of Iranian pragmatists, particularly Rafsanjani, to improve Iran's ties to the West in the aftermath of the war.[52]

It cannot be argued that the Guard's Lebanon contingent organized the bombing in violation of the wishes or orders of the senior Guard leadership. Rather, the bombing represented the concerted action of the entire Guard structure and its radical allies in Iran. Iranian pragmatists had specifically ruled out direct retaliation for the U.S. downing of the Iranian airbus but no Guard leader ever ruled out such retribution.[53] Moreover, organs of the Guard's network in Europe, such as the U.K.-based "Guards of the Islamic Revolution," even claimed direct responsibility for the Pan Am 103 bombing.[54] (In the early 1980s, the "Guards" blew up the car of a German businessman whose company had sold missiles to Iraq and which hijacked a jet in an attempt to free five persons imprisoned in France for the attempted assassination of former Iranian Prime Minister Bakhtiar.[55]) The claim demonstrated that many or all Guard subunits were aware of and involved in the Pan Am plot. The Guard's active involvement in the bombing again demonstrates its willingness to interfere in Iranian politics and to act directly against the wishes and interests of its pragmatic civilian superiors when doing so furthers hardline revolutionary principles.

Another major example of the Guard's politicization occurred in the radicalized political atmosphere in Tehran which resulted from Khomeini's early 1989 death sentence against author Salman Rushdie. According to the Iranians, the Pakistan born Rushdie had slandered Islam in his novel *The Satanic Verses*. The generally moderate Deputy Foreign Minister Mohammad Javad Larijani, an advocate of improved ties to the U.S., was forced to resign under pressure from radicals, and Revolutionary Guards allegedly beat Iran's moderate Ambassador to the United Nations in New York, Mohammad Mahallati, upon his return visit to Tehran.[56] The Guards accused him of insufficient commitment to the revolution's principles.[57]

In the beating of Mahallati, as in other cases, there is no evidence that the zealous and undisciplined Guards who committed this action against Mahallati belonged to a particular faction within the Guard. The Guards who perpetrated the action were not arrested or tried and there was no public denial of the affair on the part of the Guard leadership. Rather, the incident appeared to be a logical consequence of the radicalized atmosphere surrounding the Rushdie affair, in which the Guard clearly supported and declared its willingness to implement the death sentence against Rushdie.[58] Even if the Guards involved did not receive specific orders from Guard headquarters to undertake the action, they clearly believed that the beating of Mahallati would be supported at the highest levels of the Guard. The action fit a consistent pattern of Guard efforts to undermine pragmatists in the Foreign Ministry and thereby ensure a radical foreign policy. The pressure exerted by the Guard and its radical allies on the Foreign Ministry has even, on occasion, been sufficient to necessitate public statements of support for Foreign Ministry officials by senior political leaders.[59]

These examples suggest that actions which may be incorrectly attributed to continuing Guard factionalism actually demonstrate the durability of the Guard's uncompromising revolutionary ideology and continuing politicization. Not only do the above events support the assertion that the Guard has not matured into a professional armed force, but the manner in which these actions were undertaken distinguishes the Guard from its counterparts among other revolutionary armed forces. With the possible exception of the French revolutionary army under Napoleon, who used the army to seize direct control of the revolution, other revolutionary forces have generally intervened in internal politics at the behest and on behalf of civilian factions which supported the army's institutional interests.[60]

When they did so, other revolutionary armed forces did not intervene in internal politics on purely ideological grounds as has the Guard. Even the French revolutionary was driven more by the ability of its leaders to equate personal gain with the success of the institution than by pure ideology. The key strength of the French army lay in its unleashing of the inherent military talents of the non-aristocratic officers who were long subordinate to the less competent but better connected aristocratic officer corps.[61] The two French revolutionary forces which represented truly revolutionary elements—the middle class based National Guard and the lower class dominated People's Armies—were abolished or lost their social identity. Because of the war against the conservative European powers, the National Guard was eventually opened up to mass recruitment, thus diluting its middle class composition and position as an armed protector of middle class interests.[62] The People's Armies, which were synonymous with revolutionary terror and vengeance, were abolished when they emerged as threats to the control of the national revolutionary leadership.[63]

Resistance to Professionalization

If the Guard's political actions were motivated by ideology, they were facilitated by its corresponding resistance to professionalization. The lack of professionalism may help explain why several instances of Guard interference in politics can be confused with factionalism; both factionalism and ideological politicization, although different attributes, outwardly manifest themselves in similar manners. Both often result in unanticipated, spontaneous, politically significant acts carried out by small groups of Guards or Guard subunits.

An overview of relevant overt comments by senior Guard leaders further supports the argument that, while Guard factionalism has declined significantly, ideologically motivated resistance to professionalization remains. In the early years of the revolution, when the Guard was sharply factionalized, denunciations of this factionalism came from within the Guard itself. For example, the Guard's first operational commander, Abbas Zamani, publicly cited Guard factionalism as a major reason for his resignation in May 1980.[64] Kazem Bojnurdi similarly claimed that factionalism was his primary reason for declining the invitation to succeed Zamani as Commander.[65] However, as the Guard consolidated organizationally and factionalism within it visibly declined, public comments by

Guard leaders about factionalism within the organization—even in the form of denial—ceased.

While Guard coherence has increased over time, a reading of the statements and actions of senior Guard leaders reveals no corresponding commitment to professionalization of the organization. To the Guard leaders, professionalization would imply a virtual abandonment of the ideological and political values they have fought for since they were young urban guerrillas battling the Shah. Even in approving the establishment of formal military ranks in the Guard, the Guard leaders never indicated that they viewed the establishment of ranks as part of a broader professionalization process; it has also been said that acceptance of ranks was a concession by the Guard leaders to the political leadership and did not represent an intent by the Guard leaders to increase Guard professionalism.[66] They claimed that ranks were necessary if Guard commanders were to deal with foreign military officers on an equal basis and to help differentiate the capabilities of individual Guards.[67] Moreover, in contrast to the admonitions of civilian leaders, no Guard leader has ever called on rank and file Guards to refrain from interfering in politics. To the contrary, the consistent willingness of the Guard leaders to assert their political views have encouraged the rank and file to do likewise.[68]

The resistance to professionalization by the Guard itself contrasts sharply with the overtly expressed efforts by pragmatic civilian leaders to professionalize, and therefore hopefully depoliticize, the Guard. On several occasions, most notably in connection with the post-Iran-Iraq war gathering of Guard commanders in Tehran, both Ali Khamene'i and Rafsanjani have urged the Guard to improve discipline, establish a clear hierarchy, and to refrain from interfering in politics, such as elections.[69] Even Ayatollah Khomeini, who generally encouraged the Guard's ideological fervency but who wanted a stable Islamic government, told the Guard on a few occasions not to interfere in politics.[70] The 1988 injunction against Majles candidates using the Guard insignia in their campaigns provides yet another, albeit indirect, example of civilian efforts to curb Guard political involvement.[71]

That political leaders have called for Guard professionalization but not its greater unity provides further evidence that it is the Guard as a whole, and not zealous factions within it, that are responsible for the Guard's interference in politics. It is precisely because the Guard is relatively united in its propensity toward political involvement in support of the hardline agenda that the civilian leadership has sought to rein in the Guard. If politicization were limited to only small factions within the Guard, the civilian leadership undoubtedly would have perceived a less urgent need to attempt to depoliticize it.

Conclusion

As an organization, the Revolutionary Guard has become more cohesive, but its increased unity has not translated into increased professionalization. The Guard is a uniformly radical organization, and its interference in politics is a result of the ideological radicalism of the organization as a whole, and not the work of minor, uncontrollable Guard factions. Cohesiveness is a necessary but not sufficient condition of military professionalism. It is self evident that an army lacking in internal discipline and clear lines of authority cannot be professional. Professionalism, however, is a broader concept which implies that an armed force accepts restraints and limits. The recognition of limits, however, fundamentally conflicts with the revolutionary ideology of Khomeini and the Guard, which seeks to overthrow, rather than work within, established political arrangements throughout the Middle East. Military professionalism requires that an armed force base its decisionmaking on rational, pragmatic, and objective factors rather than emotional or ideological impulse. However, the available evidence, such as the desire to continue the war in 1988 despite overwhelming military odds, indicates that the Guard places ideology over rational calculation.

Another hallmark of professionalism is obedience to civilian political authority regardless of the regime in power or its policies, and the refrainment from involvement in politics. The Guard, however, has consistently asserted that it views political involvement as not only legitimate, but an integral part of its mission to defend the Islamic revolution. This politicization and ideological fervor have produced several notable examples in which the Guard has acted against more moderate civilian superiors. These actions were not the work of individual Guard factions, but reflected the wishes and policies of the whole organization, including the Guard leadership. Of course, in the absence of a revolution against the current regime, this proposition cannot be fully tested; however, analysis of the available evidence suggests that the Guard would fight to the death against any attempted overthrow of the current regime. For the most part, the Shah's more "professional" army, in contrast, made its peace with the new rulers in Tehran in 1979.

It cannot be argued that the demands of the war against Iraq delayed Guard professionalism. In the cases of the Guard's revolutionary armed forces counterparts, professionalism not only proceeded but was, in fact, accelerated by revolutionary war. Moreover, since the war with Iraq ended in 1988, there has been virtually no effort by the Guard leadership to professionalize the organization, even though the Guard seeks to acquire and master the use of sophisticated weaponry, including advanced fighter jets and submarines.[72] The contradictory evidence of this assessment is the announcement of ranks in the Guard and Basij in 1990, apparently at the urging of the civilian leadership and the 1992 appointment of Hosein Jalali, a regular military officer, to lead the Guard Air Force.

Notes

1. Samuel P. Huntington, *Political Order in Changing Societies* (New Haven and London: Yale University Press, 1968) pp. 22-4
2. Katharine Chorley, *Armies and the Art of Revolution* (Boston: Beacon Press, 1973) Chaps. 11, 12
3. Ibid
4. "Iran Guards Leaders Slain in Violent Purge," Washington Times; March 23, 1989, P. A7
5. "Islamic Revolutionary Guards Corps (IRGC)," in *Iran Almanac 1987* (Tehran: Echo of Iran, 1987) P. 124
6. Ibid
7. "Organisation of Mujahedin of Islamic Revolution," Tehran Iran Press Digest; March 5, 1985
8. Who's Who of Revolution," in *Iran Yearbook 1988* (Tehran: Echo of Iran, 1988) P. 570
9. "Organisation of Mujahedin of Islamic Revolution," op.cit.
10. "Lebanese Weekly on Hashemi, McFarlane," in FBIS; November 5, 1986
11. Ibid
12. "Article Recounts 10 Years of Khomeyni Terrorism," Paris Lettre Persane in French, No.46, June 1986, pp. 6-10
13. Ibid
14. Ibid
15. "Why Khomeini's Designated Heir Quit," Washington Post; April 10, 1989, P. D8
16. "Son of Khomeini Gains in Authority," New York Times; May 22, 1989, P. A1
17. "Organisation of Mujahedin of Islamic Revolution," op.cit., P. 4
18. "Iran Islamic Committees Criticized by Premier as 'Rule of Revenge,'" New York Times; April 25, 1979, P. A1
19. "Islamic Revolutionary Guards Corps (IRGC)," op.cit., P. 124; Nikola Schahgaldian, *The Iranian Military Under the Islamic Republic*," (Santa Monica, Calif.: Rand Corp., 1987) P. 66
20. "Mahdavi Kani Maneuvers Up Iran's Political Power Ladder," Christian Science Monitor; December 9, 1981
21. "Infighting Among Ruling Clergy Reported," Christchurch The Press in English; January 18, 1984, P. 18

22. Schahgaldian, op.cit., pp. 120-1
23. "Voice of Moderation Emerges as Iran Edges into New Era," Washington Post; October 24, 1988, P. A1
24. "Divided Iranians Seem Unable to Settle on Firm Policy Course," New York Times; October 10, 1989, P. A1; "Khomeini's Son Urges No Concessions on Hostages," New York Times; March 14, 1990, P. A10
25. "Who's Who of Revolution," in *Iran Almanac 1987* (Tehran: Echo of Iran, 1987) pp. 300-472
26. "Larijani, Mahallati Reported Under Arrest," London The Times; April 17, 1989, P. 12
27. Ibid
28. "Lebanese Weekly on Hashemi, McFarlane," op.cit.
29. "Rafsanjani Losing Influence Over Shiite Militants," Washington Post; January 8, 1990, P. A17
30. "Bush Took Bogus Call On Hostages," Washington Post; March 9, 1990, P. A1
31. "Washington Wire," The Wall Street Journal; April 27, 1990, P. 1
32. See Chapter Five
33. "Iran Bans Opposition Party, Arrests Eight Members," Washington Post; June 16, 1990, P. A20
34. "Tehran Sees a Rare Sign of War Dissent," Washington Post; May 17, 1987, P. A31
35. Ibid
36. "IRGC To Share Military Experiences," Tehran IRNA in English; February 27, 1990 in FBIS; February 28, 1990, P. 56; "Election, Expectations for New Regime Viewed," Tehran Pasdar-e-Eslam in Persian; August-September, 1989, pp. 44-47 in FBIS; September 26, 1989
37. Jonathan Adelman, *Revolution, Armies, and War: A Political History* (Boulder, Co.: Lynne Rienner Publishers, Inc., 1985) P. 205
38. "Absent Minister Holds Key," London The Times; June 2,, 1987, P. 6
39. "5 U.K. Diplomats Expelled for `Suspicious Acts:' Move Seen as 'Minimum Response,'" London Press Association in English; 6 June 1987 in FBIS; June 8, 1987, P. 51
40. "Absent Minister Holds Key," op.cit.
41. "Tehran Attempts to Balance Guards' Zeal, Dangers of War," Washington Post; August 23, 1987, P. A1
42. Ibid
43. "Three Recent Attempts to Kill Rafsanjani," Kuwait Times in English; January 11, 1989
44. "Iran Guards Leaders Slain in Violent Purge," op.cit.
45. "President Reportedly Escapes Assassination," Paris AFP in English; July 1, 1990 in FBIS; July 2, 1990, P. 41

46. "IRGC Commander on Supporting U.N. Resolution," Tehran Domestic Service in Persian; July 21, 1988

47. See Chapter Three

48. "Closing in on the Pan Am Bombers," U.S. News and World Report; May 22, 1989, P. 23

49. "U.K. on Alert for New Iranian-Backed Terrorist Squad," London The Sunday Telegraph in English; March 12, 1989, P. 1

50. "U.S. Aide Defends Lockerbie Stand," New York Times; November 21, 1991. p. A14

51. "Israelis Remain Convinced Syria Downed Flight 103," New York Times; November 21, 1991. p. A14

52. "Closing in on the Pan Am Bombers," op.cit.

53. "Iranian May See Quake as Opening to the West," New York Times; June 28, 1990, P. A16

54. "Islamic Revolution Guards Again Claim Plane Bombing," Beirut Voice of Lebanon in Arabic; December 30, 1988

55. Ibid.; "Iran's Agents of Terror," U.S. News and World Report; March 6, 1989, P. 21

56. "Why Khomeini's Designated Heir Quit," op.cit.

57. Ibid.

58. "IRGC's Reza'i Comments on `Satanic Verses,'" Tehran Domestic Service in Persian; February 15, 1989

59. "Iran President Backs Foreign Minister Ahead of Peace Talks," Reuters, April 14, 1989

60. Roman Kolkowicz and Andrzej Korbonski, eds., *Soldiers, Peasants, and Bureaucrats* (London: George Allen and Unwin Ltd, 1982) Chaps. 5, 6

61. Adelman, op.cit., Chap. 3

62. John Ellis, *Armies in Revolution* (London: Croon Helm Ltd., 1973) Chap. 4

63. Richard Cobb, *The People's Armies* (New Haven and London: Yale University Press, 1987) pp. 543-66

64. "Commander of Iranian Guards Resigns," Washington Post; June 18, 1980

65. "I Have Conditionally Accepted Command of Corps," Tehran Islamic Republic excerpted in Tehran The Flame; July 1, 1980; "In Brief," Tehran The Flame; July 1, 1980

66. "IRGC Official Interviewed on Restructuring," Tehran Domestic Service in Persian; January 16, 1990; "The JDW Interview," Jane's Defence Weekly; November 16, 1991. p. 980

67. "IRGC Official Interviewed on Restructuring," op.cit.; "Armed Forces After Ceasefire," Tehran Echo of Iran; October 18, 1988

68. "Which Official Determines Iran's Foreign Policy," Tehran Echo of Iran; January 5, 1989, P. 7

69. "Hashemi-Rafsanjani Speaks on Future of IRGC," op.cit.; "Khamene'i Addresses IRGC Seminar," Tehran IRNA in English; September 15, 1988

70. "Iran Guards Leaders Slain in Violent Purge," op.cit.

71. "Majlis Candidates Warned on Use of Insignia for Publicity," Tehran Domestic Service in Persian; April 2, 1988

72. "Iran's Rebuilding Seen As Challenge to West," Washington Post; February 2, 1992. p. A1

7

Conclusions and Prospects

According to systematic criteria of institutionalization, the Revolutionary Guard has successfully completed a transition from an ad hoc, disorganized patchwork of revolutionary militias to one of Iran's most powerful and durable revolutionary institutions. However, unlike revolutionary armed forces forged in other major social revolutions, the Guard's institutionalization has not destroyed its ideological fervor. Moreover, the Guard has assumed the role of guardian of revolutionary purity to a greater degree than several of its historical counterparts. The Guard's tenacious hold on its ideological principles, and corresponding resistance to professionalization, runs counter to the theses of Chorley[1] and Adelman[2] that professionalization of revolutionary armed forces is virtually inevitable as an endstage of their institutional development. The concept of inevitable professionalization can be considered a subset of Weber's theory of the "routinization of charisma,"[3] in which ideological fervor invariably becomes dampened as institutionalization progresses.

Even though its revolutionary zeal remains, the Guard's institutionalization cannot be questioned. The Guard has proven a highly adaptable and resilient organization—according to Huntington, the first major criteria of institutionalization.[4] In its eleven year history, the Revolutionary Guard has parried political challenges not only from the liberal-nationalist and moderate politicians (below Khomeini) that governed Iran during 1979-81, but even from its erstwhile political allies such as Rafsanjani, who had worked well with and supported the Guard throughout most of the war against Iraq. Internally, the Guard has maintained its ideological character despite absorbing new social groups outside the core of lower middle class militants that formed the organization. These less ideological groups include conscripts, needed to fill the Guard's ranks during the war; "opportunists," attracted to the Guard's prestige and material benefits; and many of the Guard's technical experts and bureaucrats.[5] The Guard has also been able to work with Iran's regular military without adopting that institution's professional traditions or tactical and strategic doctrines. Moreover the Guard has shown itself able to adapt to new missions; initially an internal security force, it developed a military component when the war broke out. When the war—the Guard's prime source of influence and prestige ended—the Guard accepted a deterrent mission and it has played a major role in civilian reconstruction.

The Guard has similarly displayed Huntington's second criteria of institutionalization—complexity.[6] From a chaotic and disorganized political militia, the Guard has developed a well-defined organizational structure in conjunction with the expansion of its functions. The Guard's military component, at least in form, approximates that of a conventional army. The Guard established a Cabinet level Ministry to manage its wartime expansion. (The ministry has now been merged with that of the regular military.) In addition, a separate, if less visible or well defined, component was set up to handle the Guard's export of the revolution activities.

The increasing complexity of the Guard's organizational forms, however, has not translated into conventionalization or professionalization of its institutional character. The Guard's military force never abandoned its ideologically motivated unconventional tactics or moderated its maximalist war goals, even if political leaders imposed a cessation of hostilities. The Guard's export of the revolution apparatus, although more structured now than when the Guard assumed this function in 1982, is an organizational expression of the Guard's most hardline, ideological principles.

The Guard has also proven autonomous—a third major hallmark of institutionalization—in that it has largely resisted penetration and control by outside social and political groups and factions. Unlike many other Middle Eastern militaries, especially those of Syria, Iraq, and the Persian Gulf monarchies, the Guard is not dominated by any clan, family, or civilian political faction. The Guard has resisted civilian penetration and control over its internal affairs primarily by ensuring that the clerical oversight apparatus has remained either weak or in the hands of its allies. For example, the strong and effective radical, Abdollah Nuri, was replaced as Representative to the IRGC by the somewhat more pragmatic but far less forceful Hojjat ol-Eslam Araqi, who was too politically weak to effectively control the Guard leaders.[7] The Guard, as well as the Komitehs, periodically have cracked down on violators of Islamic behavior codes even though pragmatists such as Rafsanjani have tried to loosen such strictures as a means of encouraging popular cooperation in rebuilding the economy.[8] The Guard's autonomy has enabled it to undertake significant military and export of the revolution operations which, although not always directly in violation of specific orders, have appeared to undermine the policy goals and directions of clerical leaders below Khomeini.

As for the fourth and final measure of institutionalization, coherence, the Guard has similarly made substantial progress, although some vestiges of Guard factionalism remain. The Guard factions that competed with the Mojahedin of the Islamic Revolution for leadership of the early Guard have all virtually disappeared. The minor factionalism that remains within the Guard reflects the increase in the Guard's social diversity that has resulted from its wartime expansion rather than the existence of narrow, personally based groupings within the Guard. For example, the group of more moderate Guards that Rafsanjani was able to assign to Lebanon in early 1990[9] was almost certainly drawn from the pool of opportunists and conscripts the Guard needed to replace its heavy manpower losses during the war. Although the numerous examples of Guard interference in the political process may appear to represent the work of militant factions within the Guard, these actions have been supported by the highest levels of the organization and have reflected the ideological passion of the Guard as a whole. It is the entire organization that has resisted professionalization, not merely subsets within it.

According to these criteria, the Guard has demonstrated itself stronger than other revolutionary institutions in Iran. For example the Islamic Republican Party (IRP) was insufficiently adaptable or coherent to assume new functions, such as popular mobilization and interest articulation and aggregation, after it had fulfilled its initial role as channel through which the revolutionary political elites assumed their governing positions. It was disbanded in 1987. Even the institution of velayat-e-faqih (rule by the supreme Islamic jurisprudent), the institution created for and most closely identified with the charismatic leader, Ayatollah Khomeini, has been severely weakened by Khomeini's death. Khomeini's successor as velayat-e-faqih, Ayatollah Ali Khamene'i, has had to share power with the politically skilled President Rafsanjani and there have been reports that Rafsanjani's political allies are trying to undermine Khamene'i by insinuating that the position of supreme religious leader may eventually be eliminated.[10]

The Komitehs (revolutionary committees) which, like the Guard, constituted a revolutionary security force to consolidate clerical control, have not displayed nearly the institutional strength of the Guard, even if they, too, have retained their radical, ideological passions. The regime's decision and its ability to merge the Komitehs with the conventional security forces (police and gendarmerie) demonstrates the relative institutional weakness of the Komitehs.[11] Their lack of major participation in the war effort left the Komitehs without the unifying effect and prestige that service in the war had on the Guard, and Komitehs now have only about 16,000 employees nationwide.[12] (Far less than that of the police and gendarmerie, as well as the 300,000 man Guard.) Moreover, the Komiteh leadership has been far less powerful relative to civilian political leaders than have the Guard leaders; realizing he could not block the proposal, national Komiteh commander Seraj ad-Din Musavi resigned his post when the Komiteh-police merger was being debated.[13] It is especially significant that the Guard was able to defeat a comparable attempt by the civilian leadership to merge the Guard with the regular military in 1988-89.

Historical Parallels

If the Komitehs in Iran have retained their ideological character but not their institutional strength, revolutionary armed forces created during other major social revolutions have become powerful institutions but at the expense of ideological fervor. In contrast to the Guard, the French revolutionary army, Soviet Red Army, and Chinese People's Liberation Army became professionalized relatively shortly after the revolutions in which they were created. These forces based their organization and decisionmaking on rational and scientific rather than emotional criteria. They also swore fealty to the civilian leadership regardless of its policies and ceded the role of ideological guardian to other groups or institutions.

The chronological rapidity with which these other revolutionary forces professionalized refutes, to a great extent, the counterargument that it is only the Guard's young age (12 years) that accounts for its lack of professionalization and that, given time, the Guard, too, will become professionalized. However, it can be shown that time is less important in professionalization than the political dynamics of the initial formation of the revolutionary force and the exigencies of fighting revolutionary war. The Guard's counterparts were largely professionalized at the same chronological age as the Guard is now. The Guard has resisted the professionalizing effects of its revolutionary war (against Iraq) to a far greater degree than its counterparts resisted those effects in their revolutionary wars.

At the time of the restoration of the monarchy, the French revolutionary army was barely older than the Guard is now, yet the French army was fully professionalized in the course of the wars of the revolution. Even the "levees en masse," which were used to bolster the army's manpower and can be compared to the Guard's use of the Basij volunteers, do not necessarily detract from the argument that the French revolutionary army was professional. Ellis argues that, far from turning France into a "nation in arms," the levees en masse, used to bolster the army's manpower, relied heavily on conscription and did not represent a massive outpouring of popular revolutionary fervor, even if the levees did have substantial popular support.[14] The structure of the prerevolutionary army was never abolished or subordinated into a new revolutionary army, but rather the old army structure was preserved to the greatest extent possible in order to maintain discipline and control over the armed conscripts.[15] The French revolutionary army was therefore a larger, more enthusiastic, and militarily more effective version of the old army.

Paradoxically, the French revolution and subsequent wars actually facilitated rather than obstructed army professionalism. The principle of aristocratic exclusivity was ended in 1790, opening up the officer corps to talented and professional soldiers rather than a privileged but less competent elite. The Napoleonic officer corps was firmly supportive of the revolution, but officer support was based at least as much on self interest and perceived career opportunity as on fundamental ideological commitment. After Napoleon's takeover—and even though his ascension represented the uppermost extreme in military involvement in politics—professionalism was valued even more highly because Napoleon himself was a supreme example of a military professional. Moreover, the revolution was at least partly a product of rationalist and enlightened intellectual thought, and the belief in scientific and objective factors rather than revealed knowledge. Thus, the very basis of the revolution itself, when applied to the French revolutionary army, could only hasten the drive for professionalization. The Revolutionary Guard, in contrast, was a product of an exactly opposite process—a revolution against pragmatic objectivity and in favor of charismatically inspired emotional and religious passions.

The Soviet Red Army similarly was professionalized by the time it was chronologically as old as the Guard is now. This rapid professionalization was necessitated by the civil war against the remnants of the Czarist army during 1917-20. Like the French revolutionary army, the Red Army was created from the structure of the old army, and many officers, non-commissioned officers (NCOs), and rank and file soldiers of the Czarist army were incorporated into the new Red Army. Among revolutionary elements, the Red Guards, the Bolshevik militias that helped the Party seize power in 1917, and peasant volunteers joined the new army as well, stiffening the loyalty and ideological commitment of the holdovers from the old army. The commissariat system and party cells began to infiltrate and take hold of the new army shortly after the revolution.

Specific decisions of the political leadership also contributed to the rapid professionalization of the Red Army. As People's Commissar for Military Affairs (essentially head of the Red Army), Leon Trotsky, supported by Lenin, forcefully advocated professionalism at the expense of revolutionary purity as the optimum means by which to ensure the security of the revolution against its internal and external foes. In the formation of the Red Army and in fighting the civil war, Trotsky's view won out over those of others, including Stalin, who advocated guerrilla tactics, a thorough purge of former Czarist officers, and the primacy of unit commissars over the officers.[16] Those proposals advocating conventional, professional organization, tactics, doctrine, recruitment, promotion, and internal hierarchy were consistently adopted by the party leadership.[17] For example, the radical, anti-professional principle of election of officers by the rank and file was abolished in 1918.[18] Once in power and facing

Hitler's war machine, even Stalin recognized the value of a professional Red Army and he replaced many of the old party stalwarts with the more competent, experienced commanders needed to defeat the German army.

In the case of the Red Army, therefore, as in the case of the French revolutionary army, professionalization was achieved shortly after the revolution. Ideology was dampened by the preservation of old army structures and command elements and sacrificed by national leaders in order to achieve the objective efficiency and effectiveness needed to defend the revolution and the nation. Both of these factors, those both external and intrinsic to the organization, were absent or weak in the case of the Guard.

The People's Liberation Army in China followed a different developmental path than that of the French revolutionary and Soviet Red Army in that the PLA was formed in order to help bring the Communist Party of China to power rather than to secure its accomplished victory. Once the Communist Party finally triumphed in 1949, the PLA was already well established and well organized. The Korean War, which began shortly after the Communist takeover in China, furthered the process of professionalization in the PLA. Because it defeated and eliminated rather than superimposed itself on a preexisting army, the PLA, like the Guard, was composed almost exclusively of revolutionary fighters.

During the struggle against the Nationalist armies of Chiang Kai-Shek, Mao Zedong apparently delegated considerable operational authority to commanders, and emphasized military competence.[19] In the Korean War, the PLA commander in Korea, Peng Teh-huai, abandoned traditional guerrilla tactics, modernized the PLA's logistics system, and increased emphasis on firepower—all hallmarks of greater professionalization.[20] According to Adelman, ". . . a professional, modern, and powerful Chinese army emerged from the Korean War in 1953 to replace the primitive guerrilla force that entered the war in 1950."[21]

The transformation of the PLA from a highly ideological and politicized to a more professional force was evidenced by its behavior in the Cultural Revolution of the late 1960s. In 1967, instead of intervening to bolster radical elements as ordered by Mao, many PLA units acted to restore local political stability by containing the excesses of the radical, armed, Red Guards.[22] In doing so, the army gained substantial political influence but forfeited any possible claim to the role of guardian of the ideological purity of the Chinese Communist revolution. Like a professional force, the PLA, reluctant to intervene in an internal political struggle at all, had opted for stability. Although it did intervene, it must be noted that this intervention was at the behest of the civilian leadership, and not self generated. The PLA's role in the Cultural Revolution was at the behest of Mao, who trusted the PLA more than he did the less controllable Red Guards.[23] By contrast, the Revolutionary Guard, although its political involvements have been less direct, has undertaken its political activities largely on its own initiative.

The Guard is able to act of its own volition because it is not penetrated or controlled by a highly disciplined, structured, party apparatus such as exists in the Soviet Union and People's Republic of China. This autonomy on the part of the Guard can be traced to its initial formation. Unlike the Red Army or PLA, the Guard was not created by the civilian revolutionary party. The Guard had its own independent roots in the revolution. Its precursors fought with Khomeini and the revolutionary clerics, but the Guard militias entered the revolutionary movement of their own accord, with their own agendas, and with their own independent command structure.

As further comparison, the Guard was able to emerge as guardian of the revolution's ideological values as well as security because it had no strongly unified civilian party claiming to represent ideological orthodoxy. Such parties existed in the case of the Red Army and PLA, thus leaving these armies no opportunities to claim the role of revolutionary vanguard. In Iran, however, revolutionary purity was defined by the charismatic leader, Khomeini, and not by the divided revolutionary clerical establishment as a whole. Therefore, those hardline elements, especially the Guard, which consistently upheld Khomeini's hardline vision could best claim to represent ideological purity. The role of ideological vanguard did not flow from structural or institutional position alone.

The French revolutionary army, Soviet Red Army, and PLA emerged from their revolutionary wars as professionalized forces, but the Guard, although less politically active since Khomeini's 1989 death, is little more professional now than before the war with Iraq broke out in 1980. It is more organized, cohesive, and well armed, but it is not professional and it has retained its highly radical, ideological character. It lacks the major hallmarks of a professionalized force—military decisionmaking on the basis of scientific and objective rather than emotional or ideological criteria and loyalty to the civilian leadership regardless of its policies. A corollary of the generally apolitical nature of a professional force—and a trait exhibited by the Guard's counterparts but not the Guard—is an unwillingness to engage in the suppression of civil unrest. The Guard's failure to meet the criteria of a professionalized force and the durability of its ideological commitment can be demonstrated through an examination of its actions, particularly those which occurred toward the conclusion of the Iran-Iraq war and since the ceasefire in 1988.

Continuing Radicalism

Strong evidence for the ideological rather than scientific basis of Guard decisionmaking is provided by the continuing domination of the Guard by radical ideologues. Despite accepting blame for several of the major battlefield defeats that forced Iran to accept a ceasefire, the radical Mohsen Reza'i still commands the Guard, and his hardline proteges such as Rahim Safavi, and Ali Reza Afshar remain in key positions. Hardline Reza'i allies Ali Shamkhani and Abbas Mohtaj have gained control of Iran's regular Navy and former Guard commander in Lebanon, Hosein Dehqan, was until recently commander of the Guard Air Force.[24] The only major Guard leader who lost his position as a result of the war defeats was, paradoxically, the least radical and most pragmatic of all—former Guard Minister Mohsen RafiqDust. However, he now heads a revolutionary institution, the Foundation for the Oppressed, that has worked closely with the Guard and he has apparently regained some military procurement responsibilities in the armed forces general headquarters staff.[25]

The Guard's unorthodox warfighting tactics and strategies did not fundamentally change throughout the war, even if its military organization and cohesiveness did mature during the conflict. The Guard employed its characteristic, high casualty human wave offensives spearheaded by lightly armed Basij volunteers up until the end of the war. When recruitment fell off as a result of the heavy casualties taken in its offensives (especially the 1987 Karbala 5 assault), the Guard's failure to shift to more conventional, artillery and armor-based tactics undoubtedly contributed heavily to Iran's defeats in 1988. The Guard is now increasingly working with and looking to procure conventional heavy weapons, such as advanced aircraft, and, in any future combat, it would likely make greater use of conventional tactics than it did during the Iran-Iraq war.

Some of the Guard's naval activities in 1987-88 similarly demonstrate the pre-eminence of ideology and politics in Guard decisionmaking during the Iran-Iraq war. Most notably, on April 18, 1988, Iranian naval vessels, commanded by or on orders from the Guard, counterattacked against the overwhelmingly more powerful U.S. Navy, which was conducting a retaliatory strike off the Iranian coast.[26] The Iranian naval assault, which would almost certainly not have been launched against such odds by a more professional command structure, resulted in the loss of about 20% of Iran's major naval warships.[27]

Perhaps the most telling example of the Guard's willingess to place ideology over objective military considerations was its opposition to accepting a ceasefire in July 1988 following successive battlefield defeats. Despite losing all the positions captured from Iraq during the war, the reentry of Iraqi forces into Iran, and the virtual collapse of its units, the Guard leaders and rank and file wanted to continue the war and even still believed that victory was ultimately possible.[28]

The Guard also belies its unprofessionalism in its consistent involvement in politics, often in contradiction to the policy directions set by its civilian superiors. As explained above, the Guard has gone far beyond its counterparts in other societies in the degree to which it claims the role of bastion and protector of the ideological purity of the revolution and the policies of the late Ayatollah Khomeini. Although waning popular enthusiasm for the revolution has weakened the Guard's influence and opportunities for radical political behavior, there are still several recent examples in which the Guard has acted to implement a radical policy line even, and sometimes especially, when doing so undermines or countermands the orders of political leaders.

A prime target of the Guard's political involvement has been President Ali Akbar Hashemi-Rafsanjani, whose willingess to sacrifice ideology to achieve pragmatic objectives fundamentally conflicts with the Guard's philosophy. After the war, credible reports emerged that the Guard had attempted to assassinate him because of his role in ending the war and his related efforts to weaken the Guard (a major opponent of the ceasefire).[29] Another apparent attempt by the Guard on Rafsanjani's life was made in the aftermath of the June 1990 earthquake in Iran. The Guard was, in part, reacting to Rafsanjani's attempts to use the earthquake and Western emergency relief to improve political ties to the West.[30]

The Guard has also promoted its radical agenda less directly, if not at least equally violently. In an effort to block any post-war rapprochement between Iran and the West, and to obtain revenge for the U.S. downing of an Iranian Airbus in July 1988, the Guard commissioned the bombing of an American commercial jet, even if international investigators now believe that Libya was primarily responsible for the actual placement of the bomb aboard Pan Am Flight 103 in December 1988.[31] In early 1989 the Guard beat up a Foreign Ministry official who it considered insufficiently revolutionary.[32] The Guard supported its ally and protege, Hizballah, in that group's conflict with the rival group Amal in Lebanon during 1987-1990 even as Iran's Foreign Ministry, other pragmatic Iranian leaders, and Syria were trying to broker ceasefires and a permanent settlement between the two Shia groups.[33] (It appeared as though the Iranian negotiators did not want repeated violations of the ceasefires nd that the Guard, in backing up Hizballah, was acting against its civilian leaders' wishes.) Militarily, after gaining control of the regular Iranian Navy in June 1990, the Guard, through the longtime Guard leader and now regular and Guard Navy Commander Ali Shamkhani, threatened to prevent Iraqi warships from sailing in the Persian Gulf, and Iran is widely reported to be seeking to procure modern submarines.[34] Shamkhani's threat was virtually simultaneous, and contradictory, with Rafsanjani's efforts to advance a final peace settlement with Iraq.[35]

Internally, the Guard has continued to support and participate in ideo-logically-charged anti-U.S. demonstrations, such as those commemorat-ing the takeover of the U.S. Embassy in 1979. The Guard still uses the Embassy compound as a training ground, command post, and a distribu-tion center for the anti-U.S. propaganda it publishes.[36] Moreover, in clear contrast to its professionalized foreign counterparts that are reluctant to engage in the suppression of civil unrest, the Guard continues to be not only willing but eager to violently suppress popular opposition to the regime and the principles of the revolution. In 1991, it has done so repeat-edly in the face of anti-regime demonstrators protesting poor economic conditions. In addition to putting down demonstrations, the Guard, as well as the Komitehs, have cracked down on violators of Islamic behavior codes even though pragmatists such as Rafsanjani have tried to loosen such strictures.[37] A truly professional force views its mission as protection of the nation and not in determining internal political outcomes. To the Guard, there is no such distinction, and it therefore displays no hesitation in involving itself in internal affairs, with or without invitation or orders from civilian authorities.

Further evidence of the Guard's continuing radicalism was provided by its actions during and just after the 1991 Persian Gulf war. Rafsanjani and much of the civilian leadership were trying to steer a neutral course in the U.S.-Iraq conflict, probably to gain financial and political benefits from the West when the war ended. In statements during the allied air war against Iraq, the Guard leadership generally acknowledged that Iran should remain neutral but they abhorred the killing of fellow Muslims in Iraq by coalition bomb attacks. It is consistent with its past ideological positions that the Guard was critical of the United States yet not more supportive of Iraq. Iraq had been the Guard's mortal enemy for eight years and the Guard still harbored hopes of fulfilling Khomeini's vision by overthrowing the Ba'thist regime in Baghdad, or, alternately, establish-ing an Islamic republic in Shia southern Iraq.

After the war, and despite Rafsanjani's efforts at restraint, the Guard supported its proteges—Iraqi Shia guerrillas belonging to the Supreme Assembly for the Islamic Revolution in Iraq (SAIRI) in the post-war rebel-lion against the Iraqi government.[38] It is possible that Rafsanjani's appar-ent opposition to Iran's intervention in southern Iraq accounts for the Guard's failure to intervene more directly and forcefully. The leader of SAIRI, Muhammad Baqr al-Hakim, attributed the failure of the Shia rebel-lion to the lack of sufficient support from Tehran, an apparent reference to Rafsanjani's opposition to helping the rebellion. Moreover, although the Guard remained viscerally anti-American, it was far too weak to risk a battle with the U.S. troops then occupying southern Iraq. (In July 1991, the Guard did undertake a minor naval attack against a U.S. ship in the Gulf, the U.S.S. La Salle, although it was reported that the Guard later "apologized" for the attack.)[39]

Prospects for the Revolutionary Guard

The Guard is likely to remain a highly ideological and relatively unprofessional force for the foreseeable future, but the current, less radical political climate in Iran will likely further weaken the Guard's political influence in the regime. The Guard's ideological commitment is still strong, but Iranian society and politics have become less ideological since the end of the war and the death of Khomeini and pragmatic politicians have ascended despite opposition from the Guard and other radicals. For now, Rafsanjani has successfully articulated the case that Iran must moderate its policies to attract the Western investment and credit it needs to improve the population's standard of living. The post-Khomeini regime has approved limited borrowing from the West; Rafsanjani has engineered the release of the American hostages in Lebanon despite radical opposition; and several prominent radicals and Guard allies, such as Ali Akbar Mohtashemi-Pur, Behzad Nabavi, and Abol Qasem Sarhadizadeh were excluded from the post-Khomeini Cabinet or lost their bids for seats in the Majles in April 1992.[40] Moreover, whereas at the height of the war the Guard and radical politicians drove the policy agenda, the radicals are now in the negative role of attempting to obstruct compromises initiated by more moderate leaders.

There may even be the first signs that the waning of revolutionary fervor in Iran is impacting the Guard internally. The early 1990 approval of ranks in the Revolutionary Guard—and the 1992 appointment of regular military officer Hosein Jalali to head the Guard Air Force—may represent recognition on the part of the Guard that ideological fervor alone can no longer ensure organizational loyalty or attract recruits.[41] However, given the continuation of radical actions and statements by the Guard—albeit less frequent than at the height of the Guard's power during the war—the approval of ranks represents weak evidence that the Guard's ideological character is giving way to professionalization. Moreover, it has been reported that the Guard accepted ranks in order to appease the civilian leadership, which has sought to professionalize the Guard.[42] That the civilian leadership was able to effect some internal change within the Guard does, however, represent some erosion of Guard autonomy.

Given the Guard's continued radicalism in a moderating Iran, it is essential to project its future role and activities. First and foremost, the Guard is unlikely to assemble its forces in an all-out bid for direct political power in Iran. However, if the clerical regime as a whole were threatened by popular opposition, the Guard could take control in order to put down a major revolt. In the absence of such a popular uprising, a coup against the clerical leadership would violate Khomeini's legacy of clerical rule, and violating Khomeini's ideals is tantamount to countermanding the very ideology on which the Guard's own legitimacy rests. Moreover, even in its crusade to maintain the purity of the revolution, the Guard has not threatened or demonstrated a desire to take power itself. Rather, the Guard has generally acted indirectly—supporting its radical political allies and undertaking politically motivated military and export of the revolution operations in order to embarrass pragmatic and moderate civilian leaders.

However, if Rafsanjani or other pragmatic political leaders try to compromise the principles of Khomeini and the revolution or weaken the Guard directly, a Guard assassination attempt against these leaders cannot be ruled out. If such an assassination attempt were to succeed, the Guard would likely help elevate its radical political allies such as Mohtashemi-Pur or Ahmad Khomeini to power. More likely, however, is the possibility that the Guard may arrest or detain lower level pragmatists and Rafsanjani aides as a means of intimadating the Guard's internal opponents. Even it does not act violently or directly against Rafsanjani and other pragmatic leaders, the Guard is likely to continue to mobilize support for radical policies and politicians and to undermine pragmatic political leaders where possible. The Guard leaders will likely continue to issue hardline statements, recommend radical policy options, and participate and rally the public in official demonstrations, such as those held on the anniversary of the U.S. Embassy seizure and the death of Ayatollah Khomeini. In return for its cooperation or acquiescence in pragmatic policy initiatives, the Guard will likely demand additional weapons purchases or the placement of Guard commanders in key positions in the regular military as a means of gaining control of the regular forces.

The Guard's primary weapon for undermining Iranian pragmatists, however, will continue to be the use of overt or covert military or terrorist actions intended to derail progress toward compromise with Iran's adversaries or injure its normal relations with friendly or neutral governments. For example, the Guard retains its extensive covert network abroad with which it can continue to assassinate Saudi diplomats.[43] Iranian embassies in Lebanon, Pakistan, Syria, Thailand, Ethiopia, and throughout the Arab world, Asia, Africa, and Europe contain current or former Guards who continue to report to senior Guard commanders and Guard allies in the Foreign Ministry.[44] Because of this extensive network, a Guard-inspired operation such as another bombing of a U.S. commercial jet cannot be ruled out, nor can a terrorist attack on facilities or politicians inside the

United States; in 1987 the FBI announced that members of the Guard had entered the United States as students.[45] The Iranian Navy, which is controlled by the Guard, has acquired modern submarines; an attack on a U.S. or other Western ship cannot be ruled out, if only to reverse any emerging rapprochement between the United States and Iran. The Guard may replay the "Chaplin Affair," intimidating foreign diplomats in Tehran in retaliation for Western punitive acts against Iranian agents abroad. In late 1991, the Guard may have been responsible for placing pressure on the Swiss Embassy in Tehran in retaliation for Switzerland's arrest of an Iranian suspected of involvement in the August 1991 assassination of former Iranian Prime Minister Shahpur Bakhtiar (an assassination that may have been carried out by Guard agents).[46]

The Guard is also likely to continue arming, training, and fighting in support of Hizballah in Lebanon despite the apparent efforts of Iranian pragmatists, in concert with Syria, to effect a withdrawal of the Guard from Lebanon. A more extreme but less likely possibility is that the Guard, to prevent an improvement in U.S.-Iranian relations, will encourage Hizballah to resume the taking of American hostages in Lebanon.

There is also a possibility that the Guard, in the wake of Iraq's military weakness resulting from the 1991 Gulf war, will try to fulfill Khomeini's unfinished agenda of establishing an Islamic republic in Iraq. There are reports that Iran is undertaking a major conventional buildup and it is possible that, once the buildup is complete, the Guard will push for direct military action against Iraqi forces as a means of fulfilling Khomeini's goals.[47] Similarly, the Guard may give greater support to Shia rebels in Southern Iraq as well as increasingly powerful Islamic fundamentalist movements in Algeria, Tunisia, Jordan, Egypt, the Muslim republics of the former USSR, Afghanistan, and the West Bank and Gaza. There are reports that the Guard is already establishing a significant presence (1,000-2,000 Guards) in the increasingly Islamic fundamentalist Sudan, setting up camps to train the Sudanese army and "Islamic fundamntalist militants from Algeria, Tunisian, Egypt, and the Persian Gulf region."[48] In a late 1991 interview, Reza'i said the Guard's role is "helping Muslims everywhere, since we are an Islamic army," and, referring to the Guard's close relationship with Pakistan, "if there is unity between Iran, Pakistan, and Afghanistan, this will strengthen Muslim solidarity and enable the peoples of Soviet Central Asia and Kashmir to join in."[49] Iran has already become highly active in establishing political and economic ties to and promoting Islam in the Muslim republics of the former Soviet Union[50] and it is possible that the Guard will militarily support Islamic militants who might try to wrest power from the secular elites that dominate the republics. Islamic movements are becoming increasingly powerful in several of the republics.

The Guard may also seek to capitalize on the resentment of religious conservatives in Saudi Arabia toward the U.S. military presence there. The Guard could also exploit resentment in Kuwait, Bahrain, and Qatar against the defense pacts those countries have signed with the United States. Such activities, however, would aggravate tensions between the Guard and Rafsanjani, who has been trying to use the split between the Gulf states and Iraq to improve Iran's ties to the Gulf states and obtain financial aid from them. The Guard undoubtedly contributed to Iran's decision in 1992 to seize virtual control of Abu Musa Island, which it shared with the United Arab Emirates—a move that set back an improving relationship between Iran and the Gulf states.

Future expressions of the Guard's politically and ideologically motivated radicalism, such as those postulated above, will likely take place even, and perhaps especially, if the Guard continues to lose out in the political process. That the internal political context within which the Guard is operating is increasingly less radical and favorable to the Guard does not automatically translate into the Guard's political quiescence or greater professionalization. Rather, the diminished revolutionary fervor among the population and the resulting ascendancy of pragmatic political leaders limits the Guard's ability to undertake its radical activities openly and with civilian sanction. In response, the Guard may increasingly operate outside the political system and it may undertake operations more bold, violent, and radical than those it advocated when Iran's revolutionary sentiment ran higher and the Guard's influence in the government decisionmaking process was greater.

Notes

1. Katharine Chorley, *Armies and the Art of Revolution* (Boston: Beacon Press, 1973) Chapters 11, 12

2. Jonathan Adelman, *Revolution, Armies, and War: A Political History* (Boulder, Co.: Lynne Rienner Publishers, Inc., 1985) pp. 203-5

3. H.H. Gerth and C. Wright Mills, *From Max Weber: Essays in Sociology* (New York: Oxford University Press, 1946) pp. 51-5

4. Samuel P. Huntington, *Political Order in Changing Societies* (New Haven and London: Yale University Press, 1968) Chapter 1

5. See Chapter 3

6. Huntington, op.cit.

7. "Khamene'i Appoints New IRGC Representative," Tehran IRNA in English; June 26, 1990

8. "Aftershocks in Tehran," *Newsweek*; July 9, 1990, P. 39

9. "Rafsanjani Losing Influence Over Shiite Militants," Washington Post; January 8, 1990, P. A17

10. "Iran's Leaders Achieve a Subtle Balance of Power," New York Times; July 24, 1990, P. A3

11. "Bayan on Merger of Law Enforcement Forces," Tehran Bayan in Persian, No.2; Jun-July, 1990, pp. 16-17 in FBIS; August 28, 1990, pp. 73-5

12. "Majles Commission Debates Security Forces Merger," Tehran Resalat in Persian; May 26, 1990, pp. 5-11 in FBIS; June 21, 1990, pp. 48-51

13. "Khamene'i Names Kalantari IRC Commander," Tehran IRNA in English; June 20, 1990

14. John Ellis, *Armies in Revolution* (London: Croon Helm, Ltd., 1973) pp. 95-7

15. Ibid, pp. 101-2

16. D. Fedotoff White, *The Growth of the Red Army* (Princeton, Princeton University Press, 1944) P. 53; Ellis, op.cit., P. 181

17. Ellis, op.cit., P. 187

18. Ibid, P. 189

19. Adelman, op.cit., pp. 161-2

20. Ibid, P. 167

21. Ibid

22. Ellis Joffe, "The Military as a Political Actor in China," in Roman Kolkowicz and Andrzej Korbonski, eds., *Soldiers, Peasants and Bureaucrats* (London: George Allen and Unwin, 1982) P. 145

23. James Hsiung, *Ideology and Practice: The Evolution of Chinese Communism* (New York and London: Praeger Publishers, Inc., 1970)

24. "Mohtaj Named Commander of Naval Forces," Tehran Jomhuri-Ye Eslami in Persian; April 19, 1990, P.4 in FBIS; June 8, 1990, P. 37; "Air Force Commander's Resignation Reported," London Keyhan in Persian; May 3, 1990, P.2 in FBIS; May 14, 1990, P. 49

25. "Iran After Arms," Middle East Today, No. 194, February 6, 1992.

26. "Signs of Split Seen in Iran's Counterattack on US Navy," Christian Science Monitor; April 20, 1988, P. 7

27. Ibid

28. "U.S. Rejected Proposed Sale of F-5's to Iran," Washington Post; October 20, 1988, P. A1

29. "Three Recent Attempts to Kill Rafsanjani," Kuwait Times in English; January 11, 1990

30. "President Reportedly Escapes Assassination," Paris AFP in English; July 1, 1990

31. "Closing in on the Pan Am Bombers," *US News and World Report;* May 22, 1989, P. 23; "U.S. Measures Iran's New Radicalism," Christian Science Monitor; April 18, 1989

32. "Why Khomeini's Designated Heir Quit," Washington Post; April 10, 1989, P. D8
33. "Thousands Demonstrate Against Pasdaran Presence," London Keyhan in Persian; August 2, 1990, pp. 1,3 in FBIS; August 28, 1990, P. 71
34. "Navy to Bar Iraqi Frigates From Gulf," Tehran IRNA in English; June 12, 1990; "Iran's Rebuilding Seen as Challenge to West," Washington Post, February 2, 1992. p. A1
35. "Mohtashemi Accuses Leadership of `Demagoguery'," Paris AFP in English; July 18, 1990
36. "Slow Day at the Spy Shop in Tehran: Is it a Sign?," New York Times; June 29, 1990, P. A3
37. "Aftershocks in Tehran," op.cit.
38. "U.S. Threatens to Down Any Iraqi Combat Aircraft," Washington Post, March 16, 1991. p. A1
39. "Iranian Attack," London Times, July 15, 1991. p. 11
40. "Freed Hostage Reports Seeing 3 Others in Lebanon," New York Times; August 26, 1990, P. 6; "Rafsanjani Sweeps Out Hard-Liners," Washington Post; August 20, 1989, P. A1
41. "IRGC, Basijis Titles, Ranks Announced," Tehran Jomhuri -Ye Eslami in Persian; May 7, 1990, P.2 in FBIS; July 25, 1990, pp. 60-2
42. "The JDW Interview," Jane's Defence Weekly, November 16, 1991. p. 980
43. "Reporter Names Iranian Diplomats as Intelligence Agents," London Al Dustur in Arabic; February 12, 1990, pp. 8-9 in FBIS; March 30, 1990, pp. 69-72; "Al Dustur Claims Envoy Bangkok Intelligence Agent," London Al Dustur in Arabic; January 22, 1990, P.3 in FBIS; February 20, 1990, P. 73
44. Ibid
45. "Iran Guards in U.S., FBI Says," New York Times; March 9, 1989
46. "Iran Restricts Envoys of the Swiss, Who in Turn Close Their Embassy," New York Times, December 30, 1991; "Iran: People's Mojahedin Accuse Pasdaran of Bakhtiar Murder, FBIS, August 12, 1991. p. A7
47. "Iran's Rebuilding Seen as Challenge to West," Washington Post, February 2, 1992. p. A1
48. "Iran Shifting Its Attention From Lebanon to Sudan," The New York Times, December 13, 1991. p. A7
49. "The JDW Interview," op.cit.
50. "U.S. to Counter Iran in Central Asia," New York Times, February 6, 1992. p. A3

Bibliography

Theoretical Works

Adelman, Jonathan *Revolution, Armies, and War: A Political History* Boulder, Co.: Lynne Rienner Publishers, Inc., 1985

Almond, Gabriel and Sidney Verba *The Civic Culture* Princeton: Princeton University Press, 1963

Barnes, Samuel "Ideology and the Organization of Conflict: On the Relationship Between Political Thought and Behavior" *Journal of Politics* Vol. 28, No. 3, 1966

Brinton, Crane *Anatomy of Revolution* New York: Vintage Books, 1965

Chorley, Katharine *Armies and the Art of Revolution* Boston: Beacon Press, 1973

Cohan, A.S. *Theories of Revolution: An Introduction* London: Thomas Nelson and Sons Ltd., 1975

Deutsch, Karl W. "Social Mobilization and Political Development," in *American Political Science Review* No. 55, September 1961

Durkheim, Emile *Suicide: A Study in Sociology* Glencoe, Illinois: Free Press, 1951

Eisenstadt, S.N. "Initial Institutional Patterns of Political Modernization," in *Civilizations* Nos. 12, 13 1962, 1963

Eisenstadt, S.N. "Institutionalization and Change," in *American Sociological Review*, Vol. 26, No. 2, April 1964

Ellis, John *Armies in Revolution* London: Croon Helm Ltd., 1973

Enayat, Hamid *Modern Islamic Political Thought* Austin: University of Texas Press, 1982

Finer, S.E. *The Man on Horseback: The Role of the Military in Politics* London and Dunmow: Pall Mall, 1962

Gerth, H.H. and Mills, C. Wright *From Max Weber: Essays* in *Sociology* New York: Oxford University Press, 1946

Halpern, Manfred "Middle Eastern Armies and the New Middle Class" in John Johnson ed. *The Role of the Military in Underdeveloped Countries* Princeton: Princeton University Press, 1962

Harries-Jenkins, Gwyn and Jacques Van Doorn eds. *The Military and the Problem of Legitimacy* The International Sociological Association London and California: Sage Publications, 1976

Huntington, Samuel P. *The Soldier and the State* Cambridge, Mass.: Harvard University Press, 1959

Huntington, Samuel P. *The Changing Patterns of Military Politics* New York: Free Press, 1962

Huntington, Samuel P. *Political Order in Changing Societies* New Haven and London: Yale University Press, 1968

Jaguaribe, Helio *Political Development: A General Theory and a Latin American Case Study* New York: Harper and Row, 1973

Janowitz, Morris *The Military in the Political Development of New Nations* Chicago: University of Chicago Press, 1964

Janowitz, Morris *Military Institutions and Coercion in the Developing Nations* Chicago and London: University of Chicago Press, 1977

Johnson, John *The Role of the Military in Underdeveloped Countries* Princeton: Princeton University Press, 1962

Khuri, Fuad "Civil-Military Relations in Modernizing Societies in the Middle East" in Roman Kolkowicz and Andrzej Korbonski *Soldiers, Peasants, and Bureaucrats* London: Allen and Unwin, 1982

Parsons, Talcott *The Structure of Social Action* New York: McGraw Hill, 1937

Parsons, Talcott *Essays in Sociological Theory* Glencoe, Illinois: Free Press, 1954

Perlmutter, Amos "Civil-Military Relations in Socialist Authoritarian and Praetorian States; Prospects and Retrospects," in Roman Kolkowicz and Andrzej Korbonski eds., *Soldiers, Peasants, and Bureaucrats* London: Allen and Unwin, 1982

Perlmutter, Amos and Valerie Plave Bennett eds. *The Political Influence of the Military* New Haven and London: Yale University Press, 1980

Przeworski, Adam "Institutionalization of Voting Patterns, or Is Mobilization the Source of Decay? in *American Political Science Review*, 69, 1975

Pye, Lucien "Armies in the Process of Political Modernization" in John Johnson ed. *The Role of the Military in Underdeveloped Countries* Princeton: Princeton University Press, 1962

Pye, Lucien *Aspects of Political Development* Boston: Little, Brown, and Co., 1966

Rappoport, David "The Praetorian Army" in Roman Kolkowicz and Andrzej Korbonski eds., *Soldiers, Peasants, and Bureaucrats* London: Allen and Unwin, 1982

Starbuck, William "Organizational Growth and Development," in James March, *Handbook of Organizations* Chicago, Rand McNally, 1965

Tilly, Charles "Does Modernization Breed Revolution?," *Comparative Politics*, April 1973

Tilly, Charles *From Mobilization to Revolution* Reading, Mass.: Addison Wesley, 1978

Weiner, Myron and Joseph LaPalombara *Political Parties and Political Development* Princeton: Princeton University Press, 1966

Works on Iran/Middle East

Abrahamian, Ervand *The Iranian Mojahedin* New Haven and London: Yale University Press, 1989

Ajami, Fouad "Iran: The Impossible Revolution" in *Foreign Affairs* Fall 1988

Akhavi, Shahrough "Institutionalizing the New Order in Iran" in *Current History*, 86, 1987

Akhavi, Shahrough "Elite Factionalism in the Islamic Republic of Iran" in *The Middle East Journal*, 41, 1987

Ashraf, Ahmad and Ali Banuazizi "The State, Classes and Modes of Mobilization in the Iranian Revolution" in *State, Culture, and Society*, 1, 1985

Bakhash, Shaul *The Reign of the Ayatollahs* New York: Basic Books, 1984

Benard, Cheryl and Zalmay Khalilzad *The Government of God: Iran's Islamic Republic* New York: Columbia University Press, 1984

Constitution of the Islamic Republic of Iran reprinted in *The Middle East Journal* Spring 1980

Cottam, Richard *Nationalism in Iran* Pittsburgh: University of Pittsburgh Press, 1964

Cottam, Richard *Khomeini, the Future, and US Options* Policy Paper 38, The Stanley Foundation, December 1987

Graham, Robert *Iran: The Illusion of Power* New York: St. Martin's Press, 1980

Halliday, Fred *Iran: Dictatorship and Development* New York: Penguin Books, 1979

Helms, Christine *Iraq: Eastern Flank of the Arab World* Washington, D.C.: The Brookings Institution, 1984

Hiro, Dilip *Iran Under the Ayatollahs* London and New York: Routledge and Kegan Paul, 1985

Iran Almanac 1987 Tehran: Echo of Iran, 1987

Iran Yearbook 1988 Tehran: Echo of Iran, 1988

Kazemi, Farhad, "The Iranian Revolution: Seven Years Later" *Middle East Insight*, 5, 1987

Kazemi, Farhad *Politics and Culture in Iran* Ann Arbor: Center for Political Studies, Institute for Social Research, University of Michigan, 1988

Keddie, Nikkie *Iran: Roots of Revolution* New Haven: Yale University Press, 1981

Keddie, Nikkie and Eric Hooglund eds. *The Iranian Revolution and the Islamic Republic* Syracuse: Syracuse University Press, 1986

Kessler, Martha *Syria: Fragile Mosaic of Power* Washington, D.C.: National Defense University, 1988

Khomeini, Ruhollah *Speeches and Declarations of Ayatollah Khomeini* Berkeley: Mizan Press, 1981

Kramer, Martin *Shi'ism, Resistance, and Revolution* Boulder, Co.: Westview Press, 1987

Kramer, Martin "Tragedy in Mecca" in *Orbis*, No. 32 Spring 1988

Ledeen, Michael *Perilous Statecraft: An Insider's Account of the Iran-Contra Affair* New York: Macmillan Publishing Co., 1988

Menashri, David "Iran" in Colin Legum et. al. eds. *Middle East Contemporary Survey* vol. III New York: Holmes and Meier, 1978-79

Mitchell, Richard *Society of the Muslim Brothers* London: Oxford University Press, 1969

Mottahedeh, Roy *The Mantle of the Prophet: Religion and Politics in Iran* New York: Simon and Schuster, 1985

Ramazani, R.K. *Revolutionary Iran: Challenge and Response in the Middle East* Baltimore: Johns Hopkins University Press, 1986

Report of the President's Special Review Board (The Tower Commission Report) US Government Printing Office, 1987

Sciolino, Elaine "Iran's Durable Revolution" in *Foreign Affairs* Vol. 61, No. 4, Spring 1983

Sick, Gary *All Fall Down: America's Tragic Encounter with Iran* New York: Penguin Books, 1986

Simpson, John *Inside Iran* New York: St. Martin's Press, 1988

The Iran Hostage Crisis: A Chronology of Daily Developments Report Prepared for the Committee on Foreign Affairs, US House of Representatives Congressional Research Service, 1981

Wright, Robin *Sacred Rage: The Wrath of Militant Islam* New York: Simon and Schuster, 1985

Wright, Robin "A Reporter at Large" in *The New Yorker* September 5, 1988

Zonis, Marvin *The Political Elite of Iran* Princeton: Princeton University Press, 1971

Works on the Iran-Iraq War and the Iranian Military

Afshar, Haleh "The Army" in Haleh Afshar ed., *Iran: A Revolution in Turmoil* Albany, State University of New York, 1989

Chubin, Shahram and Charles Tripp *Iran and Iraq at War* Boulder, Co.: Westview Press, 1988

Cordesman, Anthony *The Iran-Iraq War and Western Security 1984-87* London: Jane's Publishing Co. Ltd., 1987

Cottrell, Alvin J. "Iran's Armed Forces Under the Pahlavi Dynasty" in George Lenczowski ed., *Iran Under the Pahlavis* Stanford, Calif.: Hoover Institution Press, 1978

Entessar, Nader "The Military and Politics in the Islamic Republic of Iran" in Hooshang Amirahmadi and Manoucher Parvin eds., *Post Revolutionary Iran* Boulder, Co.: Westview Press, 1988

Hiro, Dilip *The Longest War: The Iran-Iraq Military Conflict* London: Paladin Books, 1990

"Iran" in *Defense and Foreign Affairs Handbook 1989* Alexandria, Va.: International Media Corp., 1989

Kazemi, Farhad "The Military and Politics in Iran: The Uneasy Symbiosis" in Elie Kedourie and Sylvia Haim, eds., *Iran: Towards Modernity: Studies in Thought, Politics, and Society* London: Frank Cass, 1980

O'Ballance, Edgar *The Gulf War* London: Brassey's Defence Publishers Ltd., 1988

Perron, Ronald "The Iranian Islamic Revolutionary Guard Corps" in *Middle East Insight*, June-July, 1985

Rose, Gregory "The Post-Revolutionary Purge of Iran's Armed Forces: A Revisionist Assessment" in Iranian Studies, Vol. 17, Nos. 2-3, Spring-Summer 1984

Schahgaldian, Nikola *The Iranian Military Under the Islamic Republic* Santa Monica: Rand Corp., 1987

Vought, Donald "Iran" in Richard Gabriel ed., *Fighting Armies: Antagonists in the Middle East - A Combat Assessment* Westport, Conn. and London: Greenwood Press, 1983

Zabih, Sepehr *The Iranian Military in War and Revolution* London: Routledge, Chapman, and Hall, 1988

Works on Other Revolutionary Armed Forces

Adelman, Jonathan *Communist Armies in Politics* Boulder, Co.: Westview Press, 1982

Cobb, Richard *The People's Armies* New Haven and London: Yale University Press, 1987

Colton, Timothy *Commissars, Commanders, and Civilian Authority: The Structure of Soviet Military Politics* Cambridge, Mass. and London: Harvard University Press, 1979

Hsiung, James *Ideology and Practice: The Evolution of Chinese Communism* New York and London: Praeger Publishers, 1970

Joffee, Ellis "The Military as a Political Actor in China" in Roman Kolkowicz and Andrzej Korbonski, eds., *Soldiers, Peasants, and Bureaucrats* London: Allen and Unwin, 1982

Jordan, James "The Maoist vs. the Professional Vision of a People's Army" in Amos Perlmutter and Valerie Plave Bennett *The Political Influence of the Military* New Haven and London: Yale University Press, 1980

Kolkowicz, Roman and Andrzej Korbonski, eds. *Soldiers, Peasants and Bureaucrats* London: Allen and Unwin, 1982

Pang Yu Ting, William "The Chinese Army" in Jonathan Adelman, ed., *Communist Armies in Politics* Boulder, Co.: Westview Press, 1982

Richelson, Jeffrey *Sword and Shield: Soviet Intelligence and Security Apparatus* Cambridge, Mass.: Ballinger Publishing Co., 1986

Richelson, Jeffrey *Foreign Intelligence Organizations* Cambridge, Mass.: Ballinger Publishing Co., 1988

Werth, Alexander *Russia at War: 1941-45* New York: Carroll and Graf Publishers, Inc., 1964

White, D. Fedotoff *The Growth of the Red Army* Princeton: Princeton University Press, 1944

Whitson, William ed. *Military and Political Power in China in the 1970s: Organization, Leadership, Political Strategy* New York: Irvington Publishers, 1972

Index

Ayatola
US - Iran
Iraq war?
resent this.
why spread?
why radical